IN A YOUNGER VOICE ▪

CHILD DEVELOPMENT IN CULTURAL CONTEXT

Academic Motivation and the Culture of Schooling
Cynthia Hudley and Adele Gottfried

Perfectly Prep: Gender Extremes at a New England Prep School
Sarah H. Chase

Children of Immigrants: Academic Attitudes and Pathways During Middle Childhood
Cynthia Garcia Coll and Amy Marks

In A Younger Voice
Cindy Dell Clark

Forthcoming Books in the Series:

Destiny and Development: A Mayan Midwife and Town
Barbara Rogoff

In A Younger Voice ::

Doing Child-Centered Qualitative Research

Cindy Dell Clark

OXFORD
UNIVERSITY PRESS
2011

OXFORD

UNIVERSITY PRESS

Oxford University Press, Inc., publishes works that further
Oxford University's objective of excellence
in research, scholarship, and education.

Oxford   New York
Auckland   Cape Town   Dar es Salaam   Hong Kong   Karachi
Kuala Lumpur   Madrid   Melbourne   Mexico City   Nairobi
New Delhi   Shanghai   Taipei   Toronto

With offices in
Argentina   Austria   Brazil   Chile   Czech Republic   France   Greece
Guatemala   Hungary   Italy   Japan   Poland   Portugal   Singapore
South Korea   Switzerland   Thailand   Turkey   Ukraine   Vietnam

Published by Oxford University Press, Inc.
198 Madison Avenue, New York, New York 10016

www.oup.com

Oxford is a registered trademark of Oxford University Press, Inc.

Library of Congress Cataloging-in-Publication Data

Clark, Cindy Dell.
In a younger voice: doing children's qualitative research/Cindy Dell Clark.
p. cm.—(Child development in cultural context series)
Includes bibliographical references and index.
ISBN 978-0-19-537659-3
1. Child development—Research. 2. Qualitative research. I. Title.
HQ767.9.C56 2010
305.231072′1—dc22

2010009166

9 8 7 6 5 4 3 2 1

Printed in the United States of America on acid-free paper.

To Richard Bruce Dell

With whom I traversed childhood
and who helped me make my way,
a friend given by nature indeed.

ACKNOWLEDGMENTS ⠶

The publication of this book marks for me the consummation of a decade of university teaching. The halls of academe where I've dwelled are predominately paved with established, well-worn avenues of research. I admit to wandering off upon unbeaten paths, partly because I am in the habit of peering through a wide interdisciplinary lens, but also because I strive to make known children's voices and perspectives. As I strayed and meandered to give voice to children, however, I found myself in worthy company, in the form of excellent guides and helpmates.

Penn State Brandywine was my academic home for 9 years, where the library and its librarians consistently gave me sustenance. Cynthia Lightfoot from Penn State Brandywine and my other PSU faculty colleagues provided me with appreciated broad-mindedness and collegiality as I began the work on this book.

I have also benefited from a home away from home at the Center for Children and Childhood Studies, at Rutgers University Camden. Myra Bluebond-Langner, who founded the Center, on many occasions has been to me a one-woman support group. Her generous and steadfast belief in this project has sustained me more than she knows.

As chair of the Section on Children and Youth of the American Sociological Association from 2007 to 2008, I was enveloped by some of the best child-centered scholars ever to keep field notes. Thanks to the members of that section for accepting my companionship within the new sociology of childhood.

If I had fairy dust to sprinkle, I would scatter some on my generous and patient husband Bill, who has steadfastly supported this book, and my longstanding quest to bring into better focus each child's eye view.

Fairy dust would also be strewn upon Peggy J. Miller, who first encouraged me to send a manuscript to the Child Development in Cultural Context Series at Oxford University Press. Peggy is proof that brilliance and achievement coexist with being a fine and charitable human being. I am grateful to her, to her series coeditor Cynthia Garcia Coll, and to Lori Handelman and the others at Oxford University Press in helping to bring this book into your hands.

Over decades of applied and academic research, thousands of children have shown me how to refine my skills of child-attuned qualitative inquiry. I thank these young and once young informants for their tutelage. This book is meant to pass along my learning in the expectation that in generations to come, children's voices will be heard near and far as a matter of course.

CONTENTS ⠶

Sidebars

IN A YOUNGER VOICE ⚏

1 ::

Introduction: Valuing Young Voices

"Was there ever any domination which did not appear
natural to those who possessed it?"
—JOHN STUART MILL

Recently, under a shady tree near my front yard, two gracious young ladies from my neighborhood drank tea. The tea was not real and the young ladies were pretending, but I could tell a lot about how they thought grown ladies conduct themselves, during a social rendezvous. When you have seen children at play, you probably have marked, too, how children role-play behaviors of adults. They dress up in mom's shoes, dress, hat, and dangly purse and mimic her words and actions. They deliver dad's lines and behavior with uncanny enactment. Teachers, doctors, and other adult authority figures are taken up in play. Performances reveal children to be attentive observers of adults' voices and behaviors. Children are prone, as well, to caricature as they exaggerate and improvise adults' entitlements and prerogatives.

It is in its own way remarkable that adults don't return the regard towards children's direction; American adults aren't prone to capture with enacted drama what children say and do. The disregard by not playing out children's roles is consistent with the limited ways in which most adults relate to children. Take politicians' treatment of children in America. Politicians kiss babies, but generally don't take the next step to listen to school-age citizens before they make policy. Persons like Mr. Rogers, a man more tuned in to children than the average adult, have been ridiculed for honoring make-believe and being scornfully child-resonant.

At the outset of my child research career over a quarter-century ago, I was forewarned that children made difficult subjects. They would be hard to interview and would be inscrutable to interpretation,

3

I was counseled. With equal assurance, others told me that children are preternaturally honest, given to the sort of unbridled truths told to the fabled naked emperor. When Art Linkletter interviewed children on his 1950s television show, children were forthright, which Linkletter (2005) exploited for laughs. (In fact, children were strikingly honest on the show, but only because they seemingly hadn't mastered social norms for what to disclose.)

Art Linkletter: *What does your dad do around the house to help your mother?*

Boy: He makes cocktails.

Art Linkletter: *Where does the tooth fairy get his money?*

Girl: He steals it from my mom's wallet at night.

Over hundreds of studies, I have found that children are comprehensible, when a researcher approaches them in child-relevant ways, as this book documents and details. I also have found that children are about as honest as adults, although they certainly parse the world and see experiences from distinctive angles and sometimes don't know adults' norms for socially appropriate disclosure.

This book is your invitation to do qualitative research with children that amplifies their voices, to reap the benefits of knowing children better. Adults share the world with children and have broad-reaching impact on children's lives. Yet adults' associations regarding children are often unexamined, and many times adults miss out on children's perspectives. Examples of this are easy to identify across varied contexts. Consider popular culture, for example. Adult American marketers, who were my colleagues in applied work, proved to have limited insight into children's proclivities; they didn't foresee in advance the intense and lasting popularity among children of the mega-hits, Teenage Mutant Ninja Turtles, Power Rangers, Pokémon, or Harry Potter. Many adults puzzled over the lasting media success of Barney, the downsized, huggable dinosaur. Mature scriptwriters have omitted Rudolph from movies showing Santa's reindeer, yet young moviegoers think the omission is jarring (Clark, 1995). Fully grown professional artists depict the Easter Bunny as an anthropomorphic being with human-like behaviors, although children envision otherwise. In a study I conducted with 5- to 8-year-old kids (Clark, 1995), the Easter Bunny was portrayed (orally and in drawings) as a nature-derived non-anthropomorphic rabbit with neither human clothing nor humanoid residence, neither language nor upright posture. School administrators recently have made dramatic reductions in recess time among children in the United States, failing to altogether appreciate the upside of child-directed free play to American children. Upon investigation, recess, rather than being at cross-purposes with academic learning as administrators suppose, has been found to enhance classroom learning habits, such as the habit of staying on task without fidgeting (Jarrett et al., 1998). Play by children that lampoons adult authority (via mockery of adults) has been censored as well, disregarding how meaningful such play is for children in coping with everyday age-based inequities, subjugation, and subordination (Factor, 2009).

There are also more somber circumstances of adult–child disconnection. Not too many decades ago, it was treated as common sense in medical circles that infants did not require anesthesia because they did not feel pain. Children's pain continues to be underestimated or oversimplified by medical personnel (Kortesluoma, Nikkonen, & Serlo, 2008; Woodgate & Krisjanson, 1996). Fortunately, researchers in Finland and elsewhere have taken the time and effort to monitor minors' perception of their pain, using qualitative methods such as journal-writing (Polkki, Pietila, & Rissanen, 1999), metaphors (Kortesluoma & Nikkonen, 2006), visual rulers (Polkki, Pietila, & Vehvilainen-Julkunen, 2003), focused interviews, or picture drawing (Kortesluoma & Nikkonen, 2004). Great strides have been made in understanding and managing the pain that is experienced by the young through these child-relevant methods.

When a youngster is being treated for life-shortening cancer, adults are prone to err regarding how much a child understands about his own prognosis and options for treatment, which can lead to poor communication with the youngster whose life is on the line (Bluebond-Langner, DeCicco, & Belasco, 2005). Better understanding would be a way for the treatment team to facilitate more comfortable and candid exchange (Bearison, 1991).

Among living children, conceptions of illness can run counter to adults' constructs. Young children's notions of chronic illness encompass not just a medically diagnosed condition but additionally the *treatment* and its significance. The inhaler is a synecdoche for asthma, an inherent part of having asthma, just as the syringe is a rudiment of child-defined diabetes. As one youngster indicated the central role of treatment in defining illness, "Diabetes means you have to have shots" (Clark, 2003). In health education, mature medical professionals draw from the canonical biomedical model in which treatment is assumed to be a positive (since a counterforce to disease), but this can contrast with youngsters' framing of treatment as an implicated part of being ill, not necessarily cast in positive terms. Improved knowledge of kids' conceptions could enhance clinical relations, communication, and adherence.

Sick or healthy, children raise issues of dependency for adults. Adults often view vulnerability and submission as fixed, self-evident aspects of childhood (Frankenberg, Robinson, & Delahooke, 2000) rather than as artifacts of adultism. Adults view kids as totally dependent on elders. This overlooks that the young have complex and dynamic relationships with adults, including inverted roles of caretaking. Children, for example, are known to support parents in various ways during adult traumas of divorce, illness, grief, or poverty (Morrow, 1996; Ridge, 2003). Immigrant children serve as cultural and language brokers for their elders (Orellana, 2001). In some places and times, children act as armed warriors, as an active response to the circumstances in which a child finds himself (Rosen, 2005). Assuming that adult relations with children are a top-down dependency misses how variegated adult–child relations can be.

Adults' views of children are frequently misbegotten or biased. Research sometimes ventriloquizes children rather than directly consulting children, using adults as proxy to report on child experience. Relying on mature proxies (parents, teachers, etc.) to give accounts of youthful experience is an unfortunate concession, since adult proxies lack a direct line to children's experienced meanings; youthful meanings are often divergent from those of adults. To fully understand the young, their trajectory, or their sociocultural engagement, children need to be firsthand sources in studies.

The aforementioned television host Mr. Rogers, who regularly met with and listened to preschoolers as a way to refine how to communicate with them, knew the value of hearing children's voices. He knew that children's own reports were essential for understanding and connecting with a young audience. Fred Rogers' strong appeal to young children often mystified or amused adults, but there was no hidden trick to it. Fred Rogers simply cared enough to meet with children and to summon ways to convey meanings that resonated with them.

Adult bias about children comes in for mocking in a satiric newsletter article published years ago by Jordan Smoller (1988). The essay satirized common adult views of children, by treating childhood as if it were a disease classification. Smoller wrote, tongue in cheek, that children's differences from adults make up a "syndrome" in need of "treatment," characterized by: "1) congenital onset; 2) dwarfism; 3) emotional lability and immaturity; 4) knowledge deficits; and 5) legume anorexia." Smoller jested that effective protocols of treatment for this "syndrome" (that is, a fixed set of essentialist traits) have been elusive; even the expensive and drastic intervention of schooling could not reverse the "child" condition, Smoller lampooned. Smoller's send-up, titled "The Etiology and Treatment of Childhood," jested about the intellectual practice of discerning childhood as an enduring set of deficit traits relative to adults, as a connotation of age-based inferiority. The spoof treats adultist notions as laughable, in the process highlighting that children in fact are dynamic creatures who are not necessarily "dwarfed" or handicapped versus adults. Interdependent with adults, children indeed can be seen as imbued with initiative, impact, and some forms of power. They are not static chips off the blocks of elders, nor are they mere constellations of age-based traits. Adults ought to bear in mind the socially situated, relational, and variable ways in which children exist in context (Frankenberg, Robinson, & Delahooke, 2000), and the complex, dynamic connections children have to others.

American adults living alongside children tend to see childhood through a lens of idealization, a sentimental kinder-utopia. The late Sharon Stephens (in Malkki & Martin, 2007) referred to this as "the private, safe, happy, and innocent 'garden' of childhood." Associated with idealized, utopic views of children are emblematic images: circus clowns, teddy bears, undersized dinosaurs, and the like. Each of these symbols is whitewashed and made diminutive in its cultural appropriation for children. Bears teddy-ized are rendered unthreatening and huggable. Dinosaurs are friendly and toothless, even purple. Clowns laugh off negativity and have fun, no matter what. In the circus, the expression "send in the clowns" refers to the way clowns amuse an audience to divert attention during a calamity. Coincidentally, modern hospital clowns do funny tricks as diversion for gravely ill children (Blerkom, 1995). Tied in meaning to childhood and its supposed kinder-utopia, clowns act as counterforce to life's strains and sorrows. At the dark and fearsome festival of Halloween, adults lampoon and caricature emblems of death, festooning the family home with skeletons, ghosts, graves and ghouls. This is a way to associate death with the innocence of kinder-utopia, rendering even mortality carefree by association with children (Clark, 2005). A grown-up lens on early life is a kind of escapism into a zone where the existentially threatening becomes not only neutralized but made to seem approachable and playful, a turnabout as much for the benefit of big folks as small. Made possible by the assumption that children are naturally innocent, the things around children are naturally innocent by association.

But, lest it be forgotten, the utopia is chimerical. Despite children's assumed innocence, adults often discount or indirectly disparage children. The terms "childish," "immature," "little," "babyish," or "juvenile" are used as epithets. In some institutions, American children are under the dominion of adults and have little input on how the institution operates. Children have to accept consequential decisions adults make for them in families, in medical settings, in places of education, in religious activities—through a power structure taken by adults as the natural order of things. In school, children have rules that govern when they can talk, when they should use the toilet, when they can move about, whether they can carry contraband items (gum, stickers, sweets, etc.), and even whether it is permissible to carry an inhaler that would give relief from asthma (which some schools prohibit carrying) (Clark, 2003). Elementary-schoolers, according to prohibitions, must ask permission to visit the school nurse, to call home, to get something from their locker, and so forth. As Foucault might have predicted in the face of such uneven relations, even preschoolers are known to rebel and make trouble in the midst of their powerless status (Leavitt, 1991; Miller & Ginsburg, 1989; Sutterby, 2005).

One might argue that children are fittingly under adult control as it is adults who care for young dependents. This view bears weight, in that adults have the responsibility to "raise" children into acculturated persons. A pillow I once saw, in embroidered motto, stated the case: "Children are adults under construction." Still, there are two flaws with the "adults under construction" argument. First, if the main crux of adult–child relations focuses on adults shaping children toward maturity, then relations with the child as a person in the here and now are crimped; this is comparable to defining workers mainly in terms of retirement, or women's rights being premised on women becoming more like men (Benporath, 2003). Second, the caretaking justification of adult control would have to be premised on a society in which adults do fully care for the child populace. At the present time the commitment of my own country, the United States, to all of its children is questionable. One in five American children grows up in poverty, often living in neighborhoods of violence and stress, facing disproportionate health risks and recurrent trauma. The foster care system is atrociously flawed. Countless priorities are more valued than children, as evidenced in polluted air, child war victims, inadequate schools, poor quality childcare, neglect and abuse, low media standards, infant mortality, unpaid child support, and more. Around the globe, most children grow up in the antithesis of utopic conditions, ravaged by severe poverty, war, disease, abuse, exploitation, or discrimination—in short, in circumstances that are desperate. U.S. pundits and politicians condemned Sesame Street television productions for introducing in South Africa a TV character suffering from AIDS. The character was meant to appeal to the young audience in AIDS stricken South Africa (a move considered out of keeping with pundits' utopian expectations for children's TV). Media expert and physician Gabriel Vigotti (in Knowlton, 2006) defended the idea that children's television should address locally relevant, if dystopic themes.

> There are very few kids that have an easy and great life. In most of countries, a great percentage of children are really living in poverty, in war situations, in abuse situations, in deprivation, discrimination of any type (cultural, religious, etc.) and they're facing that all day. So I think it would be a betrayal of the rights of a child not to address those issues.

As I write, the United States stands alone among organized nations, in having balked at formally acknowledging children's rights by ratifying the United Nations Convention on the Rights of the Child, protecting children from neglect, cruelty, exploitation, and ensuring them access to education, recreation, adequate nutrition, medical care, and preferential triage in crisis. Two of the arguments that have been used to oppose U.S. backing of the UN Convention on the Rights of the Child reveal harsh attitudes by adults in power (Clark, Paramo, & Rosen, 2007). First, in some states, proponents of capital punishment have sought to protect the option to execute minors, prohibited by the Convention. Second, it has been argued that the military should retain the flexibility (prohibited by the Convention) to draft minors into service at a hypothetical future time. Even if not the majority view, these do not seem like reasons based in elders' overriding caring intent.

As evidence of the complex ways that adults perceive their relation to children, adults sometimes treat children as a group to be symbolically protected from behaviors adults regularly practice. Obesity, material overconsumption, and violent media narratives (to name a few examples), affect both adults and children, but many of elders' proposals for change are focused on youthful behavior only, rather than everyone's. Foibles are problematized in the younger generation, leaving adults' similar behaviors less scrutinized. This is, of course, a generational double standard, even if it has caring strains. Children serve as a symbolic point of leverage for elders, a way to transform in the younger generation what adults dislike in themselves and society, as a kind of seedbed for adults' social engineering. An advocacy organization arguing for a "commercial-free childhood," opposes child-targeted marketing as harmful to children (Linn, 2005). Yet consumption by children happens in interaction with adults. Adults sometimes shop obsessively or tolerate financial problems from excessive consumption. Don't these adult problems tie to the ways children consume? A government drug czar calls attention to rising teen drug abuse yet ignores the fact that adult drug abuse is rising, too (Males, 2007). The common tagline "Do as I say, not as I do" might serve as a shorthand for the adultist double standard; the same sentiment exists in the assumption behind intervention programs that pinpoint youth as a specific audience. Ironically, many of the behaviors which adults are err to (alcohol abuse, smoking, obesity, overspending, etc.) seem to be behaviors that youth or teens become heir to, since many youth model what they see adults do. Failing to address adults along with kids may diminish the impact of educational interventions, no matter how caringly intended they are. As a policy practice, treating children as the designated drivers meant to reform society's unhealthful behavior raises probing questions—first, about whether children are being singled out as moral scapegoats, and second, about the functional efficacy of solving social problems through youth alone. Obesity (Ebberling, Pawlak, & Ludwig, 2002) and fat intake (Laroche, Hofer, & Davis, 2007) have proven family ties, as do other unhealthful behaviors.

Prevailing theories of child development permeate modern notions of childhood, even as adults tend to overlook the systematic way that adults have shaped or structured these theories (Denzin, 1973). Children have had little or no part in the fashioning of developmental theories, much as natives of developing cultures had little part in early anthropological theorizing, or women had little part in early psychoanalytic theorizing. In the international field of children's studies, it has become a familiar complaint that developmental theories place children on a trajectory toward adulthood, thereby accentuating adult concerns rather than children's felt experience (Lee, 1998). (Imagine what our theories might be like if instead, development was traced in terms of structures *lost* over the course of childhood, and what adults therefore *lack* relative to children.) Orthodox developmental theory describes children as incapable, unfinished, and somehow lesser (or at least less "developed") than adults (Waksler, 1991). Put another way, children are treated as human becomings, rather than as human beings (Qvortrup, 1987). Traditional theories of socialization treat the young as heading towards maturity, and as passive recipients of sociocultural input, a view that foregrounds the power of adults to reduplicate culture through children while it ignores children's active participation in cultural discourse.

In the last two decades or so, a vanguard of scholars (e.g., Christiansen & James, 2000; Corsaro, 1997, 2005; Corsaro & Miller, 1992; James & Prout, 1997; Waksler, 1991) has championed the child-centered mode of inquiry, acknowledging that children have agency and that children's voices should be integral to research and interpretations about children. These scholars, allied to interpretive modes of inquiry, have found that children play an active role in their own enculturation and contribute on their own to the shaping of cultural discourse. The American scholarly zeitgeist is gradually becoming more receptive to child-centered ideas, although the orthodox developmentalist view continues to hold sway in U.S. academic enclaves. (Europe, Australia, and Canada have had relatively more progress in establishing academic recognition for child-centered research.)

I am confident that investigators can and will learn how to open a path to regard children more on their own terms and from their "eye-view." This book intends to support and encourage researchers in efforts to directly and openly engage children, a methodological commitment that could help to build evidential and theoretical knowledge that is child-relevant. The implied call to action is in some ways no different than earlier calls that supported gay and lesbian studies, African-American studies, and women's studies. Children, akin to those other groups, have been marginalized and discounted in social science research, in line with a cultural tendency to naturalize children's descendant position. By a concerted effort to reexamine elders' stereotypes, research can be grounded in the experiences of children, as they interact as complete social beings.

In the final analysis, what is needed is the double vision to see both the child's and the grownup's vantage points. Society's construction is co-construction, with children as active partners along with adults. Therefore, adult perspectives and child perspectives are both worth knowing and calibrating. The child-centered approach adds to and renovates orthodox developmental theories by taking into account the multi-voiced (not just adult-voiced) and dynamic nature of human discourse and meaning. Since children are an active part of social dynamics, we need to know about children's pivotal behaviors and conceptions. Adults, who interact with children in influential ways, retain importance in the child-centered paradigm. But adults' influence has become less lopsided. The orthodox idea that adults socialize passive, receptive youth has had its bias revealed.

There are ample precedents and guideposts for conducting child-centered research, thanks to the extensive work in Europe, Canada, Australia, and elsewhere. Outside the United States, the child-centered turn has been catalyzed by the implementation of the UN Convention on the Rights of the Child, which grants to children a voice in their affairs.

Qualitative child-centered inquiry, rather than quantitative research, is the central thrust of the child-centered movement and this book. Qualitative methods have been especially important to the child-centered research movement, as an approach that seeks to avoid imposing on children adult-derived constructs. Qualitative research leaves room to uncover unknown strands and chards of meaning, that children disclose when space and means are made for them to communicate. Contrasting qualitative approaches with quantitative ones, the latter use research designs discernibly shaped by adult study designers. Quantitative instruments have a disciplined structure that leaves less space for children's unanticipated, volunteered felt meanings. As scholars refine child-centered qualitative methods, we are increasingly able to organize inquiry around children's meanings, experiences, and worldviews. In turn, this provides child-relevant input for theorizing and understanding children's experience.

The worth of child-centered inquiry has been felt upon programs and policies. It would be hard to imagine having successful social programs or public health interventions for children, unless child-centered methods were activated to inform policy with child-relevant understanding. Interventions intended to implement policy must motivate and engage the young audience being addressed, for as mentioned earlier, children's views are not photocopies or faxes of adult understandings. Even adults who are in charge of children cannot be assumed to know what will motivate or inform the young without probing children's thoughts and experiences directly. The stakes are to produce policies reflective of children's lived realities (Leonard, 2005), a goal methods like the ones described herein are intended to accomplish.

This book provides a methodological game board for doing qualitative research with children—a template of the options and ways to maneuver in carrying out investigations that are child-involving and child-amplifying. Chapter 2 will take a glance at the roots of child-centered inquiry, and the way its branches extend into research ethics and applied research. Chapters 3 through 6 will then pursue particular ways and means of fielding child-centered qualitative studies: participant observation, individual interviews, focus groups, and visual methods of inquiry. Chapter 7 will deal with the analytical process and reporting of a child-centered project, followed by conclusions in Chapter 8. Together, these chapters carry a larger message about young persons—to inspire and empower us all to listen afresh to younger voices and to take seriously the things we hear.

I do not mean to gloss over an obvious perplexity; at what point in the age span is someone a "child"? Defining a "child" is a culturally variable matter. Some cultures, for instance, reckon age beginning at conception, others at birth. Although the UN Convention on the Rights of the Child fathomed a child to be any human below the age of majority—generally below the age of 18 years—the age parameters of a "child" are admittedly fuzzy. This book foregoes the temptation to set sharp drop-off points as to who is considered a child. Clearly, though, age matters in shaping qualitative research. Infants and toddlers generally are not cut out to be forthcoming interviewees. Many of the methods in Chapters 4, 5 and 6 will be appropriate most of the time starting at some point between age 5 to 8 years. Infants and toddlers can be studied using ethnography (Chapter 3), a method suitable for a broad range of ages, across childhood and into the teen years. Some of the tools described as useful for children of school age prior to adolescence (in Chapter 4, 5, and 6) can be adapted for adolescent inquiry, too, with adjustments such as foregoing drawing or doll play or other "outgrown" activities. The conclusion (Chapter 8) includes specific suggestions for methods to use with teens, in a hypothetical policy-related study. As that chapter notes, adult methods of qualitative research can often be adapted for use with teens, who have verbal proficiencies that make inquiry less daunting than for younger kids.

In cooking, a soufflé is more difficult to do well than a scrambled egg. In qualitative inquiry on youthful perspectives, children prior to 13 or 14 years are soufflé informants, with a more intense level of difficulty compared to teenagers; indeed, the younger the child the more intense the challenge. But even a soufflé is not so difficult once the basic principles and how-to's are understood. This book, I hope, will provide the know-how to make shorter work of the "soufflé" that is child-centered inquiry. Hearing children's voices can be more than an exotic delicacy but part of standard fare in a menu of important discovery.

2 ⠿

Child-Centered Inquiry: A Chronicle

The real act of discovery consists not in finding new lands
but seeing with new eyes.
—MARCEL PROUST

Child-centered inquiry is a new kid on the block, among approaches for studying children. This young upstart field occupies in America a growing but as yet relatively peripheral sphere of children's research. It is an exciting movement, one still unfolding. How did this innovative paradigm of child-centered inquiry originate? What is its expected influence? Instructive for understanding child-centered inquiry are two aspects: (1) the supporting "roots" or foundations that underpin the child-centered field of study, and (2) the spreading implications for related "branches," including such domains as research ethics and child participatory research.

⠿ Roots

Scholars studied children throughout the twentieth century, but the move toward a child-centered paradigm is fairly recent. It was during the 1980s and 1990s that the child-centered research movement took hold, through a coalescing of sociologists, anthropologists and other academic researchers across Europe, North America, and beyond (James, 2007). The emergent central impulse of the movement has been to study children as complete social actors dynamically situated in context. The paradigm set aside presumptions of an objective, static frame for viewing children. It also rejected the idea that children were of interest mainly because they are in transit toward maturation, as established developmental theory might espouse with its emphasis on unfolding or stage-like progression. The child-centered movement sought to focus on children's own ways of experiencing, in the here and now—through child-sensitive observation and witnessing. From the outset, the expectation that children can provide competent voices prevailed, carrying on a qualitative research principle emphasizing persons' subjective accounts. Intense interest in depth interviewing and group interviewing methods had expanded among scholars starting in the 1970s, in fields such as sociology, nursing and education. Qualitative research methods at that time became more well-known, and ripe for adaptation by child-centered researchers.

Child-centered inquiry took as its purview children's dynamic social environments (e.g., family, neighborhood, clinic, schoolyard), producing accounts about and by children placed in context and in practice. This contrasts with orthodox developmental psychology, which persists as the dominating field of child study in the United States at the outset of the twenty-first century. Orthodox developmental psychology seeks to identify and isolate maturing structures or developmental properties (object permanence, theory of mind, formal operational thought, attachment, etc.) assumed to supersede social context. Child-centered research, which is less concerned with the universal, developmental acquisition of capabilities, instead asks how children as active human beings, as agents, experience existence in the social present. The link between child and context is recognized and set into relief in child-centered inquiry.

In 1999 in a forward to a collection of essays on children in varied social environments, American anthropologist Robert Levine (in Goncu, 1999) praised the essays for their context sensitivity. "The contributors concern themselves ... with how the interactions, activities, and settings of childhood vary across a wide range of cultures, as well as subcultures defined by ethnicity and social class ... Rather than clinging to the standard measures favored in conventional psychological research, these ... investigators devised measures adjusted to the activities and settings on which they were working." Levine's praise of culturally situated standards bears a degree of comparison to child-centered research, within which social circumstances are assumed as a systemic context for children's engagement.

By definition, child-centered research is characterized by an emphasis on children's own concerns and salient issues. A boost in attention to kids' issues was the UN Convention on the Rights of the Child, ratified throughout Europe after being opened for signatures in 1989.

(The United States is still not a signatory as of 2009, despite influential involvement in drafting the Convention.) The Convention formalized the notion of regarding children as valued persons within society. Child-centered inquiry gained new proponents at the end of the twentieth century, especially in nations where the Convention was ratified. The surge stirred interest in policy research among the young.

To gain access to children's concerns in inquiry, an appropriate research approach became essential, one devoid of adultist slant and charged with connecting to the voices of the young. Methodological innovation and renovations proliferated to fulfill the challenge. The new methods have been guided by child-focused principles, emphasizing ways to gain access to events and ideas as experienced by the young. A focal concern in carrying out research was to foster children's airing of their own views. No one option was a dictated standard method. Approaches that invited kids to narrate, show and tell, photograph, illustrate, or to be playfully engaged were the sorts that generally gained ground, as this book will address.

In 1991 there appeared an influential article advocating the "least-adult" approach to participant observation, exemplified by a study carried out in an American preschool. The author, Nancy Mandell (1991), challenged adult participant-observers to totally embed themselves in children's worlds, and to model their behavior after children's ways so that their language and actions would align with kids' roles. Mandell practiced what she preached, embedding herself within preschoolers' peer groups and inhibiting her own adult habits of dominance. In the preschool where she conducted research, she refrained from reporting children's transgressions, played whatever the kids were playing, and wouldn't come to a child's aid by doing such "adult" things as tying shoes or pushing swings or reaching high objects. Mandell's article struck a chord with a central issue for child-centered investigators, since it addressed what practices might bring an adult into attunement with children's experiences. Mandell felt more able to notice, comprehend, and frame child-relevant meaning through the least-adult role.

Child-centered researchers have not widely adopted the full "least-adult" approach for fieldwork. Regardless, reflexivity about how adult behaviors influence interactivity with children has come to be a sustained concern of child-centered inquiry. The power and inhibition triggered by adults exerting authority over children gained prominence as a problem to be examined (Fine & Sandstrom, 1988). Adult-associated acts during fieldwork (such as coaching a team, leading a class, cutting up food for children, or enacting discipline) can imply adult ascendance and child subordination. This is thought to carry repercussions on how well a study can reveal kids' lives. Issues of age-laced identity and power, in other words, can shift the way in which meanings are negotiated between older and younger persons (Ewing, 2006). A research movement intent on doing studies *for* or *with* children, rather than merely *on* or *about* children, earnestly pondered the need for reflexivity in adult researcher roles.

The field's commitment to reflexivity didn't emerge in isolation from other influences during the late twentieth century. To start with, reflexive themes lay just below the surface in the qualitative research movement. Likewise, issues of adult–child engagement pervaded exchanges about the UN Convention on the Rights of the Child (Mishna, Antle, & Regehr, 2004). Such discussions advanced arguments about children being granted authentic voices in decision making and research alike.

The last decades of the 1900s were a time when, across the board, reflexivity and otherness had provocative scholarly panache. Interest in reflexivity generally coincided with the development of women's studies, African-American studies, and gay studies, raising awareness of delicately contingent relations between researchers and persons from marginalized groups. The latter folk came to voice dissatisfaction with outsiders who portrayed their groups in undesired ways in published research (Mihesuah, 1998). The idea that white researchers were appropriate investigators in American Indian studies, for example, came in for criticism (Mihesuah & Wilson, 2004):

> It is a cherished and unexamined doctrine ... that a non-Indian student can spend a few weeks in the summer living on the margins of an Indian community, and because of his or her training and the innate ability of whites to be objective, accurately understand what the Indians are doing and why they are doing it. One need only look at the record of the Newberry Library Indian program to see how pervasive the attitude is.

Many indigenous community members called for their fellows to conduct research within the indigenous cultural group, rather than submit to outside investigators. Native control over research questions and published outcomes was allied with native self-determination. Such a predilection applied in the case of a Maori native, Linda Tuhiwahi Smith. Smith (1999) noted that concepts of self and other, conceptions of time; rubrics of classification, and social organization could all be distorted if seen through nonnative eyes. Misconstrued understandings amounted to tacit imperialism, she maintained. A preferred alternative by some was to arrange for research to be done through involving natives themselves.

The climate of pronounced reflexivity during the late twentieth century had a significant anthropological front. Anthropologists such as Rabinow (1977) and Rosaldo (1989) recognized the "imperial" dilemma when outsiders studied another people and assumed for themselves a privileged access to explanation. This risk had to be met with countermeasures, a chief one being that outsider-anthropologists would need to carefully scrutinize their interactions with indigenous informants. To be avoided was overlooking local perspectives, and thereby ignoring the views of people essential to relevant planning. Rather, a fieldworker should own up to her subjectivity, and the particularities of her field relationships and exchanges. Researchers should be encouraged to be more self-conscious about the nuances of exchange during engagement with informants, bearing in mind that acts of exchanging meaning and knowledge are fluid and conditional.

Fieldwork, essentially a synonym for participant observation, became an important method in child-centered research, with full cognizance of reflexivity as a matter to dwell upon. Sensitivity to relationships between researcher and researched remains a dominant concern of child-centered fieldworkers (Woodhead, 2008). Chapter 3 considers participant observation and the various research roles taken by adult participant-observers as they make contact with children as social actors. In a child-centered study, the goal is to empower young voices to speak and be heard, avoiding adult encumbrance or domination.

Children are many times invited and involved as active co-inquirers by contemporary child-centered researchers. As will be discussed in a later section of this chapter, the involvement of children as full-fledged fieldworkers is a feature of some standing, since it indicates the value placed on avoiding adult-for-child ventriloquism. Involving kids as co-researchers contests adultist tendencies, in principle tilting the authority and power more toward the young and reducing adult dominion in fieldwork and/or interpretation.

A bumper crop of child-geared methods emerged from child-centered inquiry. Despite the methodological harvest, the new approaches haven't captured much attention to date within the positivist orthodoxy of developmental psychology. The child-centered versus orthodox paradigms remain essentially segregated and contested, around such areas of difference as: (1) What constitutes worthwhile knowledge about children? and (2) Should the emphasis on standardized, universalized instruments take priority over consideration of local, social dynamics tied to a child's active participation? In considering these questions, the child-centered and developmental paradigms have followed separate tracks. Divergent goals and differing methodological predilections have led to a veering off between the approaches, including in applied research.

For instance, health-care research conducted under orthodox assumptions seeks reductionist, objectively stated findings. To provide this, the controlled experiment or a standard survey instrument (perhaps one directly derived from an adult questionnaire) would be common methods to gather information. If children were unable to respond to the questions—for example a written question was beyond their reading level—adjustments such as adding illustrations or scales made of smile faces would fill the gap but leave the standardization intact. It is not a concern under orthodox assumptions that standardized measuring leads inquiry away from communications strategies that children use day to day. As a result, orthodox approaches may not align with kids' ordinary ways of signifying or sharing information.

By contrast, health-care research using a child-centered paradigm is less inclined to take a one-size-fits-all, standardized approach. It follows a more ad hoc route, perhaps through play activities as part of unstructured interviews, seeking to track with a child's particular predilections. There is more leeway to change course to fit a child's discourse or focus. Preference in child-centered research belongs to formats that are attractive, comfortable, and accommodating to the participating children, rather than those that take a standardized form. Gesture, movement, play using puppets, art techniques like drawing, clay, collage, mapping, photography, and so on, have been incorporated in studies of children, on the principle that such tactics use familiar, child-enabling strategies. Adult investigators, during a study, would be conscious of how their actions might influence the child; for example, a paper-and-pencil instrument might be regarded by a child as "schoolwork." If such school and teacher associations arise, the researcher might pause to reflect: Might this association to school cause the child to interpret this research process as an evaluative or controlling act? Tasks and roles are reflected upon and frequently changed if the inquiry confronts glitches that go against children's relevant forms of discourse and expression.

Applying child-centered principles and methods stands to benefit applied domains, as well as expanding theory and methodology. Usability engineering (a field that studies products for hazards) largely excluded children as target users until this millennium. When child-appropriate ways were employed to assess children's understanding of safety after 2000, it was found that kids' views were appreciated and valuable (Smith-Jackson, 2002). Marketers recognized the value of child-centered inquiry decades prior to the child-centered inquiry movement among scholars. The momentum is in place for children's voices to impact a stretching array of practical domains.

∷ Branches

Child-centered inquiry is by no means a freestanding intellectual project. The paradigm has origins and offshoots tied to other academic enclaves and to applied fields. Today's child-centered investigations have connections to cultural psychology, sociology, anthropology, archaeology, history, literature, geography, folklore, linguistics, education, health care, religious studies, economics, marketing, and more. Theories borrowed from other fields (such as Bruner's or Vygotsky's cultural psychological concepts emphasizing social participation and interaction in learning) have become germane for many child-centered scholars. In this sense, the line to past ideas and other work is very much continuous for child-centered inquiry. Following are a couple of important ties.

As early as the mid-1900s, *folklorists of childhood* such as Iona and Peter Opie or Brian Sutton-Smith recorded material from children's folk life. For instance, they worked amidst street life, in schoolyards, or around neighborhoods, collecting instances of children's games and humor. This work treated children's rhymes, riddles and scatological jokes as nontrivial, respectable domains of social life. These sorts of folklore accounts were child-focused in the sense of being collected directly from children, within their social milieu, on topics that children find salient and relevant.

Historians of childhood, who often trace their lineage to Aries' (1962) work on the cultural construction of childhood, have increasingly sought the viewpoints of children made available through historical evidence. Along with archaeologists, they have done some clever sleuthing to uncover what everyday life was like for children in past times. A striking example is Eisen's remarkable study of children's play during the

Holocaust (published a quarter century after *Centuries of Childhood*). Eisen's (1988) study had child-centered goals, insofar as it chronicled how children themselves dealt with and interacted in Nazi death camps. These children faced daily close encounters with death and dead persons. Eisen traced how young inmates coped through play, pretending to be guards and prisoners, acting out routines of prison life and killing. In the absence of toys, youngest prisoners used available materials, like a broken broom. They chased rolling stones or ran after rats and mice for amusement. Their pretense and imagination was in counterpoint to the misery of their daily existence. Play provided a chance for children to recreate versions of camp experiences, and thereby to regain control as they played out the domination and power of the camp guards over prisoners. Indeed, in kids' role-play, the part of a guard was an attractive role to children, since it provided a child with a role reversal countering the degradation. Eisen's work is a good example of how centering a study's attention on children within a social context can open a child-relevant window to children's ways of being (such as coping through play). Norman Denzin (1977) expressed that scholars should view children as socially interactive, agentic engagers, who act within a context of a particular time and place. The work of Eisen takes seriously Denzin's directive.

In contrast to the analytic standardization of orthodox developmental psychology, child-centered inquiry—as practiced by folklorists and historians as well as today's child-centered scholars—is interpretive and holistic. Relative to orthodox developmental psychology, child-centered inquiry seeks to arrange things in ways that correspond to kids' perspectives, considered in context rather than reduced to context-free standards.

❚❚ Applied Research

In applied consumer research in America and elsewhere, qualitative methods have been respected and widely used since after World War II, when qualitative research methods used in the war effort were thereafter turned to industry's application (Mariampolski, 2006). As unprecedented birth rates followed the end of the war, consumer research was extended to children, often using qualitative research practices that emphasized kids' views and viewpoints. Focus groups with young people, for example, were familiar tools in applied research well ahead of academics' interest in youth focus groups in the late twentieth century. There is an extensive track record in proprietary interpretive studies among young people to be found within applied consumer research. Some of the offshoots from this tradition are shared in chapters to come. (In particular *see* Chapter 5.)

It might be said that by the mid-twentieth century, consumer research had become a kind of reservoir for qualitative methods like the focus group, during the years when scholarly research (apart from participant observation) rallied around quantitative methods. When qualitative methods came into academic fashion some decades ago, tools such as the focus group were at the ready, already well-seasoned by skilled applied researchers.

I believe enhanced exchange between practitioners and scholars would be advantageous in the future, beneficial for enhancing and refining child-centered inquiry. It would be a shame if the division between theory and practice, between pragmatic and academic intentions, would forestall such exchange. Kurt Lewin once said that nothing is so practical as a good theory. The flip side of this wisdom is that nothing is so theoretically revealing as good practice. Jean Lave (1991) alluded in her work to the truth that practice leads to learning. Jerome Bruner's influences included both academic and practical fields such as education (Lutkehaus, 2008).

Know-how from applied settings need not and should not be dismissed by scholars. Applied and clinical work has been seminal to our knowledge of children, such as in the developmental theories of Freud, Erikson, and Winnicott, all deriving from therapeutic, clinical insight. Exchange of ideas between scholars and applied experts can bring ample leaps forward for child-centered research.

Such an alliance between practice and academic learning is potentially inherent in so called "action research." In action research, a practitioner such as a teacher or social services provider investigates their own practices (Goncu & Becker, 2000; Issitt & Spence, 2005; Reason & Bradbury, 2001). Valuable larger insights can be gleaned, from data gathered for practical or project evaluation purposes. The spread of information, constructs and principles can and does seep from applied to academic domains. The term "tweens," a designation for kids in late middle childhood, entered into scholarly parlance after being first coined by marketers at the McDonald's Corporation. As already mentioned, the youth focus group was refined by market researchers, and later incorporated into academic child-centered research. Fewer wheels might need to be reinvented along the way, if the path of research ranged to include both applied and academic inquiry.

Forms of child participatory action research have now been in considerable use by nongovernmental organizations. One such case originated as guidance for city design from 1994 to 1996 in a joint effort between World Wildlife Fund Italy and the UN Habitat II Conference. Children met for 3 days with adult facilitators, educators, planners and administrators to discuss issues and potential actions to be taken in urban design. The resulting ideas were embodied in a manifesto (Francis & Lorenzo, 2005). The manifesto is testament to the breadth of input children can provide even in city planning, ranging from suggestions on traffic, to use of space, to gathering spots. Their pleas dealing with available green spaces (which were expected to be reachable by public transit) included: safe and closed to car traffic; lots of natural elements; trees, bushes and high grass to hide in; many fruit trees, from which fruit could be picked; no fixed, unchangeable play structures; natural materials such as branches, twigs, leaves, mud and stones for use in building huts and hiding places; large lawns to roll on and dive upon; water for play; sloping bike paths. Finally, children counseled that such space should be commonly available, in all neighborhoods. If it were not for the proactive process that included children's participation, adult space designers would not have appreciated the crucial role of such acts as hiding in grass, rolling on lawns, picking fruit, building huts, hide-and-seek, having fun with water, and riding bikes in a place without car traffic. Urban space planning can make use of children as fully participating community members, in essence, consultants who participate in decisions affecting them.

▪▪ Ethical Matters

History plainly shows that children's inquiry deserves oversight. In the time following World War II in the United States, institutionalized children were subjected to problematic treatments in the name of medical research, including being infected with hepatitis and given a drug with side effects known to be toxic to the liver (Ross, 2006). In America, children have been, for the sake of science, injected with dysentery, inoculated with the herpes virus, and made to be pawns in trials of a polio vaccine (Grodin & Glantz, 1994). Unethical experimentation with children in post-war Britain raised parallel concerns.

The perverse practices led to condemnation upon discovery by government bodies. Regulations for research with children were enacted in 1983 by the U.S. Department of Health and Human Services, setting forth criteria required for carrying out child research. A major impact of the regulations was to emphasize adult responsibility and dominion to protect children. Adults made up the Institutional Review Boards (IRBs) that became responsible for research approval. Youth risks and well-being were entirely adult-defined. Practices used to obtain consent placed control and emphasis with adults. The crucial power giving primary permission for a study rested with parents. (Children could "assent" to a study, an announcement of agreeable participation, but this did not have equivalent status as adult "consent.") Following such stipulations, IRBs put children in the back seat in terms of understanding or having impact on decisions regarding research participation.

Since biomedicine was an important user of federal research funds when IRBs were formed, and the child-centered research movement was not in force, the adult institutions of biomedicine by default had influential thrust (with influence even outside biomedicine) on the system of review. Children's concerns about participating in research were not considered in setting up the system. Partly tracing to this omission, child-centered researchers are often critical of IRB practices—such as protocols that give the child only a minor role of assent in lieu of full consent. A consensus is forming among American child-centered scholars (and no doubt others) that rethinking of IRB routines may be in order.

There are several areas to be considered for improvement in systems of review, although my brief discussion is not meant to be exhaustive. Here is an overview of some issues unaligned with the child-centered paradigm:

- Issues remain about the assumptions under which young participants give permission for their participation.
- The manner in which children's best interests are safeguarded throughout a study is inadequate if based on rigid, fixed directives; principles ought to guide flexible decision making by the researchers in the field.
- If research is to pay honor to children's contributions, children should not be barred from receiving compensation, including monetary compensation.
- Maintaining privacy needs to be well thought through, in terms relevant to children.

The entities responsible for U.S. ethical review generally regard children in ways that echo the biomedical paradigm practiced within health care: The child is viewed as an object of the adult gaze, acted upon by events and by others, rather than as an interactively constructing subject (Christensen & Prout, 2002). The assumed passivity of the child is exemplified by the manner in which consent is usually obtained. Parents consent *on behalf of* those under 18, and the child may "assent" but is not empowered to give the deciding thumbs up or down. If children are studied in an institutional setting such as a school, camp, hospital, zoo, or care facility, adults there serve as gatekeepers who have decisive roles about children's participation. The child is subjugate to adult dominion, then, from the outset of a study, subservient to the grown-ups in charge. Adults have determining roles in setting boundaries for a research study, with a child's "assent" largely an afterthought (Epstein, 1998). Under a child-centered model of inquiry this assumption shifts; a central issue often raised in child-centered inquiry is the desirability of a child's full sign-off for the study, in keeping with the child's empowered posture in the exchange.

Taking a child-focused perspective, Barrie Thorne's (2004) ethnographic research on a school playground led her to observe that gatekeepers, who make the decisions about a study, at times lead children to be captive as objects of observation. To be sure, such a situation puts adults in an institutional role of guarding children from risk or harm, since they make the go/no go choice. Yet the judgments are based on *how adults define risk or harm* rather than based on children's definitions. Children lack self-determination, as parents or other adults are the driving force for the child to take part. The fact of the matter is that adults do not always know what will threaten (i.e. "harm") children. Shy boys or girls, for instance, may not want to take part in a group interview with strangers, but parents may arrange for such participation in a study as a presumably enriching social experience, a situation I have observed many times. Some kids might be afraid of dogs, of Halloween iconography, of sitting on Santa's lap, instances that IRB panelists may not take into account. Adults may be unaware of what participating in a study means to children. I knew a boy who volunteered for a medical trial, enthused that taking part in the trial was a way to aid research into a possible treatment for a punishing illness. When the adult researchers filled a study quota and decided not to continue the boy's participation, he was crushed with disappointment. The disappointment of *not* participating was not incorporated in the way "consent" was structured, so the boy had no protection against being cut from a study that meant so much to him. The situation did not allow for the child's meaning of participation.

The qualitative methods dealt with in this volume, such as the focus group, also can raise ethical issues that call for child consult. A research supplier once offered to children's marketers a variety of group interviews known as a "stacked" interview. In the interview, the children were interviewed around a table as a group, and then their mothers were invited to sit in the children's seats, and take part in another group discussion layered (or "stacked") upon the prior children's focus group. The problem lay in an issue of childhood privacy. Although the children did not stay to watch their mothers being interviewed, the mothers did surreptitiously watch the children (from behind a one way mirror), and were then invited to comment on what children said. Partly because researchers objected, this practice did not become an established one, since children deserve the informed consent of knowing if a parent is observing them.

It is worth adding that neither for-profit nor nonprofit investigators have a flawless ethical track record. The methods used by marketers are generally within ethical boundaries, most of the time. Conversely, medical research has been known to step over ethical lines despite being generally vigilant. Moreover, a wrong-headed purpose, pursued by a research method otherwise beyond reproach, shouldn't be used as a black eye upon a valuable method. I don't know if cigarette marketers or beer manufacturers used the methods described in this book to push their products to minors. But if they did, this simply shows that any good tool can be put to a bad or illegal purpose. A tool needs to be differentiated from its end purpose. Righteous aims can be sought with the same methods that once served corrupt or greedy motives.

In a world controlled by adults, children are often marginalized, second-class persons (and in that sense, are brethren to ethnic minorities or indigenous peoples). This impedes designing and managing research that regards each child as a full, agentic human being. It is worth emphasizing that children have secondary status in giving consent for participation. In short, ethical symmetry between adults and children does not operate (Christensen & Prout, 2002). If ethical treatment were parallel for adults and children, risks and benefits would better take into account children's meanings and expectations.

Vulnerability is a quality that ebbs and flows across social dynamics, rather than remaining fixed. Children aren't necessarily more vulnerable than adults, in all situations. A young girl wielding a gun or bomb makes nearby adults vulnerable. A boy labeled with the "special needs" distinction, ironically can expect privilege or dispensation from unwanted activities, implying a form of ironic empowerment (Frankenberg, Robinson, & Delahooke, 2000). Some of children's choices are made as an exercise of agency and independence, as children symbolically seek to counter their socially defined dependency on adults. Cigarette smoking is such an act, often done by kids out of the sight of adults and underscoring an autonomous "coming of age" for child smokers (Clark, 1999). If we are to improve public health measures against youth smoking to stave off long-term health risks, the subjective experience of young smokers is important to know. Yet because parents are permission-givers for research, this seemingly limits child informants' openness about surreptitious, private, disapproved smoking (and other parallel acts). The fixed rules of parental consent tend to assume grown-up access to what children say, in a tacit protectionism that gets applied even when kids are in the act of rebellion against protection. Adults in the United States generally assume a child's dependency and adults' superior capacity to decide. Children are in effect expected to fall in line and participate, if mom or dad grants "consent."

Children who have life-threatening brain tumors exemplify the issues involved in consent in a poignant way. Participation in a medical trial, for such children, often involves excruciating life and death choices. Yet participant observation by Myra Bluebond-Langner has shown how children facing these options are in no position, really, to exercise their own wishes, even at the end of life. Bluebond-Langner and her colleagues DeCicco and Belasco (2005) discuss the example of a 13-year-old boy whose parents were contemplating enrolling him in a clinical trial. The parents were more involved than the boy in discussions of his clinical status and options for participation. The parents persuaded the boy to take part, using language that "spun" the facts—for example, referring to the study not as a "trial" but as "treatment." Their urging led the boy to sign his assent. He signed on a consent form that omitted any space for a child's signature. (The boy put his name following his parents.) In any full sense, these actions suggest a lack of any serious room for autonomous choice by the person most directly affected, the mortally ill child. IRB procedures allocate the power to the adults, who play out their role of protector as they see fit, and the boy—whose very life was implicated—went along.

Children may find it difficult to understand all the elements of a research study (just as adults also do not always understand totally). In a genetic study, Goodenough, Kent, and Ashcroft (2003) found that procedures to be used (such as drawing blood samples) were not always comprehended well by kids. Moreover, children's understandings of procedures could be understood in ways divergent from adults' views.

A constructive suggestion for medical trials is offered by Bluebond-Langner, DeCicco, and Belasco (2005); their suggested procedure is dubbed a sort of "shuttle diplomacy," which would acknowledge the participation and agency of all the family members, child included. Shuttle diplomacy consists of: (1) a family meeting to discuss options and issues that parents are comfortable discussing in the child's presence, and (2) meetings with the parents and child held separately, to account for the child's clear agreement or disagreement. In this way, the separate voice of the child would be acknowledged and the child's intention to agree or disagree would be clarified. Even in a "shuttle diplomacy" model, the child is unlikely to exercise full power of decision; pressures weigh heavily for the parents to assert the role as responsible caretaker, while the child, to sustain the parent–child relationship (at a critical juncture), time and again goes along.

Not long ago in America, female workers who became pregnant were ordered home by their employers for protectionist reasons, through policies that denied power and agency to the expectant mother. Post women's rights movement, many women now work throughout pregnancy, a practice that has come to be taken for granted. No matter how well-intended, protectionism can hamper the empowered personhood of human beings. In medical trials or other studies of children, the young are the ones who will undergo blood tests and bone marrow extractions, be interviewed by strangers, surrender privacy, have recess under a fieldworker's scrutiny, or experience other such adjustments to their lives in the name of research. Adults should not ignore the child's stake and place in the research experience. The issue of children's full signing of consent is important under a child-centered model of inquiry, in which the personhood of the child is expressly acknowledged. If children are capable of competently speaking for themselves, and if adults are known to be less than perfect proxies who do not have omniscient access to children's subjectivity, we should consider the possibility that kids are qualified to be informed and make consent for themselves. Precedents exist, to take one example, in the study of bullying. A study by Mishna, Antle, and Regehr (2004) sought each child's full agreement as a participant, recognizing bullying as a topic in which adults may not be able to decide consent on a fully informed basis. Adults, they felt, couldn't speak accurately for what children would expect or prefer regarding inquiry into a traumatic or sensitive subject.

Ways of communicating about research participation could be devised to be more comprehensible to kids. Rather than using a written script narrating the study verbally, the description of the study procedures could involve props, pictures, and mutual conversational exchange to be sure the child understands fully. In other words, a dialogic rather than didactic approach would be relatively child-accommodating for informing a child's consent.

The child-centered approach has placed a spotlight on parallel consent processes for child and adult, and has also set off other issues. Once consent is given and a child partakes in a study, flexible handling of knotty matters may be incumbent when complex issues arise. As the study unfolds in a natural environment, protection sometimes needs to be reconciled with empowering the child. Privacy issues may be in tension with maximal participation.

From a youthful perspective, research has positive associations. Being part of a study can be an appreciated outlet of self-expression for a child, to have a say and tell one's own thoughts (Edwards & Alldred, 1999). Group studies can provide opportunities for social companionship. Yet even as children value the social opportunities afforded by research participation, some kids may still desire privacy and some kids may not. Such trade-offs and ambiguities make it unlikely that a one-size-fits-all, standardized system will optimize all circumstances. Accomplishing ethical research that does not discount children's wishes may involve a dose of astute pragmatism regarding specific situations, rather than a lock-step a priori dictation of procedures. Children's participation may need to take place amidst *situationally responsive* ethical judgments (Wiles, Charles, & Heath, 2006). Complexity calls for nuanced understanding, in an atmosphere of human respect.

Researchers living in countries that have ratified the UN Convention on the Rights of the Child have experienced an increased call for studies highlighting children's voices. In Britain and elsewhere, listening to and respecting what children have to say has broken through to have influence beyond research, on legal proceedings, delivery of services, policies, and institutions (Cocks, 2006). Once a country adopts children's Convention-proclaimed rights, terms like "child welfare" and "coercion" become laced with new meaning, coming to imply more than adult paternalism. There is a greater call to hear and catalyze children's voices about their needs. Sometimes, children may have a higher priority than total privacy, such as wanting to publicly present their ideas to City Council (Francis & Lorenzo, 2005).

Scholars have already begun to lay out alternative systems that bear on how to ethically treat children in inquiry. Harry Shier (2001) has described five levels involved to fulfill a new ethical stance toward children:

1. Children are listened to.
2. Children are supported in expressing their views.
3. Children's views are taken into account.
4. Children are involved in decision-making processes.
5. Children share power and responsibility for decision making.

Shier's five statements potentially could serve as initial ethical touchstones guiding decisions during the research process. They are the sorts of principles that could be of service, when situations crop up during research that require judgment calls, guided by ethical principles. The situational complexity of ethnographic-qualitative research with children raises a need in decision making to adjust for what emerges. Varied situations and multiple perspectives call for adaptable tools for ethical guidance. When children construe a situation differently than adults, as can certainly occur with regard to children's thinking about risk, a researcher needs flexibility in negotiating the implications. Research, as seen, should not be *on* children but *with* them and *for* them (Hood, Kelley, & Mayall, 1996). Ethical oversight fixed by administrators who operate distanced from children, without some leeway for fine-tuning by those who are close to the children affected, is harder pressed to serve children. Given the ambiguities of fieldwork with kids, rigidity needs to be replaced by the possibility to improvise and exercise professional judgment *in situ*.

Clown doctors, who perform for and with children at bedside in hospitals, have a code of ethics that guides what they do, in settings where ethical dilemmas are many. For the Canadian clown troop known as Le Rire Medicin, the ethical code sets forth boundaries around professional clown behavior. This code is not rigidly stipulated, but is seen as a resource to be judiciously applied as needed (Simonds, 1999).

The principles of clown ethics include these: The clown is to treat all children equally, without discrimination by gender, religion, race, or any other factor. The clown is to contribute to children's well-being, and not to make remarks that will be hurtful. The clown should be vigilant about a child's safety, making sure to avert harm. The clown should exercise discretion, about matters of patient identity and privacy. The clown should remain in a performing arts role, rather than becoming a confidante or friend. The clown should forego tips or pay.

Clown ethical principles grant to the clown a measure of ethical responsibility, assigning latitude to the professional who is in the field with the children. The clown, while performing, should be alert and context-sensitive in carrying out ethical goals. Professionals in regular contact with kids (child-centered researchers and clowns alike) are in a position to have a supple understanding to guide a child's ethical treatment. Vigilance about ethics is, for specialists dealing with kids, an ongoing practice of treating situations wisely, not a mindless following of a fixed dictate. The Adlers (1996) underscored this pragmatic view of ethics when they wrote, "no structure of bureaucratic regulations can substitute for the interpretive judgment of participating individuals, as children's behaviors are understood and given meaning within the context of their situations." Ethical treatment of children at its best is sensitive to children's needs even when kids strive to be self-determining. Implementation of ethical principles, to be applied while interacting with children within their environments, is worth pursuing for child-centered inquiry.

In sum, there are fundamental ways in which child-centered inquiry asks us to reconsider our taken for granted routines of ethical review and implementation. Instead of assuming adult hegemony and child subordination in matters of informed consent, a more parallel, level approach would seek the child's full consent, to be balanced in tandem with adult consent (Christensen & Prout, 2002). Once consent is given and the study is underway, there should be fluid and flexible ethical principles that specialists in child-centered inquiry can put into practice based on situational dilemmas.

An additional point concerns ethical quandaries that come up at the analysis and reporting stages. At these stages, children may have preferences that adults don't foresee. Despite the common assumption that privacy and anonymity are to be preferred in reporting findings, children sometimes want public acknowledgment. Proud of sharing their ideas, children sometimes ask that published results use a real name (not a pseudonym) alongside photos or quotations (Barker & Weller, 2003). I have had children in studies insist upon a proud, public display of their photos or drawings, which after all, is a way of giving children an amplified voice. To children, privacy can be trumped by a sense of mastery and pride. But this is difficult to fulfill if parents have been promised blanket privacy. There are also those children among the participants who want drawings or essays or other productions kept private. Other young participants may prefer that the researcher be a steward of their output, deciding what treatment to give it.

The display of children's accounts, in a publication or presented at City Hall, has been an expressed desire of children. But taking such a public step could have lasting implications. The girl whose secrets are openly featured today might find such openness troublesome once she is older. Serving children's interests about privacy merits thoughtful consideration when designing a study (Duque-Páramo & Clark, 2007).

Money can be a sticking point with IRB panels. Money is an issue touching upon issues of power and dependency in adult–child relations. To be specific, money can be a vehicle of power wielded by its possessor. At the university where I have been employed, a communicated IRB policy is that money incentives are claims of coercion upon children, and therefore it is ordinarily prohibited to compensate children monetarily. Still, incentives for kids have been common in for-profit research, such as for drug trials and market research (Rice & Broome, 2004; Wengler et al., 2002). In my experience as an applied researcher, children respond positively when receiving a monetary token of appreciation, regarding their earnings with pleasure and pride much like a beginner would regard his first paycheck, or a shopkeeper might frame and display her first cash receipt. A cash thank you has not seemed coercive, in my view, but rather an empowering token of performing a valued act of self-contribution.

Partly because IRB panelists are not necessarily selected based on direct experience with children, unfounded presumptions about children can operate, free of reflection. Unfounded presumptions about kids by elders can scuttle child-sensitive ethical aims. More training of IRB panelists about children's viewpoints regarding research participation could be of great value, for IRB panelists who are called on to review plans for children's research.

:: Youth Participation in Research

Child-centered inquiry has set out to empower and give voice to children. One way to do this has been to integrate children as a direct part of the research team. Participative inquiry invites children to move from the back seat to the front seat, and to be co-drivers of the research process. Environmental psychologist Roger Hart (2002) has praised the idea of participative inquiry for its beneficial value to both child participants and to the development of democratic community action. Hart has also identified a caveat, that participatory research should not be just a token participation in which kids parrot adult ideas; rather such inquiry should be designed to take advantage of children's able contributions, in their own voices. Hart has shown how research activities can be tools used in youth participation, for example: simulation games, role playing, brainstorming, youth clubs, letter writing, public presentations, drawings, collages, map making, youth-conducted interviews or surveys, photography and video, music, dance, puppetry, drama, festivals, parades, and competitions. In Kenya, a competition is held annually in which children reply to questions, and send in essays and drawings. The material provided by kids, dealing with environmental or development issues, is valued information by persons young and old; prizes are given to contestants and their schools (Hart, 2002).

Child participatory research has impressively wide precedents in applied research, among voluntary organizations (Alderson, 2001) and in the proactive involvement of young consumers in consumer research (Sinclair, 2004). The UN Convention on the Rights of the Child conveyed the message that children (although in many ways vulnerable) should have a role in decisions. Nongovernmental organizations such as UNICEF, Save the Children, and others took this directive seriously and involved children in action research as community researchers, in the process refining methods to improve involvement. Children in Ireland and the United Kingdom, to take two examples, have taken part in research for policy influence (Pinkerton, 2004; Tisdall & Davis, 2004).

Academic researchers have involved children as co-researchers performing a range of roles. Children, for example, have been used as peer educators who instruct their fellows or younger kids. (Note that this confers a special status on the peer educators, who take on a role of authority in disseminating knowledge to other children; in essence this is adult-like authority, conferred by the adults in charge of the study (West, 2007).) Another option has been to regard children as consultants, who are meant to comment from a vantage point reflecting their age-set. Consultation can occur during pilot "test-runs" of the study design (with child input on materials), or during the study implementation, and/or at the study's interpretive stage (Hill, 1997). Belanger and Connelly (2007) did a study with special-needs students at a French-Canadian school. Although they did not originally intend to treat the children as co-participants, they decided midstream to have the children actively participate in the study implementation, as a way to democratize the process. With the support of the children's teacher, the Canadian researchers conducted a brainstorming session to get guidance from the children about what data should be collected, and how children would signal their preference for privacy when behaviors should not be recorded. Children from time to time, over the study's course, took an active role in volunteering information, or making notes of their own about classroom life. In taking an active and substantive role however, the students did not operate on equal terms relative to Belanger or Connelly. By empowering the usually subordinate special-needs students to actively participate, the researchers made sure that their role was more than muted, but this does not imply it was totally leveled with adults.

Child-inclusive research practices can inoculate against routine social exclusions that restrict the young in decision making and counsel (Hill et al., 2004). The advantage is doubly relevant in the case of kids who are disabled, poor, or in an ethnic minority group that is systematically unrepresented in policy input. These are children for whom the channels of communication are prone to be jammed. Youth participation in inquiry is a means of compensating (at least in part) for the everyday dearth of power that filters or dampens children's free expression. Toward this empowering end, children have played roles as authors or presenters of the report.

Nevertheless, making space for children to be co-researchers on a study is complex and requires planning and concerted effort by the investigative team. The notion of children as researchers generally works against usual expectations about what children are expected to do or to attempt. A number of downsides need to be faced. First, adult community members may contest the move toward child participation if it disrupts adults' established routines. Adult gatekeepers (such as teachers, counselors, or City Council members) may prefer to contain children's involvement within adult-set bounds of convenience and/or authority. This tends to reduce children's collaboration to tokenism (West, 2007). Adults may hesitate to hand over money or supplies to children, even to children serving as co-researchers (Poole, Mizen, & Bolton, 1999). The need to train children is an additional demand.

The time to train kids may be ample; children will need to learn something about conducting the tasks they are responsible for, and about behaving ethically during research.

It should be recognized, too, that some aspects of doing research might not interest or motivate most children. Children might be satisfied to have fun and to gain attention for their views, but some might not be as motivated to "publish or perish" as research professionals would be. Young people might have little bent toward the intricacies of theoretical or interpretive analysis, which adults train (for years) to be able to do (Alderson, 2001).

In the final analysis, preparing findings or doing fieldwork that requires children to act in adult roles under adult supervision is not essentially child-centered. The adult fieldworker may not go "native" (an anthropologist's trap of identifying with those studied), but the risk may be pronounced for the child-participant to "go fieldworker" (to take the stance of adult researchers rather than aligning with ordinary kids). The point is not to placate adult investigators by having children act out an adult research enterprise, but rather to allow children to draw from *their* available repertoire in participating. In industry focus groups, recruiters of participants guard against so called "professional respondents" who enjoy the research process and seek out repeated opportunities to take part. Such respondents are thought to be prone to a role of detached commentary, rather than merely reporting experience as it is, from daily life (Greenbaum, 1998). Activities should scaffold kids to act and talk as children, not as junior versions of anthropologists or sociologists. To amplify youthful views, it is best when kids can be kids, not miniature fieldworkers.

I expect active participation of children in research projects to continue, despite some structural resistance (such as funders or gatekeepers who don't embrace the idea of children helping to plan or report studies). Such research offers an opportunity to redress power inequities, by enabling kids' active engagement. But caution is needed about expecting kids to take on mature roles in inquiry.

Action research does show that adults can be catalysts for children to actively engage, a pattern that carries over to conventional focus groups or participant observation. Every exchange with children in child-centered inquiry is part of a bona fide negotiated process that aims to respect younger people. The principle is to give children license or latitude to communicate, and not to condescend to them.

Culturally Anchored Research on Children

Considering children in sociocultural context is an important and germane aspect of child-centered research, with its emphasis on children's active participation in social worlds. All children have culture of course, so it is not necessary to study children in marginalized or exotic cultures to study processes of participation in culture. In fact, much child-centered research to date has been conducted in cultural communities where investigators and children both live.

Wherever you plan to do research, it will also be important to anchor your study in children's local cultural meanings. Local discourse, such as the conduct of talk, play, education and family activities, should be aligned with the investigative procedures. In a place where pretend play is not condoned and not common in everyday life, avoid basing an interview on pretending with props, puppets or dolls. Don't conduct a focus group in a church or classroom facility, if children are usually not given to talk freely there. Questions worth asking about the local cultural context that can inform research planning, include: What is the role of questions and answers, of imparting information, of adult treatment of children, of privacy or secret keeping? What would be the meaning of inviting youth to participate in a particular activity? What ways of communicating are on and off limits for children? A study should seek to be aligned with such aspects of social life. Or to take other examples, what would it mean to children in this social group to be asked to make a picture, to write a letter to authorities, or to participate with other children of other ethnicities or religions or gender and so on? Can one's appearance, one's parents, or one's soul be discussed without violating social norms? Forms of communicating, and topics, should be in harmony with local norms and practices.

Researchers may want to avail themselves of opportunities unique to a social group. If a village holds numerous parades in which children participate, perhaps a fieldworker could invite children to plan a parade display on the theme being researched. Debriefing on the theme could then be handled as part of planning the parade performance. If a particular food is important to establishing mutual togetherness, refreshments for a focus group might have such a menu. Natives (including kids) can and should be consulted on ideas and plans.

Community psychologists have much experience in studying diverse cultural groups, since they are motivated by the belief that social programs and policies should take into account local sociocultural realities (Hughes, Seldman, & Williams, 1993). Of course, this can be easier in principle than in practice.

Anthropologist Jeffrey Samuels (2004), upon using the method of photoelicitation or photo taking with a sample of child monks in Sri Lanka, discovered he understood less about that cultural milieu than he thought. He found that the field notes he was gathering were framed by his own, Western ideas about the monks' activities, and that he had missed aspects of the young monks' true preferences and roles. Playing cricket and other games, to his surprise, were better liked than meditation, a point he had missed among these monastic young people. He was also astonished at the many photos taken of sweeping. Snapshots of sweeping invited him to newly understand that cleansing and making the temple area attractive were central, and metaphorically significant. The use of photo taking allowed Samuels to break frame, and to reopen a new view of the monks' lives from their perspectives. (See more on photoelicitation in Chapter 6.)

Cultural systems can be elusive at times, akin to the third dimension in the science fiction classic, *Flatland*—a third dimension that those in the fictionalized two-dimensional world were touched by, but did not perceive. Culture, like *Flatland*'s third dimension, or like the water fish swim in, or the air humans breathe, profoundly impacts the activity of individuals, yet culture's substance and import can be as subtle as culture is pervasive. In orthodox developmental research, culture is made graspable through treating it as an isolatable essence: individuals get assigned a variable that indicates belonging to a certain cultural group; groups are then compared. But as a system of situated meaning and discourse, culture is not so easily pinned down and reduced. The social systems influencing and influenced by children are not, in any neat way, detachable from the child's own actions. Cultural systems pulse through and touch persons in fluid, engaged, integrated interaction. These systems are emergent, rather than reducible.

Community psychologists have criticized scholars' overdependence on fixed, comparative research approaches that focus on between-group differences in outcome variables. Hughes and DuMont (1993) commented that such methods yield little insight into the social and psychological processes that animate cultural exchange. Qualitative, holistic tools (such as focus groups, participant observation, or discourse studies) outdo reductionist approaches to facilitate learning about interactive dynamics and multivocal perspectives within a social group. It is not surprising that anthropologists' tool kits have long been outfitted with qualitative methods. Such research allows for flexible, holistic study of social processes, rather than a flattening of culture through a calculated, decontextualized reductionism.

Culturally anchored research needs to break the frame of the researcher, leaving intact the frame of the informant's vantage point. This enables children to be revealed as cultural beings and socially constituent persons amidst a particular, dynamic social world.

3 ▪▪

Observation and Participant Observation

*To see what is in front of one's nose needs a constant
struggle.*
—GEORGE ORWELL

Observation can open mature eyes to how children see things. As a university teacher, I annually assigned my upper-class child development students to observe children wishing. The students would hang out in shopping malls near a fountain or pool of water, to watch the adults and children in the mall make "wishes" (while throwing coins into the water). The rules were: Only observation could be used in the assignment: no interviewing or interacting with the wishers. The exercise asked students to classify their observations along predetermined criteria, and also to keep unstructured, open-ended field notes.

Observation alone was almost always enough to show students that wishing is laced with significance (and is not trivial, as many presupposed). Wishing, my students discerned from observing, sometimes can involve a kind of supplication-like, prayer-like posture (head down, eyes closed, attention drawn inward) in a ceremony-like ritual. Adults (who also wish) scaffold children's wish making. That is, elders guide kids in learning that wishing involves one coin at a time, no retrieval of a coin once tossed, and no divulging one's private wish. In field notes, some of the undergraduates have had the insight that wishing is an act that assumes fusion of thought and action—a kind of half-belief (Opie & Opie, 1959) in mental-physical causation that occurs among adults and children alike. Children's spoken wishes that divorced parents would reunite, or that a soldier father would come home alive from Iraq, or that the young wisher's diabetes would be cured, have been recorded by first-time observers. My students have learned by power of looking that what is quotidian and routine can hold powerful sense.

"The boy was standing at the fountain with his mother right next to him, which was interesting because he seemed to be a least fourteen. He seemed to take it very seriously. I could see his mouth move, but as if in prayer." [Student Field Note]

"A girl went through the [wishing] process, but she was speaking to her newborn brother as she was making a wish. But it wasn't her wish. I was close enough to her [to hear that] she was telling her brother she was talking to God in her head. She was about 7 or 8." [Student Field Note]

"Young girl with long curly hair comes up to [the] fountain. She has a coin in her right hand, which she holds in front of her. She says 'Mommy says I have to be good because Santa Claus is coming, please let me be good. [She] leans over and drops [the] coin in the water." [Student Field Note]

Right in the heart of a shopping mall, wishing blurs the same mental and physical lines as prayer does. Wishing converts cold hard currency (the coin tossed) toward charged purposes. Wishing amounts to an internalized beseeching, yet outer observation gave insight into its practice. A subtle and brief behavior gives off visible signs and tangible revelations about inherent meanings. Systematic observation can pick up, and help to read, these signs.

Wishing is not the only ordinary or quotidian topic which observation illuminates, as is easily demonstrated by a large body of scholarly and applied work by professional researchers. The folk psychological notion of TV watching as a passive activity (with children "glued to the set") has been overturned based on systematic observation, which has shown that youngsters viewing TV are surprisingly active, often combining TV viewing with other activities (radio listening, computer usage, magazine reading, playing with friends, eating, doing homework, and so on) (Solomon & Peters, 2005). Children's engaged watching of TV is a modulating and dynamic act, as children choose to shift attention toward and then away from television and back, in action hard to construe as passive (Anderson et al., 1986).

Contexts less familiar than shopping malls or television can be studied through observation. Observation helps to newly frame, with nuance, what is familiar, and conversely, to acquire better understanding of the foreign or little known.

Participant observation, a form of unstructured observation over time in which the researcher interacts socially with those observed, has been a methodological lynchpin for anthropologists and sociologists interested in youth's social experience, both exotic and familiar. Many valuable methodological writings have dealt with conducting participant observation, and are worth consulting despite a concentration on adults, not children (e.g., McCall & Simmons, 1969; Powdermaker, 1966; Spradley, 1979). Participant observation is perhaps the prototypical method within ethnography, a term referring to a constellation of holistic, qualitative methods ranging across participant observation, depth interviews, the use of key informants, photography and filming, and document or artifact analysis.

Early examples of participant observation with children include: Kidd's (1906) study of Kafir children, their play, and social lives, as well as Mead's (1930) widely debated study of Manus childhood. The mid-twentieth century socialization research of the Whiting team (Whiting, Child, & Lambert, 1966), while not emphasizing children's perspectives, included participant observation (called fieldwork) among its methods. Participant observation has been adapted widely for child-centered research, for it enables a situated consideration of children within a dynamic social environment, with close-at-hand scrutiny of children's roles as social actors.

For scientific investigators, observation is a primary means to knowledge. Newton's naked eye observing the fall of an apple, Lorenz seeing how graylag goslings followed after a parent or surrogate, astronomers observing the universe through high tech telescopes and robotic devices; all these investigators have built scientific knowledge through observation. Observation, especially aided by prestructured coded checklists, has been important to the traditional psychological study of infants and children; observation was influential in the work of both Piaget and Bowlby. Observation allows us to learn about children too young to express themselves verbally, including their interplay with parents or each other. Observation has led scholars to venture outside the laboratory into the naturalistic domain of children's daily lives, where they meet children on their own turf. Folklorists, in a long disciplinary tradition, have recorded children's games and lore, based on observation in children's own habitat (e.g., Opie & Opie, 1959). Environmental psychologists have used observational studies to understand how children navigate and approach settings, such as neighborhoods, cities, or parks (Spencer & Wooley, 1998). Scholars studying language practices and language socialization have derived significant learning from participant observation (Goodwin, 1990; Heath, 1983; Schieffelin & Ochs, 1986).

Close cousins related to observation are discourse analysis and conversation analysis, which have been applied in the study of language socialization and language in children, for example, by linguistic anthropologists. Discourse analysis generally takes a constructionist tact in its philosophy; natives' dynamic renditions and depictions of reality, coordinated in social communication, are a prominent subject matter. To name a worthy example, Marjorie Harness Goodwin (2006) has commandeered the study of children's language in natural settings to explore kids' cognitive and social worlds. It does not take a linguist to know (and I am not one), that this kind of closely observed study of talk is, first, an important model for the study of individuals engaged in joint cultural activity of any kind, and second, a fertile seedbed for major scholarly contributions that enlighten children's perspectives and their power relations with peers and adults.

Although academia has made considerable use of observational research to study children, the academy has no monopoly on observational research. Roger Hart, the environmental psychologist, once wrote that urban planners and designers have shown more creativity about studying children in their own environments than have psychologists (cited in Spencer & Wooley, 1998). His remark resonates with the fact that applied researchers have used observational research extensively to study children since the mid-twentieth century, and often in situations where findings are put to the test of application and follow-up evaluation. Understanding the settings in which medical care is delivered to children has been approached through observation, shedding light on children's understandings of procedures and treatments (Bernheimer, 1986). Toy makers and software developers often refine designs with the help of researchers who observe children playing with prototypes. The playthings are modified based on such observations, followed by further research. When the item is manufactured and sold, feedback accrues on the final design, in the telling form of sales and user satisfaction. Similarly, playgrounds, museums, zoos, and theme parks employ observational research to understand how children traverse and utilize each location—information that is helpful for further design. I have used observation (from a box seat looking down at the audience) to study how children behave at youth orchestra concerts for a prominent symphony orchestra, and the resulting insights were used to shape parameters for future concerts. Research on packaging may be employed to gauge if children can successfully open or use the product, or if there are safety hazards revealed when children interact with the item. When seeking a broad, inclusive and holistic view, applied research makes use of participant observation, as applied researcher Tom McGee (1997) has stated, "to get a more complete picture of the child's life and how specific products and services fit in."

Observation, then, is a fundamental tool—or perhaps better said, a roomy kit of multiple tools—for learning about children's worlds. This chapter showcases how two common observational variations are useful and enlightening in child-centered qualitative inquiry. Neither form of observing children is necessarily child-centered as such, since they can be used with adults or other analytic frameworks. But used with child-centered investigational goals, both forms ably focus on children's experiences, inasmuch as observation provides a direct view of children in action.

First, I will consider the method of *participant observation* in anthropology, sociology and education, a tool used regularly for learning about children's worlds and social encounters. Later, I will return to nonparticipant forms of *observation* in which the human researcher (such as one of my students studying wishing) doesn't interact in a direct, sustained way with the persons studied. As a variant of nonparticipant observation, I will consider the intriguing promise of observational approaches that are assisted by technological or electronic ways of recording behavior (such as video recording, audio recording, or experiential sampling using pagers).

▪▪ Participant Observation

It bears emphasis: Participant observation has assets that dovetail well with the goals of child-centered qualitative research. Features central to participant observation are its naturalism, its sensitivity to the role of context, and its emphasis on process rather than static views of behavior (Goodwin & Goodwin, 1996). Exemplifying this sensitivity to process, anthropologist Donna Lanclos (2003) carried out participant observation on Belfast playgrounds, watching, learning, and also participating in the folklore of children such as games, songs, and jokes. Her work grounded children's lore within the larger context of their everyday lives. Lanclos' focus was not on folklore as fixed artifacts, but on the process by which individuals take part in socially shared (and negotiated) folklore activities. Lanclos observed that the very social identities of children were not fixed, but flexed and morphed across varied social contexts.

Similarly, Nobutaka Kamei (2005) studied the children of Baka hunter-gatherers in Central Africa's Congo basin. Kamei regarded children's play among the Baka as situated amidst modernizing cultivation, that is, within an era of cultural change. Kamei observed youngsters' play activities as including both modernity-oriented and tradition-oriented elements. But these were highly dynamic components, pliable rather than fixed. Children made use of these varying elements in shared activities that modulated as children transmitted, acquired, or extracted play elements in an active, child-empowered, system.

The advantageous aspects of participant observation go further than this sort of sensitivity to process. Participant observation engages the researcher with the life experiences of a child in a manner that invites empathy and openness on the part of the investigator. Unlike orthodox methods of developmental research such as experiments, the participant observer innovates and navigates to give voice to children's viewpoints. More malleable than a questionnaire, the researcher essentially acts as the instrument of research, by flexibly interacting with the children and others. Many of the classic monographs of child-centered fieldwork, such as those by Bluebond-Langner (1978), Briggs (1998), Corsaro (2003), Fine (1987), and Thorne (1994), can be read as treatises on successfully making trustworthy, empowering connections with children. Adult–child alliances of such access and trust would not have been possible, without the fieldworkers' facile navigation and socially responsive interaction.

Participant observation is intended to avoid a rush to judgment, instead entailing (in its prototypical use) prolonged involvement in the field, and a discovery process that evolves rather than calcifies. Field entry can be paced providing for children to gradually acclimate to the researcher, and to build confidence for making contacts—rather than the researcher initiating all contacts (Woodgate, 2001). Emergent problems and issues can be explored opportunistically in participant observation. In child-centered research, many times the research issues involve children's instantiations of meaning. Over the course of the project, as insight into children's meanings crystallizes, elders' preconceptions may convert to reflect children's conceptions.

Lanclos (2003), in her work in Belfast, has exemplified the empathic, open-minded, inductive path of a child-centered participant observer.

She caught on to the unexpected fact that sectarianism was little mentioned by the Northern Irish children, in contrast to the widespread emphasis on sectarianism in much prior publishing about children in Northern Ireland. She found that gender was a more salient categorization actively used by children than being Catholic or Protestant. In this finding, her predilections going into the field were by and by catapulted.

Given the holistic, unstructured, and interactive nature of participant observation, it goes without saying that the fieldworker should be someone with the proclivity to enter into a socially intricate and ambiguous undertaking. Good participant observers have a knack for openness, tentativeness, and breadth of insight. Good fieldworkers are socially intelligent and also reflexive about social interaction. They are persistent and vigilant, for they need to observe carefully and relentlessly. Just as steadily, they need to document through written field notes even the most routine events.

Given that everyday life is ceaseless and pervasive, the fieldwork process can be as tedious as it is fascinating. A case in point: Amanda Lewis' (2003) school-based study of race, involving daily fieldwork as well as interviews with families, plus an expected contribution of necessary school labor (negotiated as a duty exchanged for the privilege of site entry).

> I was in the schools every day doing participant observation and scheduling interviews in the evenings with parents from all the schools. I had to schedule those interviews so they did not conflict with after-school events parents or I (or both of us) planned to attend. In addition I was spending several hours most evenings typing up field notes … People were regularly amazed that I did all I did [to help] in the school without 'getting paid' for it [per the agreement made to gain entry to the school].

An extended term of observing and recording can be a marathon testing a researcher's stamina and persistence. Fieldworkers vary in how they go about recording the detailed information they observe. Some, like Amanda Lewis, write field notes after observing, based on recall of events. Others attempt to take notes in the field, a procedure that does not seem to go unnoticed by children. Ashley Maynard always carried a notebook during her study of Zinacantec Maya kids, in Mexico (Maynard & Greenfield, 2005). Adults joked about her notebook, but seemed acclimated to it. Children were very interested in what she wrote in the notebook, and often asked her to read it aloud to them. An issue involved in taking notes in the field is that notes entail a literacy skill, making note-taking a sign of mature functioning and a skill that grown-ups teach to kids. In Corsaro's work in an Italian kindergarten, the children practiced printing words in his field notebook, and made judgments about one another's prowess at writing words there (Corsaro & Molinari, 2000). Kids also suggested information that they thought that Corsaro should record. Sometimes, they drew pictures in his notebook. The fieldworker is advised to consider how note-taking in the field will likely inflect the tone of the researcher–child relationship, and if that inflection is appropriate in a given project and setting.

When I first studied participant observation in two graduate school classes, there is no doubt that my craft of observing and taking notes became better with practice, and it has improved further since then. I came to record more overall, in more detail, as I became more experienced. The most experienced, master fieldworkers etch out their fieldnotes with finesse. Here is a fine-lined account excerpted from Bill Corsaro's fieldnotes from an Italian preschool class (Corsaro & Molinari, 2000). This circumstance occurred not long after he entered the field. Thorough fieldwork requires this sort of systematic effort sustained across the course of a study.

Renato, Angelo, Mario, and Dario [all children] are playing with plastic, grooved building materials. They hand me some of the materials and ask if I can get them apart. I accept this task willingly, but soon realize that the pieces are stuck together much tighter than I realized. In fact, I first push with all my might with no success. One of the teachers, Giovanna, now walks by, laughs, and says the children have found a practical use for me. I now realize that many of the pieces have probably been stuck together for a long time. Just about the time I am about ready to give up, I try holding one piece on the edge of the table with the other hanging over the edge. I push hard and the pieces pop apart. Angelo and Renato yell: 'Bravo Bill!' and then immediately hand me several more pieces. I easily separate the first two with my inventive method, but then I run into trouble again as several pieces will just not budge. Meanwhile the boys are copying my method with some success, so I keep at it. I then notice that Angelo and Mario are gathering up all the separated pieces and are putting them back in the box. They tell several other children that

Bill got them apart, but they are not to play with them. I wonder about this. Are they afraid that they will get stuck back together again? In any case I continue working on what has become an unpleasant task until to my relief I hear Giovanna say it is time to clean up the room.

Fieldwork's steady diet of fieldnote recording, complete with unanswered questions about children's thoughts, is a ripe opportunity for a kind of reflexivity about the research process. For in writing about events, fieldworkers are occasioned to ponder the role played by themselves, as personalities or presences amidst the social context being investigated. Corsaro's self-reflection is implicit to his account of separating materials for the children, where he plays the role of a problem solver when the children so request. He is simultaneously a part of the children's social group, some of whom cheer him on, some imitate his solution, and some stow away the materials he has fixed. In other instances a fieldworker may have overstepped the bounds of appropriate behavior, as far as children were concerned, eliciting resistance, silence, or conflict. Reflection on such difficulties is often enlightening, revealing of implicit rules of youthful social interaction that, unwittingly, the researcher violated (Davis, 1998). A mishap of this sort can act as a kind of unintentional, ad hoc, social psychology case study, revealing patterns of expected social behavior. Competent fieldworkers frequently reflect on their role in the child–adult power structure, anticipating issues that might arise and planning for the role they will play in the future.

The following excerpt, from field notes kept by John Davis, describes events when entering fieldwork at a Scottish school for children with multiple disabilities (Davis, Watson & Cunningham-Burley, 2000). As Davis reflected on his difficulties communicating with the children, he himself felt disabled as he sought to live up to his research goals. This sort of reflexivity can help a researcher to assess the status of his social relatedness, or in other instances perhaps to brainstorm about fresh fieldwork strategies.

After a very friendly meeting with the head teacher, I was thrown in at the deep end. I was introduced to the staff in the classroom and left to explain to them what I was doing there. The senior teacher and speech therapist introduced me to the children who were practicing their parts in the forthcoming school play. Unfortunately, I could neither understand the words of the children who spoke to me nor communicate with those children who did not employ the spoken word as a means of communication. This resulted in me relying on the staff to explain what the children said or signed. I found my admission into the school quite a frightening experience. On a personal basis I didn't have a clue how I was expected to behave by staff and children and I found it extremely difficult to understand if the children were happy with my presence in their class. This led to a lot of standing around, getting in the way of children and staff, until my role in the class developed. This uncomfortable experience was confounded by my academic related fear that I would be unable to fulfill the requirements of my post—to develop interactions with disabled children in order to understand their social worlds.

Participant Observers in Lilliput: Dealing with Adult–Child Issues

Adults have carried out remarkable fieldwork even when remaining in adult-associated roles. Good examples are Patricia and Peter Adler (1996) who retained their married, parental roles, while studying the peer networks and interactions of their own children's social circles. The parent-researcher approach allowed them ready access into the varied social environments of their son and daughter, who were students in upper elementary school. In a sense, the Adlers utilized the ultimate convenience sample; they observed their own and other children at home (where they welcomed all comers among their children's friends), and at school events, during carpool, at field trips, or in youth sports. The approach converted into informants virtually everyone encountered in the Adler children's lives. Revelations about the youngest Adlers popped up in the older Adlers' published writings. In an exchange illustrating that both generations of Adlers tacitly acknowledged the dual-role arrangement, Patricia Adler probed her daughter for information on a dance. When her probing was resisted, Patricia Adler explained "I'm not asking as your mother anymore. I want to know as a sociologist." (Her daughter was then forthcoming.) Patricia and Peter Adlers' project, whether as parents or as sociologists, stayed on an adult level: the adults requesting information were the same adults who enacted discipline and other forms of power. The fused roles in essence left intact the expected power dominion of the adults. (Certainly, it also complicated their parental role with trade-offs and ethical strains, when weighing between responsibilities to parenthood and to research.)

Role-fused participation is increasingly common in educational research. As part of a trend toward action research in classrooms, teachers not only teach but double as researchers. A particularly prominent example of teacher-researcher role fusion lies in the work of Vivian Paley (1990; 1993). Paley made an art of teaching kindergarten, and at the same time, harvested observations from her classroom.

I have used parent-researchers in my own research, recruiting adults with research experience to keep field notes about their own children, with regard to particular rituals (Santa, the Easter Bunny, and the Tooth Fairy) (Clark, 1995). I have also enlisted parents without research experience to keep field notes on their own child's chronic illness (Clark 2003). Having information from a parent's standpoint can be very valuable as a complement to child-focused field notes or interviews. Child rearing forms a facet of children's experience, worth being seen from the vantage point of the main caretaker. All the same, it is often forgotten that child rearing coexists with parent rearing, such as when: children serve as sounding boards for parents, help with household duties, provide amusement to parents, serve as translators to immigrant parents, influence consumption, explain an innovation of their generation, and otherwise socialize their parents (Boocock & Scott, 2005). Parent rearing is by and large too little underinvestigated, perhaps because adults generally shape research agendas, and tend to think of themselves as care dispensing rather than cared for.

Adult roles in research do not obviate the value of (or the need for) inquiry explicitly intended to explore children's worlds and vantage points. Research done with, rather than on, children, is essential and valuable. But importantly, this sort of research assumes a relative leveling of roles in interaction, rather than a total hierarchy based on power. If adults doing fieldwork stay in strictly adult roles, this sets in motion a power inequity between the child and the ascendant, adult researcher. Children stand to be intimidated by adults, even by having to look up at those very tall humans (Holmes, 1998). Children, in reaction to being subject to institutional adult domination, generally carve out opportunities to resist adult control. Child-centered research seeks to circumvent the hazards of stacked power relations between elders and children (as much as possible) to better privilege children's views (Epstein, 1998; Mandell, 1988).

Dilemmas are certainly involved. Generally, the problem of entrenched child subordination to adults can hamper a fieldworker's attempt to skirt power differences. A relevant case occurred during the reporting phase of a child-centered study (Barker & Weller, 2003). Adults calling into a radio program in which children reported on a child-participatory project seized control of the discussion (away from the children) and used diminutive and dismissive terms ("kiddies") for the child guests. This adult domination was not the outcome the researcher had intended.

In much of daily American life, elders interact with children while unconsciously suspending or modifying the golden rule. Rather than treating kids as they would want to be treated, a different sort of discourse is dispensed—one that can be dismissive, punitive or coercive (Fine & Sandstrom, 1988; Thorne, 1994). At certain times adults expect children to be standard bearers for behavior adults themselves do not keep to, such as encouraging children in Northern Ireland to adhere to complete nonviolence (Lanclos, 2003). A double standard often applies, by which children are expected to be more innocent, wholesome and untainted than adults. Although grown-ups were once children, then, adult-serving notions lead to off-kilter perceptions of kids (Fine, 1987). Adult researchers, to some extent, straddle a generational breach in which elders have a stake in how children's intentions are viewed. Child-centered research aims to lift the generational blinders and preconceptions.

Child-centered fieldwork proceeds by leaving intact the child's role, while carving out a distinctly exceptional, softened role for the grown researcher. The latter role is distinctive in, first, its degree of child-friendliness, and second, its lack of ascendancy or control over children. Bill Corsaro (2003), called "Big Bill" by the Italian kindergartners he studied, overcame his superior size to forge trusted friendships with his child informants. Whereas the Adlers studied their children's peer networks as adults with access to the young peoples' peer system, Corsaro studied the peer relationships of kindergarteners by becoming *part* of their network, a friend (albeit a "big" one) with whom kids shared experiences. I would judge from his results that Corsaro came as close to an insider's view as he could, his adulthood notwithstanding.

To achieve such friend-like status, fieldworkers generally react to children without interfering or intervening, as adults often usually might do. The road is not always smooth. Hsueh-Yin Ting (1998), in a study of a multicultural preschool classroom, followed Corsaro's method of reducing perceived authority (not telling children what to do) and seeking a friend-like role. The event described below took place during her first week of participant observation, and in an essay written in hindsight, she generously described her dilemma. N (Ting's code-name for one of the boys) resented having an observer in the room, according to the teacher.

> I am observing next to the block center. N comes up to me and punches me twice in the shoulder. His little fists do not hurt me. Not knowing what he means by hitting me, I react with a smile, trying to show him my friendliness. He comes up and punches me again. Instead of stopping him like a teacher, I decide to react as a peer might. I ask, 'Why did you hit me? I don't like that.' He says, 'I hate you.' I ask 'Why?' He replies, 'I don't know, I just hate you.' M (girl) walks by. He hugs her and says, 'I don't hate you (to M), but I hate you (pointing to me). He then moves a few steps away and shouts to the whole room, 'I hate that woman over there!' Feeling hurt and embarrassed, I don't know how to react. He finally leaves when the teacher calls, "N!"

Not only children resist initially. Attempting to level the power between children and themselves, fieldworkers often find that there are adult gatekeepers who undermine that aim, and who expect the adult researcher to fully act her age. In a school setting, there can be substantial pressure for a fieldworker to take on (adult) teacher-like roles, such as checking papers or supervising recess or dealing with parents. Mature duties can make it harder to achieve "friend-like" stature in children's eyes. Such binds are difficult to escape entirely, making it hard to imagine that an adult can fully pass as a kid, in any real sense. The crux, however, is to try for the most child-friendly posture possible. The pressure to assert adult power over children needs to be continually struggled with and thwarted, as is feasible.

Extreme advocates of child-focused fieldwork have argued for the "least-adult" approach (Mandell, 1988)—a posture in which the adult researcher takes on a strictly child-mirroring role, steering clear of any adult-inscribing behaviors whatsoever. To accomplish this totally least-adult stance, the researcher must not only turn down adult-like roles suggested by grown-ups, but must spurn adult-like requests made by the children (such as Corsaro fixing children's stuck blocks). Fixing toys, reading stories, pushing children on swings, tying shoes, letting kids sit on laps, lifting children up for a higher view, and other grown-up pretensions would be off limits, rejected because of adult-like associations. The least-adult role provides a kind of ideal type exemplifying the need to accomplish or approximate a child-compatible approach, but the purist least-adult role can be difficult to achieve in practice. Mandell, who entered a preschool class of 2- to 4-year-olds with a committed intent to be least-adult, found that even the children could persist in placing pressure on her to be adult-like (Mandell, 1998).

> Mac, David and Daniel were lifting plastic and metal boxes up. Mac was giving the orders to lift the cartons. The others were complying and talking about it. Mac says to me, 'Nancy can you lift these up?' I replied, 'They are heavy.' Mac said, 'You can lift them up, you're a teacher.' I responded, 'No I'm not a teacher.' Mac says nothing but looks puzzled. I go on. 'I just watch here, I'm not a teacher. Teachers come here every day, and I don't.' Mac listens carefully and then asks, 'Well can you lift these up?' I respond 'sure' and hand him the boxes.

One of the solid accomplishments of child-centered participant observation has been a truly professional standard of reflexivity about issues of adult–child power, a commitment to thoughtfully manage such issues in approaching children. An emerging consensus among child-centered researchers is essentially a compromise: to make a flexible alloy of "child" and "adult" orientations, tailored to suit the social context and research goals of a project. Such a compromise generally operates within the parameters of the role Gary Alan Fine (1987) has called the "friend" role—an adult, but an unusually friend-like adult, without the usual trappings of power. The "friend" is a hybrid role—an observer, yet one who is also a friendly adult who genuinely honors (and tries to back) children's practices. In the "friend" role, the researcher tries to fit into children's social frameworks by softening adult presumptions and resisting taking on power-infused adult privileges. Moreover, such a fieldworker wisely knows that children's meanings do not, and will not, map neatly onto adult meanings; she expects to recalibrate her frame of reference to grasp kids' formulations. Child-centered participant observation requires setting aside adult-given signifying structures, as the fieldworker enters into children's individual and shared systems of significance. The striving to gain understanding of things children take in stride can bring a sense of humility. Bill Corsaro, who was perceived by his Italian preschool informants as "dumb" because of his poor Italian, found that his ineptness helped to build a connection with children who shared the stumbling process of learning (Corsaro & Molinari, 2000). A researcher's inadequacies in children's eyes can be an asset for inviting exchange during explanations, and can help to soften authority and power, as in the following baseball related example from Gary Alan Fine (1987). In fieldwork in Little League, a lack of baseball prowess endeared children to Fine. Such times give a fieldworker no options but to drop adult conceit.

> An intrasquad game was organized by the coach of the Angels. Since they did not have the necessary number of players, I was asked to play center field. In the field only one ball was hit toward me and fortunately was sufficiently far from where I was standing that I didn't need to be embarrassed about not catching it, and actually made a fairly decent throw to hold the batter to a double. At bat I struck out my first time up, grounded out in my second time up, becoming known as an "easy out." Finally in my third at bat, I singled. … I was teased by the players for my lack of playing skills and had to make excuses to the coach. … [The coach said] 'Do you want to pitch batting practice?' [I said] 'I don't know if my arm is ready for it.' …My lack of skills … may have had a beneficial impact in that I was treated as more of an equal and not as a baseball expert.

There are other patterns that recur in child-centered fieldwork. Kids, in settings where they are subject to adult control, often act to protect a degree of privacy and to resist authority, including committing acts that adults wouldn't approve. To maintain an alliance with the children, child-centered fieldworkers are compelled to acquiesce when children do such things. This might include petty stealing, making prank phone calls, telling dirty jokes, ignoring directives from an adult, or disobeying a nursery school rule by urinating outdoors, all actions for which child-centered researchers have expressed no disapproval. To fortify the alliance with children, child-centered researchers avoid treading on children's interests by pulling rank (except in a situation that threatens safety). Barrie Thorne (1994), during fieldwork in an elementary school, at first felt "like a big Alice or Gulliver trying to fit into a scaled-down world," and so attempted to minimize her generational privileges. Taking notes at recess, she had to reassure kids repeatedly that she was not "taking down names" and that her writings wouldn't be used as evidence against rule-violators. Because of similar concerns, Gary Alan Fine declined to take the role of umpire in his fieldwork on youth baseball, out of concern that this would undermine his child-responsive rapport (Fine & Sandstrom, 1988).

Ideally, over time children lose track of the researcher's seniority, and come to regard him, at least in some respects, as integrated into their own circle. This process seems to be catalyzed when the researcher is able to enter into shared play or folk activities, the sorts of activities ripe with social negotiation and shared construction of meaning. Indeed, participant observation studies by Lanclos (2003), Lewis (2003), Thorne (1994), and others have showcased the school playground setting expressly, where play and folk activities (songs, rhymes, jokes, games) are windows into social dynamics. Being on a playground is an advantage for child-centered fieldwork. Playful folk pastimes (joke-telling, games involving rhymes, etc.) set into action a dialogical interplay, which helps to foster the process of exchange between the fieldworker and the children. The liminality of play serves to invert and level power distinctions. Play puts the researcher on kids' turf, in a zone of kid expertise. As Donna Lanclos (2003) has expressed it, "Folklore is a way to connect with kids in a nonhierarchical fashion that allows their concerns to come through, not just those of the adults around them."

Child-centered fieldworkers, through reflexivity, judge the goodness of fit or connection that evolves between themselves and the children. What might indicate a good fit? Inclusion of the adult researcher in child-only activities would be a good indication of rapport (Christensen, 2004). Being told secrets, and being trusted to keep them, would be another. As a sign of her close connection with child informants, Myra Bluebond-Langner (1978) had children with leukemia entrust her with the secret that their illness was fatal, even though adult caretakers assumed the children had been kept from this knowledge. Having children regard the fieldworker as a trustworthy companion during antisocial or dubious behaviors (fart jokes, rule violations, etc.) is a desirable indicator as well. Being given an affectionate nickname, or being referred to with a less formal name than other adults, is a promising indication. Conversely, what are signs that the researcher's relationship with children has elements of adult-associated disparity? Here are a few: If the children are doing an activity, such as passing out candy, and the fieldworker is excluded (Corsaro & Molinari, 2000). When passing on the school stairwell, if a child is deferential and stops to let the adult pass first, this is a way of letting rank prevail (Holmes, 1998). If the fieldworker, in collecting information from students, overhears the students refer to their answers as "school work," this could be a warning sign that an authoritative stance is taking hold, that the fieldworker is a giver of assignments akin to teachers. No one warning sign matters in isolation, but rank sensitive signals, if they persist across situations, should trigger reflection.

Linguistic anthropologist Charles Briggs (1986) has written about the sociolinguistic dimensions of the ethnographic interview. Although Briggs did not particularly have children in mind, his notions about the interview are highly relevant to fieldwork with children. Briggs, like Elliott Mishler (1986), argued that communicative strategies in research should draw from the native practices of the group under study. In other words, information gathered in research should aim to use a medium that typifies how information is exchanged in ordinary social life between insiders. Forms of discourse used by kids with one another indeed stand ready for adaptation. In fieldwork at a camp for children with asthma, my research assistant Holly Blackford borrowed from a children's folklore practice to gather information. Cootie catchers (also known as "scrunchers" or "fortune tellers") are folded paper devices used playfully by American children, with questions written on the folds of paper. Blackford adapted the cootie catcher device by writing questions on each "catcher" panel that would help to probe background information about the girls for whom she was counselor. The cootie catchers were brought out the first day of camp and distributed when the girls were becoming mutually acquainted, a fun tool for both the research inquiry and the newly arrived campers. The game-like cootie catchers set the right tone, by borrowing from a child-relevant form of exchanging information. (Future chapters will discuss many adaptations of children's sociolinguistic practices, ripe for research use.) Folk practices vary from culture to culture, of course, but the broad principle travels well—collecting information from children in a way that draws from culturally prevailing forms of child discourse is fruitful.

Schools are places where American youth try to retreat from control as they cordon off or shield themselves from the constraining push of adult authority. Adult authority can be pervasive, extending in some cases to electronic scanning of backpacks (upon school entry) to the need for a hall pass to visit the rest room. Inside school, you could ask any principal or teacher what goes on that offends authority. Text messaging is a rampant modern-day version of note passing. Playing hooky has been made to seem all the more attractive, thanks to movie depictions. Peers teach peers song parodies that target teachers or school. Bronner (1988) reports one such lyric: "Mine eyes have seen the glory of the burning of the school, we have tortured every teacher and have broken every rule."

A great deal of investigation on education has stayed on the adult side of the generational divide: using elders' interpretations and goals to analyze schooling as adults construe it. If we want to understand the full dynamics by which kids embrace or resist elements of school, child-centered fieldwork could expand our access to the flip side, the resistance mode occupied by school-captive children. Child-centered research, by following children on the path they carve out, can better illuminate children's own frameworks, involvement, reactions, and adaptations. But to do so, the methods employed need to be youth-relevant, not authority-borrowed.

Like educators, marketers too want to communicate effectively with children; for this, marketers have long relied heavily on child-centered research. The communicative process of advertising is presumed by practitioners to be a mutual act between adults and children, a dialogical process (Wells, 1965). Mapping the process requires a window into youthful responses, for the young are active participants and can put up barriers, or conversely, advocate an action. This interactive system has been presumed to operate behind many a memorable commercial or first-run product.

Dialogical give and take is at work in public and private education, too. But pedagogical artifacts (textbooks, instructional films, etc.) are not subject to the degree of child-centered inquiry that is used to study how TV programs or commercials communicate. The relative dearth of inquiry into the child side of the school experience relates to a tradition of intense and salient power relations in classrooms. At school, adults in effect "look down" at children as they seek to instruct and remediate children's immaturity (Holmes, 1998). School is carried out upon children rather than with children.

As more child-centered fieldworkers do studies in classrooms, new ways of looking at the school experience are bound to arise. Child-centered researchers, who take a child-friendly stance to better draw out children's subjectivity, can be expected to bring new child-relevant insight into educational issues, even into kids' topsy-turvy urges to resist or repel authority. Education, despite adult power, is a dialogical process that needs to be seen from a youthful, as well as educator, angle.

Participant Observation: Issues of Gender, Ethnicity, and Culture

Age or generation is not the only factor operating within the social worlds of children. Gender and ethnicity are also prominent, contributing facets of children's complex experiences.

Some researchers believe that women, in line with their smaller stature, may have an advantage as child-centered researchers (Holmes, 1998). Whether or not that is true is in doubt: "Big Bill" Corsaro and Gary Alan Fine, among other male counterexamples, have been very successful child-centered researchers. Still, gender may still play a part in fieldwork. To take one example, Thorne (1994) acknowledged that she felt closer to the girls she studied than the boys. Child-centered fieldworkers would do well to reflect about the impact of their gender on their emerging role and field relationships. Do American children seek comfort from a female fieldworker, but expect a male fieldworker to dispense discipline? Are male fieldworkers more fluent in rough and tumble play (Holmes, 1998)? Such questions, which I am not the first to raise, pose methodological issues worthy of attention.

Ethnicity is another facet of social dynamics that can impinge upon child-centered fieldwork. To be sure, child-centered researchers have shown that crossing national or ethnic lines is viable, even in the case where an adult is not completely fluent in the language used locally (such as "Big Bill" Corsaro in Italy). Nevertheless, interpreting behavior, not just being accepted in the field, is fieldwork's aim. Reckoning what children do through a mature generational lens, and at the same time through an unfamiliar ethnic or cultural lens, is demanding. Fathoming a child's unknown world as it operates within a strange culture or ethnicity is no simple matter. A risk cannot be dismissed that children may be misconstrued (Holmes, 1998). This may be why David Lancy (1993), in his discussion of rules of thumb for judging a good ethnographer, includes in the list learning the language, as well as successfully capturing native meanings. The following field note about a multicultural setting where English was the children's native language, but not the researcher's, shows how difficult it can be to comprehend children while interacting with them. Very young children still perfecting the phonological aspects of their native tongue may use pronunciations that are nonstandard and hard to decode on first hearing (even for a native), adding to the challenge of a fieldworker not fluent in their language (Ting, 1998).

> I found at times that doing research in English rather than my native language made it difficult to pick up all that children were saying. I also found that nuances of nonverbal communication made it difficult to record interactions in narrative fieldnotes ... [With video and audio recordings] I could listen to children's

conversations repeatedly, and gain understandings that initially eluded me.

Children, of course, are constituents of their culture's body of meanings. Children actively partake in and gain sway over meaning systems. As part of a culture's intricately connected whole, children intrinsically influence collective processes, even as they derive social knowledge. Veteran fieldworkers or natives of a particular community, who already understand particulars of a cultural system, may have an edge in studying how children participate, because they understand the cultural system in which the intricacies of exchange occur and in which children operate. Peggy Miller (1996), who has worked with collaborators to study children in an array of ethnic and social class contexts, has investigated personal storytelling practices by and around young children, by means of researchers taking a participatory role in a family and its community. She assigned her researchers to communities that culturally mirrored their own. The researcher who studied middle-class Chinese families in Taipei was born and raised in that city. The researcher who studied a middle-class community in Chicago, was raised in a similar community in another state. Miller thereby trusted these natives of each community to negotiate a role with the family that was culturally appropriate. Indeed, the two fieldworkers just mentioned negotiated roles with the families in distinctive ways. The American middle-class researcher evolved a role as a family friend, one who was on a first name basis with everyone in the family. Fictive kin status was granted to the Chinese researcher, whom children addressed as "Aunty," and who shared in adult privileges, such as hearing about children's past transgressions.

Jean Briggs (1998), author of an ethnographic case study of an Inuit 3-year old, did this research when she was already an experienced fieldworker who had done ample prior ethnography among the Inuit. Briggs recalled that early in her years among the Inuit, she was sometimes corrected and treated like a child by native adults because of her inexpert language and cultural incompetence. (She found this treatment gave her an affinity for children, who faced similar treatment as she did.)

During her early fieldwork, Briggs' (2008) status as nonnative many times led young persons to take advantage of her by luring her into play, in a role befitting an outsider.

Some teenagers had asked me to play Evil Spirit. This was a game in which one person—usually a child—pretended to be a *tunraq*, an Evil Spirit. The tunraq grimaced, distorted his or her body motions, and, with clawed hands, approached other children, who laughed excitedly and fled. Children and teenagers often begged me to play the tunraq role because, as a strange-looking outsider, I made a very convincing Evil Spirit. Usually I complied, on condition that we play outdoors, so that their panicky flight wouldn't overturn my oil lamp. This time, however, it was night and we were playing indoors ... the teens urged me to direct my frightening behavior toward Sauli, 'because he is easily scared.' I foolishly did so. Sauli, predictably, dove behind his companions ... crying out 'Mother! Mother!' His friends laughed uproariously ... I felt sorry for Sauli and called a halt—but it was already too late. ... The next day ... Sauli returned from hunting and complained that there was a tunraq in his belly, and that I had stolen his soul. ... [The elders] moved him away from my vicinity ... and told me not to go near him ... They eventually sent him to another community and told him not to come back until he felt better. ... Years later, Sauli still avoided speaking to me.

Despite such early missteps, Briggs gathered experience that made her a seasoned and astute interactant. With more experience under her belt, she undertook the study of an Inuit toddler. Her story reminds us that a relatively new participant observer who is a stranger in a strange land has significant challenges and risks. I think this would be especially true if the observer had never before done fieldwork among young children, and intended to study them in an unfamiliar society.

As roles evolve in fieldwork, especially relating to children, these roles can trace out the fluid connections and social webbing between children and adults, between insiders and outsiders, between the institutionally powerful and powerless, and between child siblings or peers. Navigating intricate systems of social relatedness is knotty—but at the same time richly revealing—perhaps in ways that a naïve adult outsider initially might not appreciate. Initially crossing major cultural boundaries, as a novice, raises a very high bar for a beginning fieldworker who also plans to do generation-crossing child-centered inquiry. The Gordian knot lies in the need to stretch across the age barrier, without the elasticity of cultural familiarity. The irony is that it likely demands more than a beginner's level of cultural adeptness to initiate study of the nuances of how children navigate culture.

‖ Nonparticipant Observation

As well suited as participant observation is to the goals of child-centered research, it would be a shame if that method came to monopolize the field and evolved into a reigning orthodoxy. Other methods of observation have much to offer, as do group and individual interviews. Nonparticipant, direct observation of children has proven merit, within and beyond academia.

Investigating children using human observers has long roots, tracing to such fine work as Barker and Wright's (1951) well-known study *One Boy's Day*, a round the clock account of a single child, made possible by rotating adult observers who kept in the background, and reported the lad's moment by moment behavior (on April 26, 1949) in words. The closely timed surveillance starting at 7:00 a.m., when the boy's mother said "Raymond, wake up." And less than a minute later, "Son, are you going to school today?" The record of observation proceeds minute by minute, over 400 pages of printed text, and ends at 8:32 p.m.. Raymond was in bed at 8:32, but showed that he was eavesdropping on adults' conversation, by audibly correcting his mother's statement about the timing of an illness: "Raymond set all of us right by calling from his bed that he got sick the night before the movie."

Barker and Wright's record reflected an ambitious attempt to witness and completely annotate Raymond's observable behavior, movements, and vocalizations. On the spot inferences about motives or emotions were logged. Observations were dictated into an audio recorder immediately after, and later transcribed under the supervision of the observer. In contrast to participant observation and the attention paid to the fieldworker's relationship with a child, Barker and Wright intentionally precluded any interpersonal relationship between each observer and the boy, by involving multiple observers taking turns.

At the time of Barker and Wright's classic study, tape recorders were very large contraptions. There was no such thing as voice recognition software. Room-size computers were in their initial introduction, for institutional use only. Options for recording or sorting observational records were strictly labor intensive. Imagine if Barker and Wright had access to today's recording and computational devices. Serviceable hardware devices have become small, adept, affordable, and capable of data management and easy correction. A modern-day Barker and Wright could issue their observers handheld computers or microcassette recorders, and could take advantage of electronic technology to not only transcribe, but to also sort and locate observations. Were Barker and Wright to time travel to this millennium, with its cell phone, computing, and recording technology, they likely would be surprised that there isn't far more observational study of children's ordinary lives.

In another classic study of children, Roger Hart's (1979) *Children's Experience of Place*, direct observation was combined with a number of other ethnographic methods to study children's relationship to places and locations. A pivotal method used was drive-around tours of the town made during after-school hours. Children's activities were noted and logged by location, as well as photographed. These records helped to show when and where children "broke the range" of permitted space to travel, and further, revealed where there were short cuts, habitual routes, and patterned activities. The study showed that children's physical environment is tied to children's feelings of effectiveness, and that children's fears (such as the fear of getting lost) are apt to be based geographically. The findings traced out how children's worlds operated, in practice.

Hart shared with Barker and Wright a willingness to devote steadfast and sustained human effort to observe children directly. Researchers today could accomplish Hart's "drive-around" tours with the help of a global positioning system and digital photographs, neither of which existed during the 1972 fieldwork.

In a third classic work worth mentioning, Eugene Webb (1966) and his collaborators made use of highly unobtrusive investigation through tracings, or indirect evidence left on the scene. Webb's group employed indirect ways of studying human subjects, without any direct intent to do child-centered investigation. For instance, a group of researchers visited Chicago's Museum of Science and Industry, a setting where families and children were, and still are, regular visitors. They noted that an exhibit of live, hatching chicks was surrounded by floor tiles that needed replacing about every 6 weeks, compared to other areas where the floor tiles went years without replacement. Erosion rates of floor tile became a form of indirect observation potentially indicating the popularity of the exhibit, which had many young visitors. In another indirect measurement, they calculated the length of time that people stood in front of the exhibit (above average, for the chick exhibit), yet without undue foot shuffling that might account for tile wear. I find the intriguing work of Webb and his coauthors important as a reminder that children's actions leave "tracings" that can be observed, in the same way that detectives have perfected the art of reading criminological evidence. A child's collection of picture books, even after the child is grown, leaves evidence about how much each book was handled (and perhaps liked!), by signs of wear. Child-centered historians apply particularly ingenious, unobtrusive strategies for figuring out how children lived in the past. Aries' (1962) influential history of childhood explored, among other things, the proportions with which children were depicted in paintings. Such indirect strategies have much to offer, in light of the simple fact that preliterate children don't bequeath archived written records.

Unobtrusive observation can be set apart from contrived observation, according to Webb and his coauthors. Contrived observation, such as blind "bugging," uses hardware in the place of a human observer. Applied research in recent times has made extensive use of equipment to videotape, audiotape or otherwise record naturalistic behavior, often in home or retail settings. As an applied researcher, I individually videotaped children, at home, building a plastic model car, even as each assembler commented on the building process as it transpired. I also visited homes to videotape family dinnertime. (This has been done by academic researchers recently too, as I will soon discuss.) I once invited mothers who sewed, one at a time, to meet me at their favorite fabric store, where we walked together through the store as the woman explained the act of shopping for fabric, commenting into an audio tape recorder I carried. I worked with an observational research collaborator, who used suction cups to attach a time lapsed camera to the display where coloring books were showcased in a store; the research team placed signs in the store to let people know that filmed observation was underway. The study uncovered how mothers and fathers interacted differently with the display of coloring and activity books; mothers intensively examined the coloring books before selecting one, compared to a much more minimal glance by fathers, on average. (Later we interviewed a separate sample of mothers, showing them our videotape, to find out why they thought this gender difference might exist.)

In this sort of contrived observation, investigators have generally found the informant to be surprisingly unmindful of the recorder. Often, one can visibly see (on the videotape) that informants shift into a relaxed, oblivious posture after becoming acclimated to the taping. A colleague once explained this by saying that people's lives are simply more important than any research study, so the study apparatus becomes less conspicuous in the course of going about the actions of living. Reed Larson (1989), who used electronic pagers to signal children to report on their ongoing behavior (Experiential Sampling Method), made a similar point about the pager method; children were not highly reactive to the use of pager hardware and "look puzzled when we asked if being part of the study made them do things differently during the week than they would have otherwise."

The value of recordings is that they capture the actual process of behavior, as it unfolds, revealing the logic-in-use rather than a reconstructed rationale for action. This sets the information apart from what can be learned in a conventional after-the-fact interview, or through methods that are more removed from immediate behavior (such as surveys). Better diapers, or better dishwashing products, have come from filmed observation over the diaper-changing table or the kitchen sink. The value rests in this: experience-near understandings are appropriate when studying how life is lived rather than reflecting upon it in a distanced way. Better policies, or more well-placed theories, can come from recorded facets of everyday life—in hospitals, schools, homes, or clinics. The action research movement, in places around the globe, holds more and more examples of this sort of recorded observation on a grass roots level, done to spotlight child experience.

Experience-near forms of observation, focusing on what children do during everyday activities, help us to understand the flow of children's lives in the here and now. This, of course, is the very essence of the child-centered platform. Resourceful researchers have observed children and their families in ways that incorporate video taping, audio taping, pagers, single-use cameras, digital cameras, and handheld computing devices, just to name a few. There are various research designs possible (Wheeler & Reis, 1991). Participants can report their experience at regular predetermined intervals (interval-contingent) or can be signaled by the researcher to make a recording, perhaps in response to a pager pulse (signal-contingent). A third possibility is that a predefined event be established, with recordings done each time an event occurs (event-contingent).

A scholarly example of an event-contingent recording comes from research by Elinor Ochs, one of several resourceful academics who have studied family mealtimes using both videotaping and audiotaping. (Linguists such as Ochs, of course, have an established track record in recording children's language in everyday contexts.) Children were present at the meals recorded. Ochs showed that the meal discourse revealed a role by powerful family members (especially fathers, and to a less extent mothers) to dominate the framing and unfolding of discourse. Children, although they were the subjects of others' narratives, had the least influence over discourse. Mealtime talk treated children as objects of scrutiny but not as empowered agents of narration (Ochs & Shohet, 2006; Ochs & Taylor, 1992).

At the Harvard Medical School, Michael Rich and collaborators have used videotape to explore the lives of children and teens under medical treatment. In one study, young people as young as 8 years, diagnosed with asthma, were trained to use camcorders and keep independent video diaries. The resulting visual narratives vividly showed that physician–child discourse didn't accurately reflect children's self-care in their own environment. In the course of this medical research, it was found that kids' video diaries provided a remarkable opportunity to see how children experienced asthma as a day-to-day challenge of life. Video is growing ever more pervasive in young people's lives in developed countries, with on-computer video cameras, internet sites that allow for posting video material, and the like. This trend reinforces the notion that video diaries might now be considered a youth-appropriate, even naturalistic, method (Rich et. al., 2000).

In Chapter 6, visually based methods within the child-centered research paradigm will be considered in greater depth and detail. As will be shown in that chapter, visual methods can be combined with face-to-face interviews, to provide a verbal and visual account of how children understand and interpret the recorded life events. This sort of "show and tell" braids together two threads of evidence: a visual portrayal of what children experience, and a verbal portrayal of their articulated meanings.

⁙ Avoiding Elder Arrogance

In discussing observational techniques, Weick (quoted in an article by Wheeler and Reis, 1991), has reinforced the notion that observers need to be alert to avoid a potential trap—arrogance. This is the same trap that lurks in the laboratory when researchers assume to know what their subjects are thinking. Although Weick's writing didn't single out children specifically, a child-relevant warning can be traced in three parts, borrowing from Weick. Arrogance can occur when: (1) The observer's version of a child's life is assumed to be the child's life; (2) The child's version of that same life is dismissed as invalid or "subjective;" and (3) The observer presumes to explain away the "inaccuracy" when a child experiences life in a way that did not "actually" happen (according to adult assumptions about reality). This trio of errors are made when adults, finding differences between their own worldviews and those of children, privilege the adult version as "correct" and explain away children's versions as developmentally incomplete. Weick's distortions are more likely if research does not actively honor and seek children's own accounts of their lives, which is a mandate of child-centered inquiry. Avoiding the know-it-all fallacy can be a motivating force for participant observation and nonparticipant observation, where an adult fieldworker has close encounters with children's worlds. Interviews as part of fieldwork can also be an antidote to adult arrogance, since they often arise out of what has been observed, and provide a chance to hear how children frame happenings.

Observational Research from Apprentice to Master

The trade or skill set for child-centered research might be thought of as tracing out a career chain through which the practitioner progresses. Considerations that might be weighed when undertaking research may shift, as you gain expertise. Here are a few such considerations:

Apprentice: Many of those doing child-centered participant observation previously did fieldwork with an age group closer to their own age, before undertaking participant observation with kids. If you are considering fieldwork with young children, it would be advantageous to have acquired prior experience with adults or young adults, and especially to acquire firsthand cultural familiarity or fluency in the culture where you plan to do fieldwork. Observation conducted with equipment (such as through video or other technology) may make for an easier first project in a site than would participant observation, if you have minimal prior experience in that place.

Journeyman: Assuming that you have played a successful role as a child-centered participant-observer, I hope you will be able to stay or return to the field, for there is a lot to learn about children's worlds. A challenge at this stage is gaining grant funding and publication outlets for further work. Outlets for publication may be on the rise, as reflected in some of the research described in these chapters.

Research funding, however, can be a thorny issue in the United States, where research funders have yet to fully appreciate the value of knowing children's vantage points. Although an apprentice researcher might be able to obtain funding for a dissertation project, those with more experience might discern a gap in available grants. In that case, necessity needs to be the mother of inventive approaches for supporting research. Studying one's own children or one's own culture have been tried and true practices. Work that combines paid responsibility with astute, systematic observation (such as Vivian Paley's work as a teacher) can have merit, assuming conflicts of interest from multiple roles can be managed.

Master: The accomplished skills that come with gaining complete language literacy and cultural adeptness in the field can bring about a more native-like position. This carries issues and problems, on occasion. A master is no longer a novice to the community at large, no longer corrected with sympathy for social faux pas. A researcher at this stage may come to be treated as a full community member, and expectations may increase. Jean Briggs (2008) found that her level of familiarity, after studying the Inuit for decades, led an Inuit acquaintance to persistently propose marriage to her, and to tease her in a suggestive way. Having become part of the community, she had to gingerly rebuff his overtures.

Adeptness with the culture in which children live can appreciably expand possibilities for inquiry, whether studying one's own culture, or a mastered, nonnative culture. Highly sensitive problems (death, spirituality, etc.) can be better navigated by a fieldworker who is facile in communicating with native children. Working out socially appropriate ways to delve into children's perspectives appears easier if natives' systems and sensitivities are well-known. Familiars of a culture can more boldly go into domains of children's lives with finesse, thanks to their cultural familiarity.

4 ⠶

Individual Depth Interviews

An essential part of true listening is the discipline of
bracketing, the temporary giving up or setting aside of one's
own prejudices, frames of reference and desires so as to
experience as far as possible the speaker's world from the
inside [and] step inside his or her shoes.

— M. SCOTT PECK

You can discover more about a person in an hour of play than
in a year of conversation.

— PLATO

An individual interview, like a first date, involves conversation but so much more. As daters can attest, convivial conversation is hardly a sure thing when two people meet. When an adult talks with a child, the stakes ramp up: the exchange can be exquisitely sublime, or uncomfortably tortured. Even if initial small talk suggests promise of more to be said, sustaining the momentum is no small task for two folks unmatched in age.

Over hundreds of studies, I have spent extensive time interviewing American boys and girls from varied backgrounds. My interviews have been unstructured, face-to-face, and many times with a single child at a time. In the applied research context where I worked before my academic career, interviews are routinely videotaped, audiotaped and/or observed by unseen note takers on the other side of a one-way mirror. My efforts, successful or not, were under scrutiny or at least could be revisited via recording. I could peruse the interview later, and judge if I had shown that I accepted the child, put my own frame of reference aside, and bracketed my adult assumptions (as Scott Peck's advice quoted previously implies). So much of what I know about interviewing children individually I learned reflexively, from taped review or from rereading transcripts of interviews. When I needed to correct lingering habits (one past flaw: saying "that's good," as if it were my place to validate a child's comment), I could do so. I self-corrected and tried new approaches (revised saying: "that helps me to understand, thanks"). Through gradual trial and error, I operated more on children's turf. Children seemed to trust me, to stay interested longer and communicate more. Since interviews were almost always transcribed for reporting purposes, I could measure my progress by the duration and content density of an average interview. The content expanded with experience, as did the time period I could spend with a child before her attention waned. I found that my videotaped encounters (when watched at high speed) came to have a dance-like mirroring and synchrony as the two of us, in an interview, moved and reacted in tandem. Like an experienced shopping mall Santa, I found that my ability to make sense of the wee voice of each boy or girl amply grew, with practice.

All the in situ training has not meant that I hit a home run with every single interview or child, but as they say of baseball (another difficult skill), even an outstanding batting average leaves room to grow. On a good day and a good hour, an adult like me can leap across years by spending time interviewing a fellow human being who happens to be young. Although the challenges are sometimes daunting, the humane fulfillment is unparalleled.

Not everyone is a fan of the individual depth interview applied to children. The method requires time and sustained drive both in collecting and interpreting intricate, bountiful data. Some have raised the possibility that a mature interviewer may be a more pressuring influence in individual interviews as compared to focus groups, since the adult interviewer is the child's only interlocutor (Leonard, 2005). The skill involved in moderating a group interview generally garners more star power for the moderator than does interviewing individually. A focus group seems a more impressive stunt, in contrast to the individual interview. But the fact is that a true sharing between one child and one adult can be just as challenging as a focus group.

In the hands of an interviewer able to work on a child's terrain, the individual depth interview is a penetrative form of qualitative inquiry. Individual interviews are a way to engage with each child, no matter how reticent they might be amidst young peers. It is possible to carve out a space of trust and mutuality, without dilution or interference from other children. With only one child to deal with, an interviewer can accommodate a child's own style of communicating. A fledgling artist or visual communicator can draw with markers or crayons. A restless dancer or athlete can move. Talkative kids can talk. Others can talk with their hands. There are options to pretend or reason, to go slow or go fast—tailoring the pace and communication to each child. If a child is bossy or resistant, I can yield the upper hand, zen-like—devising a way for her to express the impulse to take more control. (This is of course, a form of "stooping to conquer.") The individual interview places one child's role in the foreground. Communicative strategies are tailored to the child's comfort zone, his modes of sharing information. The child can give feedback on a piece of communication (such as a commercial or film) without the confounding "help" of others in the room. There is no one present to judge (as might another child in a focus group). The child can be totally accepted, no matter what, building the trust needed for a wholehearted connection. If a topic to be discussed is intimate or vulnerable in nature—such as illness, injury, the dark, transitional objects, adoption, or divorce—the trustworthy interviewer has a chance to hear in depth about such subjects. These topics might not necessarily be safe for youngsters to expose in a focus group with unfamiliar age-mates, or in the presence of peers who are known schoolmates or neighbors.

Some practitioners of qualitative research with young children (younger than 8 years) eschew the individual interview, instead opting for a *friendship pair* in which a child is interviewed alongside a pal. For young friends, this is thought to subvert a painfully quiet interview. But there are comparable disadvantages in a friendship pair as in any group interview. Peer influence (maximized in the established dominance patterns of a pair of friends) is one hazard. Another hazard lies in having less opportunity to find out in depth what one child understands about a topic, free of another's input. If friends are a relevant unit of analysis for the topic at hand (such as reviewing a video game meant for two to play), their joint participation makes sense. But friendship pairs are a poor crutch for topics that would benefit from intimate, solo disclosure.

Admittedly, dyadic exchange between a child and an adult can be something of an adventure sport, especially in the case of very young or taciturn kids. Interviewing skill counts. In contrast to a focus group, in a one-on-one session the interviewer is in a sense operating without the backup help of other children, who in a group can be helpful aids for advancing conversation by restating or advancing what gets said. When an adult operates as the sole interlocutor, mistakes can reverberate and might be tricky to correct, such as miscommunication or condescension that undercuts rapport.

While it is true that, during an interview, adult ways of communicating should be bracketed or set aside, I have found that my adult, analytical cognition stays intact as a back-of-mind influence on my thought process, guiding me about the content I should probe in more depth. As a researcher, I am able to stay on a child's wavelength, yet also to fully tap into how the child's comments bear on the goals of the project. This is reassuring, for when I analyze my findings, I usually find that I have pursued the avenues I needed to. I have not lost sight of the study's analytical goals. I have asked what was needed, and followed up the relevant clues a child gave me.

Generally, I aim to become quickly accustomed to a child's level of vocabulary and language (and adjust my language in turn). As mentioned, I suggest activities that suit the child's style of communication: drawing, pretending, hands-on tasks, and so on. I try to listen to the child carefully and adjust my queries accordingly. I may suggest a nonverbal way to signal an opinion, by asking a child to spread his arms apart as wide as appropriate to show a response (wide = good; narrow = bad). Another nonverbal approach is to gesture thumbs up or down. (Such gestured points can be followed up with verbal probes.) I may modify the order of my questions, to make sure the child is neither bored nor frustrated by the level of challenge. I will also check aloud with the child to see if my way of grasping things seems to be right on or far off. ("Am I getting the right idea, or not really?")

I treasure the rapport I am fortunate to achieve. No privilege is as great as sharing understanding and mutual respect with a younger human being. It makes me bigger, not smaller, as if my sense of being in some sense expands, or could it be that my arrogance shrinks?

⠓ Choosing a Method

The choice of method, between focus group or individual interview, is a topic regularly discussed among professional qualitative researchers. In fact, both these methods are variations on one idea—the "focused" interview—in which the interviewer explores a topic, actively listening to bring into focus what is germane to the interviewee(s). Children in an Irish study have indicated an equal liking for either format, individual interview or focus group (Heary & Hennessey, 2006). The individual interview allows more time and concentration to follow the arc of a single individual's views than does a group interview. This confers an advantage in studying individual representational processes. For instance, educational researcher Herbert Ginsburg (1997) is an accomplished user of individual depth interviews to explore how children dynamically encode mathematical knowledge. Ginsburg regards the method (as Piaget did) to be a powerful technique for exploring psychological processes of learning and knowing. The individual interview allows for a "clean" assessment of what ideas and reactions a particular piece of communications (a commercial, a computer program, a teaching pamphlet, a movie, a book) registers in a given child. Personal communications that are undiluted by peers' confusion or hints are often de rigueur for studies about computer programs, TV commercials, or other communications that are individually interpreted.

In a focus group, children are stimulated by and tend to "build" upon one another's understandings, which has advantages for understanding peer-to-peer influences, but disadvantages when seeking to isolate how one child encodes knowledge or makes sense of communicated material. Compared to one-on-one interviews, the mutual give and take in a focus group is known to lead to richer elaboration of each theme raised. By comparison, one-on-one interviews are more idea generating, yielding more overall themes discussed across a study, albeit less elaborative in associations about each idea (Heary & Hennessey, 2006; McGee, 1999).

In designing research, the choice between focus groups or individual interviews can be less than clear-cut. Importantly, the decision should be made in light of project goals and local cultural discourse practices. Using a cultural insider as an adviser may be crucial for anchoring to the locale an appropriate research tool. In some cases, an alternative or altered method might be preferable to either individual or group interviews.

In North America, two guidelines often seem to hold. First, American kids aged 7 years and younger are generally better candidates for individual interviews than group interviews, since the give and take of group conversation is not reliably a part of kids' discursive repertoire at that young an age. (Kindergartners and preschoolers in the U.S. generally don't sit around in groups discussing.) Second, it bears emphasizing, matters of communication may call for individual interviews in order to cleanly discern the meanings conveyed to each person, away from group influence.

Other issues to consider in deciding which method to use involve the available pool of subjects: If there are only a small number of respondents available to be interviewed, who are diverse in age and gender, disclosure may be more amenable in several one-on-one interviews.

(Focus groups ideally call for respondents similar in age, gender, or possibly other distinctions, necessitating adequate pools of qualified children to fill out a session.) Of course, there might be other options too, such as an internet-assisted focus group for older kids who are computer-proficient, even if geographically dispersed (Huffaker, 2004). Children 8 years or older who all suffer from a rare disease, for instance, might connect online for a moderated group meeting. Perhaps a bit tricky to judge in advance, another issue has to do with whether children will freely discuss a topic, in an ensemble. Sensitive topics (illness, menstruation, poverty, parental divorce, sexual abuse, sibling death, etc.) need to be considered thoughtfully: Will respondents feel comfortable discussing such a touchy issue openly in a group, or would they hold back and be circumspect (McGee, 1999)? Whether sensitive topics can be discussed fruitfully in a group may depend partly on the moderator. He or she needs to comfortably establish a zone of safety for frank sharing, as well as to handily contain insensitive statements by participants that might hamper openness. In North America, experience with support groups reminds us that group discussions can be a form of mutual support and reassurance, if the group shares common concerns, and an atmosphere of mutual trust can be sustained. Many studies of illness have used the method of focus groups among youth, employing a homogeneous sample of young sufferers who have all "been there." I have found that face-to-face focus groups discussing a mutual matter can provide a form of social support, even in cases when the participants were heretofore strangers. Adults or teens who met at focus groups I moderated occasionally exchanged phone numbers afterwards, to arrange a get-together again later.

In the final analysis, it can be hard to foresee which topics are amenable versus uncomfortable for kids in a group interview. Among American kids I have encountered, topics that children associate with their maturing selves, especially themes that symbolize aspirations to be older, may be more comfortably disclosed amidst peers than issues that are thought to be regressive, or seem "babyish." Wetting the bed, sleeping with a transitional object, imaginary companions, believing in Santa Claus, or other topics culturally equated to early childhood might be embarrassing for some school-age kids to discuss with peers, particularly with known acquaintances. Yet in an individual interview where there is no scrutiny of age-mates, school-age kids will willingly disclose to a supportive and accepting interviewer their regressive impulses. Matters of spirituality can also have an important personal dimension, revealed when a child is individually interviewed. Susan Ridgely Bales (2005), who observed classrooms of children preparing for First Communion, used one-on-one interviews (with drawings) that allowed her to see children's "unique views on the Eucharist's meaning."

Interviewing one child does tax and challenge an interviewer. The format places the interviewer as the sole interlocutor, without assistance from other children in the group to keep the conversation going or to help interpret what a speaker means to say. But an absence of peer pressure is also a plus. For myself, I find that having the child all to myself lets me take full advantage of the close private alliance we establish. But this does not mean that I have removed any social meaning attached to me, the interviewer. Children react to interviewers in a contingent way based on perceived roles, as do adults (Richards & Emslie, 2000). Unfortunately, interviewers aren't always aware of the impact of their social position and demeanor upon the cultivation of an interview. Focus group moderators may find the multiparty feedback from 6 to 8 participants to be salient, undeniable advice about how the moderator is being viewed (Tobin, 2000). A group of children may openly make alliances, resist, undermine, parody, or complicate the mature researcher's intentions. Signals from a single child may be harder to pick up.

Power dynamics and mutual influence, nevertheless, occur whether you are interviewing an ensemble or a single child. In either setting, the moderator is best off leveling power relations, rather than being perceived as a bossy teacher or authority figure. As Virginia Tech's Jan Nespor (1998) has recounted from a participant observation study, resistance or mockery are responses to a coercive style of questioning. Powerless children tend to flex what little influence they have to preserve dignity.

Jan: Calm down, I don't know what you're talking about but calm down.

Child 1:   We're setting a good example.

Child 2:   Let's give him [Jan] the wrong information, he's from Virginia Tech.

It may be difficult for a teacher to bracket all authoritative maneuvers, should the urge to protect children call forth a controlling impulse, a pulling of rank (Newman, Woodcock, & Dunham, 2006). Averting harm in the event of a power failure, seismic eruption, or a siren call to evacuate a building, calls for firmness and solid direction. Under routine conditions, though, heavy-handed dominance can almost always be avoided, when offering child-relevant activities and talk.

There is virtue, too, in flexibility. A facile interviewer tailors the discourse to empower each child. It cannot be overemphasized that the interviewer of young individuals can amplify back the child's communicative strengths—allowing one child to use visual communication such as drawing, and another verbal child to talk at will, or a restless child to get up out of their seat to pantomime. An individual interview affords the qualitative researcher full flexibility to match and modulate so as to suit each unique young person. Pacing and order of tasks can be adjusted. Youngsters with peculiarities of word use can be questioned with their own vocabulary. A reticent child can be drawn out of his shyness, coaxed at an appropriate pace. In sum, children can be scaffolded in a responsive manner, with just the right level of questioning to encourage confidence and maximum expression. There is no need to focus on crowd control (as in group interviews) so the child can be given undivided, full attention. Reaching for the approaches that seem to suit each unique youngster, a researcher can pivot in tandem with the child.

It is possible to combine methods within an overall study design, doing group interviews as well as individual interviews in order to have the combined advantages of both formats. A relevant example would be a study of mine underway, in which I am exploring what is communicated to kids by films that dramatize asthma in a stigmatized manner. The intended research plan combines both group and individual interviews. The one-on-one interviews were chosen to provide a "clean" uninfluenced account of how individuals make sense of the movie content, that is, what gets communicated to individual children. One-on-one interviews also provide a "private" context to discuss issues of stigma in asthma that might be socially compromising to divulge in a group. By doing focus groups additionally, a peer-influenced context provides a lens to watch how social give and take colors reactions to stigmatizing movie scenes; peer interaction is at the heart of how stigma influences children in their lives, their social behavior, and even their illness management. A hybrid study approach could provide depth of vantage point, allowing a triangulation across social and private aspects of meaning.

To recap, group interviews allow the investigator to see how a topic is treated in a broad context of interaction with peers. Individual interviews allow deeper, more private immersion, as the interviewer in principle adjusts the approach to suit each child. Yet commonalities between both methods (such as preparing for an interview, leveling adult-child relations, and analytical discipline) are many. Each mode of inquiry has particular affordances for empowering and learning from children. Additionally, there are times when multiple methods can add important nuance through a combined study design.

❖ Individual Depth Interviews: The Nature of Engagement

Despite the label, an individual interview is not carried out individually but in tandem. Like a teeter-totter, a one-on-one interview involves give and take as a paired dynamic, implying active mutuality between an interviewer and a child. Each child brings to the party a selfhood and a way of being in the world, at once personally and culturally shaped. To and fro, the researcher needs to interface with the contours of a child's motivation, skills, and communicative inclinations. A kind of intersubjectivity is the goal, during which meanings are conveyed through interaction. Roberta Woodgate (2001) has described a kind of transacted understanding and sustained relatedness during inquiry, bringing about a "mutually shaped reality" between researcher and child; "knower and known" are interactive and inseparable. On videotape, I can see how a child and I visibly synchronize our movements and gestures, a kind of partnered to and fro or duet.

But acts of resistance and misunderstanding also can occur. Sometimes, I have felt as though the seesaw has come to a standstill, as if someone put the exchange on hold. This sense of "stall" can be mutual and isn't always initiated by the child. There is nothing to do, but to restart the momentum.

The process calls for an interviewer who is an attentive listener, tenacious, resourceful, and willing to take risks—qualities that grow all the more important as the age of the child decreases. An effective interviewer is caring and willing to live by the "golden rule" to treat the child as he would want to be treated if their roles were switched. Knowledge of child development can be important, for having realistic expectations and reacting appropriately.

The late American television host Fred Rogers, in recording his shows, anticipated and tactfully addressed how unseen children at home would react. He would broach a difficult subject gently on his show, such as referring to a character's (Mr. McFeely's) long marriage as a mild-mannered, indirect way to bring up divorce. He knew how to meet children on their level about their own concerns in the here and now. An interviewer can do worse than invoke Mr. Roger's sensitive qualities.

Much can be learned from those times that go less than smoothly. Consider a home-conducted interview I did with a kindergartner I will call John Dill, whom I met for the first time at his home, one September. We had not met prior to the day of the interview.

I rang the doorbell at the Dill's home in a neat working-class neighborhood just outside Chicago, intending to interview his mother and him (separately) about the Tooth Fairy. I caught them at an exciting time, for in addition to losing a tooth that week, John had just finished his first week of kindergarten. John greeted me at the door, but not in the way I anticipated. He had a toy "Ghostbusters" gun, and pointed it directly at me, telling me from the entryway "Get out of here. I'm not talking to you." His mother dismissed him, though, and invited me in. We agreed that I would interview John's mom, but I was inclined to follow John's lead to skip our separate meeting.

I sat down across from Mrs. Dill in her family's neat and sunny living room. Our conversation lasted about an hour. Every so often, John would run in, with his toy weapon pointed forcefully in my direction. Once, he reminded his mother with indignation, "I told you she should go away." As John interrupted us, I instinctively decided to play along with him, and fell down out of the chair to the floor, pretending that I was shot dead by John's toy weapon, yelling out, "I'm dying!" John giggled with pleasure at my playing dead, a pretense that gave him the upper hand and showed me to be at his mercy. When I was done talking to Mrs. Dill, he had a change of heart about the interview, and told his mother he would spend time with me, as long as he didn't have to talk to me. I agreed, happy for the opportunity and the challenge to make a connection with him, even if nonverbally.

I gave John a drawing task, to draw a picture of kindergarten, which he did. In doing this, I followed the clinician's rule that one should start by acknowledging what seems to be imposing itself as an issue (Greenspan & Greenspan, 1991). I had a hunch that John had been overwhelmed by his first week at kindergarten, perhaps leading him to turn the tables and to refuse to be dominated by one more unfamiliar adult: me.

After the picture of kindergarten, I asked John to draw the Tooth Fairy, which he did. As John labored at his artwork, he began to speak, unasked. He invited me to his bedroom because he wanted to show me his book, *The Berenstain Bears Visit the Dentist.* I was relieved to be invited! Now, I thought, I have a chance to take the interview further. John, who was already a good reader, read to me the entire book, *The Berenstain*

Bears Visit the Dentist. I asked him if I could ask him some questions about the Berenstain Bears, thinking that this might be a topic about which he would willingly share his ideas. With his permission, I began to inquire into what the fictional Bear children might know about and think about the Tooth Fairy. John opened up at this invited pretense, even relating some of his own impressions about the Tooth Fairy. He was an articulate, intelligent 5-year-old, and taught me a great deal about the Tooth Fairy as he imagined her. I had coordinated with John's overtures (acquiescing to play dead, following his lead on the limits he set), and that worked well to draw out his participation in the end.

After 1 ½ hours interviewing this bright kindergartner (not counting the time I spent with his mother), I had to leave. But John followed me outside as I walked to my parked car. As I slowly drove away, John was standing on top of his backyard Jungle Gym, a tall perch from which he could be seen to smile down in my direction, to wave good-bye and to watch me drive away. I smiled and waved too. Since then, John has always been my touchstone for the fact that the best interviews can come from the greatest challenges.

Lene Tanggaard (2007) compared the individual depth interview (performed with any age group) not to a seesaw but to a crossing of swords, a Foucaultian metaphor that highlights the struggle for ascendancy and power, both conscious and not. Sword crossing was an apt metaphor for John's case. John was willing to engage me only after he had a turn at pretend domination, through which he likely sensed my willingness to be playful and respectful. I let him express himself through art, about a salient new experience (kindergarten). He then was willing to volunteer ideas about my proposed topic, the Tooth Fairy, by offering to share a well-liked storybook about dental matters. Allowing myself to be vanquished by mock gunfire, and after that to follow John's lead, I succeeded because I stooped to conquer—listening closely at each step and incorporating John's sharing into my subsequent interrogatives. An interview in which there seemed to be no hope of cooperation at the outset, came around to a point of genuine rapport as I was able to be flexible and accepting of John's resistance, and respectful of his limit setting. In the end, we both disarmed and were the better for it.

It is a truth of many societies that children regularly have conversations with adults that place the children at a power disadvantage. Medical interviews by allopathic physicians, for example, largely leave the child out of the conversation, as the medical personnel and parent(s) usually dominate the exchange. In a Netherlands study, children's contributions to their outpatient pediatric encounters were limited to 4% of the overall discourse (van Dulmen, 1998). A pattern of adult domination holds in other contexts, as well. Many U.S. children receive verbal feedback, directions, or critiques from parents yet are warned not to "talk back." Teachers or educational examiners test children's knowledge seeking brief answers to narrow questions, but don't let children frame what they think is relevant. Ed Elbers (2004) has described a personal instance, from observing his daughter's visit to an ophthalmologist.

> Claire was aged 3 years 6 months and there were a number of reasons why we wanted her eyes tested. In order to test a person's eyesight opticians usually use letters and numbers of decreasing size. Children who are not yet able to read have to say what simple pictures depict (e.g., a house, a duck, or a flag) ... Her younger sister Elisa accompanied Claire. Each time the optician pointed to a picture there was a long silence before Claire answered. The silences lasted so long that her sister started to give the answer before Claire had said anything, therefore, Elisa had to be to be taken out of the room by a friendly nurse. Even then, the pattern repeated itself: long pauses, a hesitant answer, and often an answer that was wrong. Instead of a duck, the answer was a swan and instead of a flag, a boat. ... Why did Claire find it so difficult to give the right name? ... I concluded the reason could be found in my daughter's perception of the situation. She preferred a more complicated answer rather than a simple interpretation—hence "swan" instead of "duck." Claire must have thought: it cannot be this easy, the optician's request must require something more difficult. ... She failed to understand that the task was very simple for somebody with good eyesight. The optician had neglected to make this clear to her.

In situations in which deference to adults is normative, children who hesitate (or who respond contrary to adult expectations) do often find that adults interpret they are unable to solve the problem in question. Such a reaction accrues from a general tendency to treat adultness as authoritative, and childness as knowledge deficient (Benporath, 2003). In the absence of knowing the purposes of adult questions, children may fall back on monitoring (as best they can) what generally satisfies (or upsets) adults, making conversational moves that accommodate to the age-based power structure (Lamb & Brown, 2006).

One of the most important principles for the child-centered interviewer, then, is to break the usual norms in order to power share with the child. Also the child will need to be tipped off to the rather unusual rules and goals governing this exceptional situation—an interview. My way of explaining an interview to a child is to remind them that they are experts at topics about which grown-ups know little: certain media characters, games, toys, etc. I explain that in the interview they will be teaching *me* about something kids know more about than grown-ups. The point I want to frame at the outset is that during an interview, the researcher is the novice and the child is the expert. I also tell each child to "Interrupt me at any time, if you remember something else I should know," as a way to establish the child's dominion at commanding attention. I also tell the child to "Tell me right away if you think I am starting to get the wrong idea about something," conferring on the child the right to correct an adult. Moments when children remark on an area in which I am ignorant or in need of correcting are significant, for these times show the child realizes her ascendancy of expertise. Jan Nespor (1998) gave an account of such an exchange in conversation with several kids.

Adult (Jan):	Power Rangers, what are they? Are they a TV show or what?
Child 1:	A TV show.
Adult (Jan):	When do they come on?
Child 1:	Don't you know anything?

Another act indicative of empowerment is to give the child some latitude about where to sit. Ideally, the interviewer should sit so that any height advantage (e.g., one chair taller than the other) is not automatically given to the questioner; rather, the child's seated stature should be comparable (or above) the questioner's height. The idea of the questioner sitting on a chair, while the boy or girl sits on the floor, is too evocative of teacher–child hierarchy in the American classroom, in my experience. (But reversing these roles, by having the child in a chair, and a questioner on the floor, can draw out some children by setting up a context in which the adult lowers herself to learn from the child.) Overall, I like being seated in chairs better than on the floor, since it is less reminiscent of preschool and therefore (to the elementary school crowd) less condescending in association. Sitting at a table has the advantage of providing a ready surface for drawing, sorting, driving pretend cars, and so on. Using a chair furnishes other advantages too, since a chair is a kind of natural container (assuming it does not swirl or have wheels) that cuts down distraction and restlessness by limiting wandering. Akin to a kind of childproofing, sitting in chairs can free the interviewer from having to pull rank to keep a restless child in range. An option taken by some interviewers is to leave the location to sit (floor or chair) a choice left up to each child (Epstein, et al., 2008).

As the interview gets underway, give tactful feedback, when that is needed. Avoid telling a child to speak up. If the child articulates unclearly, the feedback should put the onus on the questioner not the child: "My ears are very slow today and I can't hear very well. Can you tell me that again, maybe a little louder?" As Wilson and Powell (2001) have emphasized, the interviewer seeking clarification should confess that need to the child, rather than leave the child thinking their explanation was faulty. "I'm not sure I understand, you said they lived on the moon...?" If the researcher is to grasp the child's view, the child needs encouraging signals to talk freely, to challenge, to reframe, to correct, and to condescend (to the adult).

Hence, moments of scorn and amusement at my ignorance are evidence that the child has been empowered, and understands that I am, in some ways, a novice. Another sign I am glad to see, for it indicates a kind of alliance, is when the child prefaces a volunteered comment with the preparatory question: "You know what?" My reply "What?" leads to a disclosure by the child—in a discourse pattern driven by the child's overture ("You know what?") not just my promptings.

Don't get me wrong, kids know I am (lets face it) an old lady. But they also come to realize that they have information or knowledge I need—and that they can contribute in their own, age-appropriate and individually comfortable way. I am not discarding adultness in order to interview a child, I am throwing aside the hierarchical dominance generally wielded by grown-ups. In its place, I am an audience raptly attending to the things children say, especially if they voluntarily bring up an issue, unprobed.

⠶ Guidelines for Interviewing

Individual depth interviews are hardly predictable. Discourse is subject to cultural variations. Children have idiosyncrasies. There is no standard playbook to memorize. Still, some provisionary tips may provide some guidance if used with care. Following are selected suggestions, which combine my ideas with those from Herbert Ginsburg's (1997) book *Entering the Child's Mind*. (Ginsberg's suggestions, ones I share, are marked with an asterisk.) Note that these are suggestions based on experience with North American children. Apply a liberal dose of forethought as to whether a suggestion is appropriate to a dissimilar cultural setting.

1. **Don't invite multiple kids when you intend to interview only one.** In the United States, children who agree to be interviewed generally do show up, barring a virus outbreak or blizzard. Overrecruiting, and then rejecting some kids, is not a kind system. If an "understudy" is needed, be sure the child knows in advance that they will be an understudy.

2. **Check out the equipment and setting beforehand, if possible.*** An interviewer needs to devote their attention to the child. If a piece of equipment fails to operate the way it should (such as a videoplayer, video camera, etc.) the interviewer risks losing momentum and flow between himself and the child. With very young children, getting attention back after it's lost can be a poor proposition. Prior to the interview, organize the materials to be used so that everything can be accessed with ease.

   Another piece of advice is to check the room for anything hazardous or distracting that may need to be moved elsewhere. If the interview is conducted in a child's home, of course, you won't be able to do this. But if you are in a public facility and can do so, keep out of the way things that could be unsafe, or that you don't want the child to rifle through at the wrong moment.

3. **Spend time with the child to get to know them at the outset.** I usually don't start in on the main interview (unless the child mentions the topic) until the youngster is relaxed and engaged. Start by finding out about their family, pets, well-liked activities, movies or TV programs, or how they celebrated a recent holiday or birthday. Ask about the sports insignia on their hat, or the rap group on their t-shirt. A really good icebreaker is to ask about the young person's birth order and their siblings. "Tell me what it's like to be (the oldest/the youngest/the middle/the only one)." "Do you like being the oldest/the youngest/the middle/ the only one?" Children often have a lot to say about the privileges and problems of their sibling position. Learning all about a child's passionate interest (a hobby, sport, friend, or

vacation place) is another excellent lead-in. This initial conversation can establish that you (the interviewer) are not judgmental and that you are truly fascinated by the child. The warm-up process may take a longer time if the child is initially reticent. With time, you can almost see a child relax as she talks and finds herself on safe ground. At the point when a child settles in, it is also a good time to respectfully double-check if the child needs to visit the rest room, in case they were too timid to say so before now.

4. **Provide privacy.** Not having the parent in the room is a good starting rule, for parents are known to make interfering in-roads, to worry judgmentally about a child's "good" performance, and to even answer on behalf of their son or daughter (Wells, 1965). In home-based interviews, the layout of a particular home at times can make it difficult to cordon off the parent to give the child autonomy; if the parent is busily engaged nearby, this likely would be better than letting mom or dad sit directly amidst the conversation. Negotiate, if possible, for an enclave providing private disclosure; the less interference from adults you can manage for the child, the better. Children don't always see things in a way that puts adults (or others) in a positive light, so telling their views in confidence is important.

5. **Clearly explain the interview process.*** Ginsberg wisely points out that the depth interview is likely to be a game that children have never played before. Explaining the nature of the interview is an ideal opportunity to explain that the child has authority and power, not just the adult (Wilson & Powell, 2001). I prefer to compare the interview to school only by contrast. I'll ask, "Did you ever notice that teachers ask questions they already know the answer to?" "Well, the questions I'm going to ask I don't know the answers to, because only you know these things, not me." Asking a child to describe what happens in a video game, or to recount a favorite media story popular with kids, or to explain how to play with a dog or cat, establishes the idea that a young person has things to teach an old lady like me.

6. **Bring to the interview specific, age-appropriate tasks.*** (This is of increased importance as the age of the child decreases.) I prepare a discussion guide or outline of topics in advance, complete with possible activities. Keeping activities within the reach of a child's ability and interest is important. If a child is

going to confidently share her viewpoint, being frustrated by too arduous a task won't set the right ambience. In other words, the interviewer needs to select ways of questioning that fit the particular age and proclivity of a respondent.

Leave abstract questions for teens or adults. The younger the child, the more concrete the prompts will need to be: props, models, or pictures can make for a more tractable inquiry. For a study of retail outlets, I have brought along a toy car, and a set of pictures on stands that included the logos of popular retail outlets for a certain product. The child could make a pretend "street" out of the pictures and could drive the car up and down the street, pretending that the people in the car stop to visit certain stores, in the process narrating what those places are like. Children as young as 5 years make use of this palpable, hands-on approach. A 12-year-old might find manipulating a toy car to be babyish, however, so an alternative use of the pictures could be marshaled for use with older kids, perhaps sorting the pictures as he verbally explains the features that set each retail outlet apart.

A treasure trove of possible tasks are coming to the fore from child-centered investigators. McCabe and Horsley (2008) have written a book of exercises to use in evaluation studies with young people, ranging from making art for a CD cover related to a topic (used with teens), to collage making, to pretending to look through a telescope (made from a cardboard tube) as a way of focusing on how something is seen. Another task to concretize ideas is a timeline used in an Australian study of transition to school. Dockett and Perry (2007) described how kids marked along the timeline points at which decisions were made by they themselves, or decided by others for them. Even verbatims from research can by drafted as material for interviews with kids: Quotations taken from what children said in a previous study (excerpted and read aloud) served as prompts to elicit fresh reflective reactions in another study (Forsner, Jannson & Sorlie, 2005).

Overall, teenagers have a cognitive capacity for many adult-like tasks, such as asking them to think aloud about interior processes of deciding (Branch, 2000). This contrasts with children 11 years and under, who usually benefit from concretized and game-like activities, including: bringing an item from home for showing and telling, pretending a phone conversation, dictating or writing a pretend letter or diary, ventriloquizing for a photo, using a mask or hat to role play, imagining what might be happening in a picture, responding through (or to) a puppet (Epstein et al., 2008), pretending to pack a bag for a destination, interacting with a replica, playing card "games" with pictures, or making an artistic representation. The very process of stating a preference can be made tractable with the right question: instead of asking for an oral report of a child's favorite item from an array, I'll give a child a sticker that looks like a trophy (or a star), and ask the child to place the sticker on the best one. This action serves as a starting point for talking about the "winning" item. ("What part makes it a winner?" or "What part makes it deserve a trophy?") Actions can energize communication for younger persons.

Almost every step of the interview can be made involving, even determining a randomized order for exposing stimulus material. As a way to randomize the upcoming order, I might hold behind my back two items, one in each hand, and ask the child to pick the next one we'll talk about ("Pick a hand, any hand"). Or I might fan and hold out cards to be discussed, magician-style, and invite the child to pick any card. The child has the power to determine the very flow of the interview, albeit by chance. Even sorting cards can be made more sportive, by treating the cards in an active and exaggerated way. Let the child throw the rejects or "wrong" items on the floor. Or slide a card across the table to the child rather than placing it in the child's hand. Throwing down cards on the floor, or sliding them across the table, makes sorting them more lively and less "lame" (to quote a youthful derogative). So too does treating stimulus material like a deck of cards—spreading them out face down as if for a game of Solitaire, or dealing them into two piles for exchanging, or turning them up one by one, to be slapped by the child, like Slapjack. Just as education can be edutainment, an interview can be, and probably should be, *interplay*.

With preadolescents, tasks that involve direct manipulation or visual props are generally advantageous over vaguer verbalizations. To be avoided, especially with youngest kids, is asking a child to listen to question after question, for an entirely talk-based interview.

Aligning the tasks to a respondent's age, then, is key, even while getting the needed information about the topics in question. The best-laid plans for activities, of course, are flexible. I retain the option to deviate from a planned outline, as needed, for particular children who don't take to the intended tasks. (A child may not like to draw, may tire particularly quickly, may need to move about, and so on.)

7. **Start and end with an easy task.*** Many interviewers like to begin with drawing, a nonverbal task that can be child empowering. (See Chapter 6.) Drawing gets the ball rolling without undue verbal pressure. Moreover, it is usually best not to dive in too quickly to directly ask about introspective, emotionally charged issues. Such issues will come out unaided during visual tasks much of the time. Visual approaches often exhibit a propensity to draw out emotional expression, as play therapists can attest. When the time is right, puppets or play figures can also be helpful ways to approach emotional areas delicately. Losing a tooth, for example, involves elements of trauma for quite a few children (bleeding, loss of a body part, worry about one's future ability to eat, etc.). In asking kids about the tooth loss experience, I made use of a cardboard toothless "puppet." Instead of asking a child to revisit the experience of losing a tooth directly, I could instead ask him or her to use the puppet (of the same gender as the child) to act out and tell what it is like to lose a tooth (Clark, 1995). This indirect approach, through ventriloquizing, generally was more child-compatible than direct questions. It also fit the general rule of thumb that young children succeed more when tasks are concrete rather than abstract.

Ending on a note of confidence (through a task the child can manage without difficulty) is a way to support a child's sense of success as she exits the interview.

8. **Vary the tasks over the course of time.*** The attention span of a child is not infinite, but fatigue can be held at bay if the activities employed are varied. Monitoring a youngster's attention or involvement level, and shifting tasks as attention *starts* to fray (not waiting too long) is the trick. Allowing the child to lose interest completely could take inattention beyond a point of no return.

All methods will not work with all children. If a child doesn't take to a task, having a variety of tasks in mind, or ways of adjusting a task, will enable rebound. Multiple tasks make for a more facile interview.

9. **Sensitively make your way within a child's zone of proximal development.** After an initial easy task, the level of challenge can be increased to what the child seems capable of doing. An adept interviewer can support the child's efforts when challenged, but still avoid the temptation to lead or direct. If the child has several pictures to look at one by one, for instance, but seems to have trouble focusing, the interviewer might remove remaining pictures from view, and continually point to the image the child should consider. Rephrasing a question in a simpler way, excluding terms that might be unfamiliar, is another act of scaffolding.

   To repeat, increase the level of challenge in questions or tasks over the course of time. Then, back down to easier activities or questions if the child shows frustration or withdraws. There is a balance to be achieved: work up toward a "ceiling" or asymptotic level of challenge, but don't push too far. The idea is to match each child's mettle, to tailor the level of difficulty within a comfort zone. On the occasion when you meet with an articulate, forthcoming boy or girl, take advantage of the opportunity to ask more difficult and deeper questions. Kids who talk with comfort and aplomb can be challenged to provide helpful insights and interpretive direction, thanks to their verbal confidence. Still, nobody should be pushed to feel incapable. Revert to easier or different tasks as needed to accommodate a child's communication.

10. **Show sincere human warmth.*** Good interviewers of children are gentle, even if this is sometimes mocked in general society. Mr. Rogers was lampooned in urban legends, credited with a supposed aggressive or dark side. There were rumors that he wore sweaters to hide his edgy tattoos. An urban legend had it that Rogers had been a marine sniper in Vietnam with numerous kills. *Saturday Night Live* parodied Rogers as a less than innocent person, as did *The Tonight Show*'s Johnny Carson. It was as if adults gained by mocking the gentle man Rogers appeared to be on his TV show.

   Good individual interviewers take a cue, all the same, from traits seen in Mr. Rogers: gentle yet protective, empathic yet responsible, attentive in the moment, and ever patient.

An interviewer ought to deal with the child in front of them, letting each child know that the inquirer understands and accepts their angle on things. If a child is getting out of bounds (such as rocking the chair so violently that they could fall and get hurt) an interviewer is gently reliable—stepping in without taking over, perhaps with a task that will distract the child, or perhaps by tactfully inviting the child to sit somewhere else, since that chair is "tipsy." An approach that shows warmth is appropriate. Cool, unfeeling objectivity or assertion of control works against the goal of achieving connection and understanding.

11. **Monitor the child's affective state.*** Throughout, while listening to what the child is saying and showing, more than content should be monitored—but also the child's affect: anxiety, glee, disinterest, tiredness, pride, delight, frustration and so on. Sometimes the affect will reflect a feeling about the content of what is being said or shown, and sometimes it will reflect a feeling about the interview process. At times, clues to how a child is feeling will be nonverbal, at other times verbal. Occasionally, the interviewer may need to clarify how the child feels by asking. Either way, it's best to monitor mood as carefully as other communication, for it may be central to the meta-message being conveyed. Monitoring mood is also valuable for keeping the interview on track. Bored children can play a new game, anxious children can be given reassurance or encouragement, delight can be celebrated, exhaustion can lead to wrapping things up more quickly.

12. **Encourage, don't belittle.*** An attitude of calm reassurance should go along with warmth. The tone should be respectful. Sometimes adults, in the presence of a child, adopt a kind of saccharine tone that implicitly infantilizes a child, using the tonal patterns of motherese (the tones used by mothers when addressing a baby). In a pitch that starts high and moves lower, such adults might say, "Oh, isn't that a cute drawing of a house!" or "Oh look at your little hiking boots!" or (in exaggerated interrogative) "Do you have to go to the bathroom, sweetie?" Those whom I've observed using such a tone didn't seem to be consciously aware of the belittling insinuation. Aware or not, the voice I am talking about demeans by accentuating the difference between an adult and an oh-so-diminutive child.

Ideally, an interviewer's voice should come from a place of respect and equity. A lively tone of voice is helpful, but an infantilizing or disrespectful tone is not.

13. **Seek to understand, rather than judge.** Viewers who have watched my interviews occasionally make evaluative judgments about each child: This one was a troublemaker, that one was articulate, and so forth. I think the impulse to judge or evaluate each child is greater when observing than when interviewing, due to vantage point; the viewer isn't interacting face-to-face and engaged in a reciprocal process. Still interviewers may sometimes have lapses when an unsettled tension comes between the interviewer and the child. George Devereux described that the study of humans can be impeded by anxious arousal coming about between subject and observer. Rather than fully witnessing the child, evaluative reactions can disrupt the reciprocal process in the dyad. Devereux (1967) recommended self-reflection about one's relationship to the informant, as a counterpoint to such struggles. It is important not to lose sight that there are inevitably differences between an adult and a child. Otherness is unavoidable (Lahman, 2008). What is also inevitable is a need for ongoing reflection to allow for a level of sharing and equity despite the generational divide.

14. **Help the child to self-reflect.*** The younger the child, the harder it will be for them to answer questions asking them to reflect on their own experience. Children may not be able to step back and make a reaching interpretation, unaided, about the impact of a trauma, for example. But as mentioned previously, if asked to imagine about a puppet or play figure having the same experience, they can often reveal such information, indirectly.

15. **Look and listen.** Active listening is more than listening. Children communicate on more than one channel. Mirroring their gestures can be just as important for reflecting back to them as using their words. If the child is struggling or confused, this may be tipped off by their nonverbal expression, not by what they say.

16. **Pick up the child's language.*** Use the terms that kids use. In my project on Halloween, kids seldom used the term "jack-o'-lantern" or the term "vampire" when looking at representations of these items. They more often said "pumpkin" or "Dracula" as the terms. Stores, even ones beloved by children,

are sometimes called by idiosyncratic terms, such as calling "Toys R Us" by the name "giraffe store." (The store symbol is a giraffe.) One kindergartner with asthma I interviewed used the term "asthma" to refer to his inhaler. I try to compose my questions using the same sorts of words as the child. It's so important to me to get the vocabulary right that I sometimes unobtrusively jot down any idiosyncratic words, names or phrases that the child mentions, so that I won't forget what term to use with the child at a later point in the interview.

Don't expect preliterate children to deal well with written language. I once had to explain to a client, who wanted me to show kindergartners unfamiliar cereal boxes with names, that the names might as well be in Russian for most 5- and 6-year-olds. With that reminder that literacy is not inborn, my client concurred on not showing the boxes with names.

17. **Repeat and explore.*** I refer here to repeating or paraphrasing what is said by a child, and probing it further. Follow-up probes should be as concrete as possible, such as, "What's the best part about ____?" rather than the more vague question, "Why?" A fruitful way to ask a question is by waiting until the child mentions a topic, and then incorporating the child's way of talking about the topic, pursuing the needed information. (For example, in a study of American Independence Day, this would involve asking the child about the holiday, and waiting until the child mentions fireworks ("the fire show"), and then broach questions about fireworks with reference to "the fire show.") Staying on a child's train of thought, as much as possible, and picking up issues and terms on the fly, as children mention them, can be a good game plan.

18. **If you must hint, do so carefully.*** Don't be tempted to put words into kids' mouths except as a last resort. Sometimes the best way to probe, when you're forced to give an example or hint, is to make a purposefully wrong suggestion (e.g., about the building materials for a gingerbread bread house: "Is it made of rocks from the moon?"). Children usually delight in correcting the foolish interviewer on their fanciful or false idea—so this sort of probe can sometimes trigger the answer without being biased or leading.

19. **Experiment.*** Trial and error is a child's abiding mode of being; an interviewer would do well to emulate that spirit of taking a

chance on a new approach to see if it might help. Many of my best innovations initially occurred to me and were tried on the spot, during interviews. If nothing seems to be working, not much is lost by taking a new angle. There is a well-known story that circulates about Thomas Edison. At his lab, his technicians had tried hundreds of different ideas for filaments for the light bulb. Not discouraged, Edison regarded these misfires simply to be part of a long process of invention. Doing individual interviews with kids often requires a similar commitment to try, fall down, get up, try again, and eventually find a way forward to communicate.

:: Interviews and Intersubjectivity

No matter how many tips and tricks an interviewer puts to use, in the final analysis the adult interviewer is not determinative of an interview's outcome. Young interviewees are actively instrumental in their participation. Intersubjectivity implies mutual subjective involvement, an emergent effort between both parties. The teeter-totter metaphor is apt, for the interviewer and interviewee together negotiate a topic, with give and take involved in driving the action. The interviewer and interviewee likely are aware of one another as initiating and responsive persons, but the interview ultimately is cultivated *ensemble*, in interaction. The parties are coupled. Their synergistic interplay may turn out to be for better or for worse. The interviewer has a responsibility to their pairing, but cannot dictate the outcome fully.

Humans are remarkable in their capacity for mutual exchange. Ritual, dance, singing, play, attachment, language and more depend on it (Collins, 2004). In my experience, when the interview arrives at the sweet spot when the child and I are functioning like a connected system, it's palpable. Perhaps the child remarks, "You know what?" as an active invitation to instruct me. Perhaps the child and I start to draw upon a common set of terms, terms that we improvise in concert. Mutual playfulness may overcome us, as we role-play or make faces or joke. In the process we are *jointly* discovering what's true or should be true, much as actors do as they listen to and play off one another in a scene. Even a child who balks or challenges can still be in his way making contact; there are no difficult children in my way of seeing things—but there are children whose actions show they have difficulties to air.

Cultural psychologists Shweder and Haidt (2000), writing about people in general, have treated the capacity for intersubjectivity as an *emotional* interface, one that both connects and challenges.

It is one of the great marvels of life that across languages, cultures, and history, it is possible with sufficient knowledge, effort and insight, to truly understand the meanings of other people's emotions and mental states. Yet one must also marvel at one of the great ironies of life—namely, that the process of understanding the consciousness of others can deceptively appear to be far easier than it really is, thereby making it even more difficult to achieve a genuine understanding of "otherness."

Empathic sensing of a child's emotions in an interview is not a pre-formed, ready-made talent or gift. Empathy is dialogic. Understanding another is a process of responsiveness, not detection (Hollan, 2008). Being openly receptive to emotions and moods can help, just as opacity to emotional experience hinders. But there is no systematic assurance of fully understanding someone younger, any more than there is assurance of melding with the mind of someone culturally "other." The emergent, dynamic interaction of a face-to-face interview can't be mechanically imposed. An interviewer attempting to connect and comprehend is engaged in a mutual human process, which may yield bits of insight rather than fully blown understanding. (Fortunately, the bits of insight from each child may accrue child by child across a study, providing a more ample view overall.)

When the partner in the conversation is a child, routines for starting and ending can help to anchor the process. To reiterate, at the start I try to get a sense of how verbal a child is, or whether he fidgets so much he might benefit from play that allows him to move while we communicate. If a child seems tense at first, I'll back into the topic slowly and allow her more time to relax. A distractible child is a sign to keep stray material out of the way. Starting the interview with a drawing, as Bales did in her First Communion study, can offer clues that particular children might lean toward visual communication. (Confident and able sketchers often excel at varied visual tasks.)

Altering the sorts of activities in an interview can extend attention, but a child's attention is not everlasting. After a valiant effort at explaining, a tired child may yawn, look away, or even lay their head down on the table. With experience, an interviewer can judge when the exchange has gone past the point of no return.

When time comes for leave taking, I like to make sure the child knows they have helped. Clapping my hands in a circle motion (a "round" of applause), or placing a star (or trophy) sticker where they choose (hands, forehead, shirt, etc.) are ways to express a heartfelt show of gratitude. Sometimes, when the topic we've discussed has depressing overtones (such as illness or hunger) or scary features (such as Halloween or car crashes), I try to finish the interview with an encouraging or positive activity, a question or task that dwells on possibility or strength rather than vulnerability.

One point is worth emphasizing about individual interviews with kids: this is an occasion for an adult inquirer to encounter each child's otherness. I don't believe an adult can deny their grown-up nature, but neither do I have to take a judgmental and controlling adult role. Be and let be. Don't order a child to sit still, to use proper language, to refrain from putting his hair in his mouth. Even if a child lacks conversational fluency or mature propriety (Lamb & Brown, 2006), neither do adults know how to behave in children's systematic ways. Bracketing adult expectations, in the attempt to connect with each child, can be hard to get used to but has an upside: there is fun and learning to be had.

∷ Setting

Interviews may take place away from the child's natural habitat (such as a market research facility, at a clinic office or university), or can also take place in a home or school. School settings are not uncommon. Still, I am concerned about insinuations of adult power associated with formal school settings, especially classrooms. Schools are places where children are expected to say what adults want them to say, warping the angle of sight on their views. School discourse carries power inequities, especially where teaching takes place. Places of recreation, such as a playground, may be less restricting in association.

Home interviews benefit from happening in a child's comfort zone. In the comfort of home, children are relaxed and are likely to feel on a more equal footing with the interviewer. But a home is not a controlled environment in any sense. Siblings may scramble about. It may be difficult to arrange for a child's privacy, as parents or others may want to stay close by. Telephones and doorbells ring. Pets get out of cages. Unexpected visitors stop by.

When I am doing an interview in a child's home, I often plan to talk with one or both parents, too, separately from the child. If that is the case, I try to bring a movie on DVD that lasts about the length of the parental interview. A movie will keep all the children entertained while the parent talks with me. Children might decide to watch a DVD of their own, or to do some other activity, which is fine.

On occasion in a residential interview, it can be difficult to give the child seclusion from others. Siblings or friends may interrupt or make ploys for attention. I try to find something for the other kid or kids to do (such as a drawing related to the topic of the interview), and ask them to go elsewhere to do the activity. (I always bring along coloring and activity books, to offer to young bystanders as a pastime to do elsewhere, if needed.) If a parent wants to keep tabs on the interview, I suggest that the parent set about at some activity nearby, rather than hover—for the sake of the child's comfort and privacy. In some studies, I have brought a written survey for the parent to do while I interview the child, a diversion of parental attention as well as a source of data. I do check with each person at all points when others might be present: Is it okay with you if we talk while he/she is here?

Once the family has met me or witnessed my interaction with their child, parents often feel more comfortable letting me talk to the child privately, such as in the child's bedroom. In fact, a woman I interviewed with several very young children and a new baby once left me in charge, to watch her kids while she went out with the baby to buy milk; after this test as a babysitter, she was quite comfortable letting me interview her son, in a room sequestered from interruptions. Gaining this sort of trust is precious.

In a vivid essay about conducting individual interviews in children's homes, MacDonald and Greggans (2008) describe the "chaos" that sometimes overwhelmed them when they were researcher-guests in family homes of kids with cystic fibrosis. Children were sometimes on the move, during interviews, rather than sitting quietly to respond to questions. One boy rolled around the floor and bit the cable of the tape recorder. Another 16-year-old boy was interviewed in a room where family, friends, and pets hovered about. One of the energetic dogs of this teen sat uninvited on the interviewer's lap throughout the interview. The teen's mother, holding an armful of laundry, stood right in front of the interviewer, blocking her line of sight to the interviewee. A sister played with marbles nearby, and a courting couple went in and out of the room. Rapport was difficult to obtain with so many intrusions and so little privacy. In fact, the teen interviewee later declined to continue with the study.

Explaining to the family that a young informant should have some privacy is not only an ethical matter, but a relational one. Although privacy may be less significant in some other societies, in the American way of thought it signals to the child that during the interview she will occupy a position of respect and singular attention. Finding private space is thus worth some effort. The back yard (where parents can look on from a window, yet not be intrusive) can be a good resolution (though sound intrusions such as overhead planes or barking dogs do sometimes surface). Young neighbors who drop in can play with siblings elsewhere, watch a DVD, enjoy a coloring book, or some other diversion provided by the interviewer.

The advantages of home can be well worth dealing with unexpected contingencies. There is no substitute, really, for seeing a child on her own turf. At home a child feels less inhibited. She can fetch her own books, toys, or household items as aids for explaining. When interviewing chronically ill youngsters, I had a chance to see how the supplies used to treat illness took up substantial space, often an entire cabinet, in the kitchen. I could see asthma triggers present in some homes of kids with asthma, such as a parent's package of cigarettes in the kitchen or cat hair on the child's possessions and bed. In a study of plastic car models, I could see the space available for the child to do the assembly, usually limited to a corner of a crowded or much-used table in the hustle-bustle of home. In a study of a holiday such as Halloween or Easter, I could see the decorations and paraphernalia for celebrating.

In short, my sense of children's lives has been enriched by individual interviews done at home. I have seen how houses are reordered during years of child rearing to make way for toys and play. I have seen how, on the home front, children are honored with laudatory schoolwork on the refrigerator and trophies on the mantle and birthday party paraphernalia. The rest of American society may not regard children as policy priorities or persons of influence, but in the homes of families, children—and all the chaos they entail—are given space. When I am discouraged about children's place in American priorities, I have a compensating sense that that the nuclear family, as a rule, bends with children's ways, adapting and relishing what children bring to life.

Individual Interviews from Apprentice to Master

No simple matter, the nuances of individual interviews are learned along a career chain, through which the practitioner moves link by link. Relevant issues tend to vary with one's place along the chain.

Apprentice: If you are a relative beginner, some degree of anxiety about doing individual interviews with children is a positive sign that you recognize this is a more difficult challenge than sometimes realized. If you have interviewed adults, or have consulted handbooks about interviewing adults (cf. Seidman, 1998), this is helpful but may fall short of getting the hang of children's interviews. A suggestion to consider is to work with a coach, perhaps as an extension of taking a class in children's qualitative research. Another possibility would be to invite a seasoned child interviewer onto your project as a consultant. A consultant can watch you interview and provide feedback.

In conducting your first one-on-one sessions with young informants, one tip is to avoid the intuitively obvious scheme for scheduling: starting with the youngest children and scheduling, based on age, until doing the last interviews with the oldest children. Instead, do the reverse; interview the oldest children first and schedule in reverse order of age, ending with the youngest. This will help to accommodate your learning curve, since youngest kids are the hardest to interview well. Many researchers who work with the young have done their initial projects with teens. Adolescents are more similar as interviewees to adults than kindergartners, and the level of difficulty is less. Unless you have relevant experience, 5-year-olds should be avoided until you are a confident and relatively fluid interviewer.

Your early success will be enhanced if you incorporate a tool (such as photoelicitation, see Chapter 6) that can scaffold the interview process and place more of the control and momentum with the child. Photoelicitation has a successful track record across many different cultural contexts. In photoelicitation, kids drive the interview process fairly actively, which takes some of the pressure off the interviewer.

Journeyman and Master: Now that your skill level has advanced, the clients or collaborators around you may take your prowess with child-centered individual interviews in stride. In other words, you may make it look easy. But as you know, this is a demanding and mentally draining sort of research. Don't be compelled into a busy schedule of interviews that leaves no breaks for you to recharge. Safeguard your capacity to listen—for fatigue matters more for child interviews than for interviews with adults. You've earned the right to build in times to rest, to be at your best for a difficult job.

5 ::

Focus Groups

Younglings, younglings gather 'round.
—YODA, IN STAR WARS

In 1991 I attended a birthday party in Manhattan to celebrate the 50th anniversary of the focus group. Present at the festivities were members of the Qualitative Research Consultants Association, a group of professional experts who moderate or lead focus groups. The term "focus group" refers to a small number of participants, led by a moderator in guided conversation, to bring into focus salient and relevant experiences, reactions, attitudes and perceptions. A renowned sociologist involved in the development of focus groups, Robert K. Merton (then of Columbia University) was present as an honored guest at the golden anniversary fete. Merton (1987; Merton et al. 1956/1990) had been involved in developing the idea of "focused interviewing" as part of his research for the 1940s war effort, when the new method figured heavily into Merton's work on radio propaganda and troop morale. Following World War II, focus groups turned civilian and were incorporated into the repertoire of audience research by commercial interests; the flexible probing of salient issues, discussed in shared conversation, proved to be enormously valuable in shaping consumer marketing and product design efforts (Hennessey & Heary, 2005). By the time focus groups reached the half century mark (at the party in 1991), the focus group had become a routine and influential staple of advertising, consumer, media, political campaign, legal and public policy research.

Focus groups have shaped the content of movies, TV, retail stores, computers, clothing, food, transportation, beverages, services, and more. Focus groups have been commissioned to anticipate solutions to problems yet to come, such as a long past project (once described to me) to explore reactions to the death of the commercial persona, Colonel Sanders, prospectively. (This study supposedly was known by the tongue-in-cheek nickname "Project Colonel Kicks the Bucket.") Focus groups have prevented many a product or ad, panned by consumers participating in focus groups, from seeing the light of day beyond the drawing board or prototype.

Because focus groups became such a valued stock in trade in trying to understand and influence adults, it is not surprising that the method was also adapted for research with children. Child focus groups provided youthful input into decisions, making focus groups an unparalleled opportunity for children to give voice to their own perspectives and be heard. From the way playgrounds are designed, to the cut and color of sneakers or inline skates, to fine-tuning the text and layout for kids' magazines or software, groups of children have had influence via focus groups. Today, many moderators do focus groups with kids online through the Internet, as well as in person. Over time, applied researchers have accumulated methodological expertise about what works and what doesn't, through conducting focus groups with profuse numbers of children.

At the time of the 1991 party honoring Robert Merton, American academe was just beginning to catch on to the broad methodological advantages of focus groups. The scholar Richard Krueger (1988), in a book on focus groups as a method of evaluation research, decried that so little methodological information had been documented about focus groups, because the largely applied method had passed down orally "from master to apprentice," and had developed in the hands of a "guild of practitioners." Focus groups have since grown far more important in scholars' research in the United States and abroad. Admittedly, though, the technique generally still plays third fiddle (to the survey and experiment) in U.S. grant funding. The recent scholarly renaissance in qualitative research, arising out of a paradigmatic interest in person-relevant, interpretive methods, has contributed to more interest and more writing about focus groups.

I learned to be a focus group moderator and analyst in an apprentice-like work context (such as Krueger mentioned), from one of the masters, Barbara Thomas, when I worked at the Leo Burnett Company in Chicago. Babs, as she was known, would pick someone whose personal qualities dovetailed with being a focus group moderator; then Babs would take the novice into her department, which had a heavy load of "group discussion" projects. (The only thing I remember about her selection of me was that, after watching me facilitate two groups, she asked me if strangers often talked to me on public transportation, which they do. I suppose that was an indicator to her of my listening proclivities.) I later left Leo Burnett to open doors as an independent qualitative research consultant, and for 15 years I was part of an informal "guild" of focus group practitioners who voluntarily interacted and exchanged expertise, provided mutual support, and collaborated on quite a few projects. Focus group moderators, even today, extensively share expertise with colleagues, although rarely in published text form. The largest proportion of moderators seem to be busy writing research reports for clients, rather than coveting public authorship. Yet an industrious minority have published worthwhile articles or books on facilitating focus groups (for example, Bystedt, Lynn, & Potts, 2003; Greenbaum, 1999; Langer, 2001).

Because I have worked on both sides of the ivory tower, I know there is much valuable learning about focus groups that developed through the oral tradition of the applied research "guild." This chapter dealing with focus groups and children will tap into practice-derived learning about children's focus groups, based on the applied context in which the method evolved. In addition, the chapter will also draw from a growing pool of academic literature on applying focus groups to children.

⠃⠃ Academic Orthodoxy and the Focus Group

Any form of data collection—be it experiment, survey or focus group—is an instance of human interaction actively engaged in (and made sense of) by the participants. Data collection is itself a social event in which participants (children included) seek to interpret what happens during research. No study of people is truly distanced from human subjectivity, since all human investigation entails interactive behavior and involves humans in meaning making. Ironically then, even research approaches that seek to hone in on particular facets of cognition simultaneously dip into systematic social meaning, since the process of measurement itself is a part of human exchange. Instruments used for research, in other words, are ever embedded in social discourse. There is no pristine or objectively decontextualized means of knowing, since all data reflect the social fabric in which research happens (Mishler, 1986). This is true for orthodox methods used by academic researchers—the survey and the experiment—just as it is true for the focus group.

Among children, structured questions in a survey preframe discourse since fixed questioning determines, before the research takes place, what is worth asking and (to a large degree) the latitude or breadth of the child's options for responding. Asthma, studied by surveys with children, has often been investigated through questionnaires while disregarding salient aspects of the illness to children: breathlessness and mortality are often unmentioned in youth-directed surveys about asthma, yet are a very salient and impactful issue to asthmatic youngsters (Clark, 2003). Experiments, for which the interchange with a child is narrowed down to particular variables of interest, while all other variables are set aside (that is, "controlled for"), vest the researcher (not the child) with determining what is made salient. Orthodox methods carry an intention that is to an extent comparable to that of surgery, presuming to extract out vital components of the child's tendencies (be they social opinions or psychological constructs) in a manner that can be read objectively and in isolation. But as in surgery, the constructs being plucked out are in fact part of complex systems that function in context-dependent ways. And since the research method is itself a context and a kind of social interaction, the surgical severing done by the method has much to do with what can be learned.

Traditional, surgery-like methods are well-funded and well-respected in the academy, part of an entrenched set of standard operating procedures. By contrast, in much applied research, findings are to be implemented in the dynamic and complex systems of children's everyday lives. In applied research, findings are valued that can be interpreted and translated into use for situated, ordinary contexts. In applied research, methods that are relevant to children's own meanings are actively sought and honored, particularly when the conducted research needs to guide the way to a desired result such as getting kids to eat more vegetables, buy more coloring books, take vitamins, request a particular fast food brand, stand up to peer pressure, exercise, go to an orchestra concert, wear a bicycle helmet, or whatever might be the goal in the applied investigation. This is why focus groups are so pervasive in applied research, even while experiments have a more limited role (mainly in product testing) compared to the academic realm. Focus groups are not reductive, and carry ecological relevance by being situated in a recognized social context, a small group.

In fact, a famous U.S. case study in market research, well-known among consumer marketing professionals, is a story told largely as a rationale for why focus groups should not be trumped by experimental product tests, in investigations. The often told tale of New Coke's failed 1985 introduction (Schindler, 1992) is a parable in market research, a justification for why focus group findings should not be disregarded, even in situations when survey findings and experimental results contradict focus groups. Coca Cola, a product with deep tradition-steeped meanings to Americans, had been reformulated and was studied using experimental taste tests, surveys, and focus groups. Tasters were surveyed with a hypothetical question, about whether they would buy and drink the soft drink if it was Coca Cola, and most said yes. In focus groups, however, a vocal minority were angry at the thought of the reformulated Coke, and said they would stop drinking Coke altogether if the change was implemented; these skeptics were able to sway others in the focus groups to a negative view of reformulated Coke. When New Coke was introduced in 1985, there was a huge backlash, a devastating public shock at the idea that Coke had been changed, just as presaged by the focus groups. Sales dropped. The chairman of the Coca Cola Co., Robert Goizueta, was not American by birth; his incomplete appreciation of cultural issues was said to have led him to accept the exhaustive survey and experimental results. Coca Cola's error is widely traced to discounting the socially relevant interpretive data gathered in focus groups. "The focus group is more than just a means of getting a quick and vivid look at consumer opinion," an analyst of the fiasco concluded (Schindler, 1992). "It is a unique source of information about how the consumer will respond in a situation where there will be an awareness of the views of other consumers." Intriguingly, an urban legend later arose that the Coca Cola Co. made the blunder on purpose, since eventually Coca Cola was able to proliferate many different Coke formulations, but tales of such a conspiracy are apocryphal.

In discussing the role for focus groups in research with children, bear in mind that the method is a prime form of research in applied settings in large part because it is *situated in social interaction*, consistent with the social nature of children's life activity. The ability to track the nature of mutual influence in a focus group can be invaluable. The socially embedded nature of the exchange is not a disadvantage relative to orthodox methods such as the experiment or survey. When children take part in a focus group, a good moderator develops a dynamic exchange between children, in which the give and take of children's shared discourse is comfortable and easy. If the moderator is pressured to make focus groups less socially influenced—by inserting into a conversational exchange the juxtaposition of individually administered paper-and-pencil instruments, or by having the moderator "poll" throughout the interview by sequentially interviewing each child, one by one—the advantage of the method is undermined at least in part. Mutual social exchange is at the heart of the focus group method, whether for children or adults.

∷ The Nature of the Child Focus Group

Charles Briggs (1986) regards interviews as sociolinguistic events, in which honoring the communicative norms of the interview is crucial to avoid tension and misinterpretation. Thus, planning research approaches should start with metacommunication, understanding the routines that normally govern communication for a particular cultural or social group. A study should seek compatibility with these unwritten rules. For instance, norms may govern whether and at what age children converse in small groups, in mutual give and take, in their everyday lives. Other questions about metacommunicative norms are also pertinent. At a given age, what are the linguistic practices of children that are appropriate for a group conversation? What sorts of information are shared in a group, and what secrets might be kept when around others? What are the norms governing expressed disagreement? What is the socially shared meaning of questions formulated in particular ways (Garbarino & Stout, 1989)? What sorts of exchange promote a shared bond among kids? How do ways of asking questions contribute to the power relationships perceived by children? For instance, teachers often ask rhetorical questions to see if children know the answer, a practice associated with the power inequity between a child and an adult. An interviewer who is unaware of metalinguistic cues when asking questions might revert to pedagogical style, an approach I have witnessed; unwittingly the moderator might be interpreted as an authority figure, even perhaps responded to with tacit resistance (Fine & Sandstrom, 1988). Interviews, including group interviews, need to be considered in the light of how children ordinarily express, trade, or share experiences with others. In interviews, children seem to reason best in informal, less constrained adult–child exchange, as opposed to formal and institutional contexts (Elbers, 2004). It is not that focus groups should transcend or get beyond usual communicative patterns. Rather, rapprochement needs to be sought between children's native practices and the dynamics of inquiry. (More will be said at a later point about the role and impact of the adult moderator.)

The guiding principle in designing research and facilitating children's interaction, then, is *to be as true and appropriate as possible to the metacommunicative norms of children in a particular cultural group.* Examples throughout this book are mainly drawn from American children. Children in other lands, or from particular American sub-cultures, may have divergent metacommunicative norms; if so, adjusting the approach taken, or rethinking the very advisability of the focus group method, is in order. Cultural variability should be kept in mind in considering the American examples in this chapter.

Literature discussing how to implement focus groups with children has been accruing across academic fields, with each entry into this quarry of publications reporting on a singular project, limited in scope. Academic researchers, who balance research activities with other demands, are prone to author methodological articles fairly soon in their learning curve. There is an advantage gained by considering the research method through the clear, fresh eyes of a relative newcomer. In academic writings on child focus groups, authors tend to bring enthusiasm and support for the method's potential; at the same time, these fresh reports convey raw, vivid commentary about the method's pitfalls. Child focus groups (like individual interviews with younger children) are akin to a high-intensity, high-impact sport, in which errors can misfire in pronounced ways. Being warned of the risks, as well as the benefits of a method, has value.

In what follows I will consider writings about focus groups with children by researchers ranging across diverse academic fields including: library science (Waters, 1996), computer technology (Large & Besheti, 2001; Large, Besheti, & Rahman, 2002), media (Goldman & Glantz, 1998; Tobin, 2000), education (Mauthner, 1997), mental health (Hill, Laybourn, & Borland, 1996), health care (among many others, Penza-Clyve, Mansell, & McQuaid, 2004; Ronen, 2001; Wee, Chua, & Liu, 2006), public health (Porcellato, Dughill, & Springett, 2002; Waiters, Treno, & Grube, 2001), and consumer research (Kenyon, 2004; McDonald & Topper, 1988). Literature about child focus groups, it is clear, spans continents, from Asia (MacMullin & Odeh, 1999) to Australia (Dockett & Cusack, 2003). Drawing from the spreading literature from academe, this chapter combines practitioners' and scholars' views, to shed full light on a versatile and dynamic method.

In my years of applied focus group research, I was one of the moderators who concentrated almost exclusively on qualitative research with children. Generally, focus groups or individual depth interviews among children (and separately, their parents) were my major professional activity for 15 years. Across scores and scores of projects, I experienced a learning curve. Some of the restraining issues I faced at the outset, when I first started to facilitate groups among children, were not as limiting once I was more fluent in children's language practices and ways of communicating. Over that decade and a half, the amount of talk that children contributed to an interview increased nearly threefold, as my ability to work with children's verbal exchange improved with practice. I also found that the maximum time that a child's attention might sustain a session extended as I grew more adept at dealing with how to keep children content, focused, and engaged. I also learned how to deal with more subtle or sensitive areas of probing. I grew in my ability to question in productive ways, partly because I came to know about children's perspectives on a wide range of subjects, and was able to understand how a child's comment in an interview on one topic might perhaps connect to other contexts and facets of life. As my fluency increased, another improvement was in my skill to monitor children's gestures and nonverbal communication. I gradually incorporated more and more gesturing and visual methods into my work with children. I was able to listen better and talk at an appropriate level, attending to subtle nuances of children's word choice and grammatical development. Like an anthropologist gradually catching on to the intricacies of communication within an unfamiliar tribe, I became more and more adept at mirroring and matching how children communicated, simply through sustained dedication to my craft. Just as would be true of any sort of communicative skill, the more I rose to the multifaceted challenge of engaging and listening in child focus groups, the more natural and apparently easy the whole process appeared, including to others. My own experience, then, suggests that more can be accomplished in focus groups with children if the moderator is seasoned. Similar to the child therapist who is able to engage in play therapy seemingly seamlessly after years of professional practice, or the facile surgeon who has done a particular procedure over and over, in the same way moderating focus groups with children is a skill that through reflexive practice and dedication can be honed and improved.

To provide know-how for strengthening children's focus groups, areas to consider include: (1) Inviting the children; (2) The setting; (3) The moderator's craft; (4) Special applications. (Interpretation issues that arise in analyzing focus group research will be considered in Chapter 7.)

Inviting the Children

In designing a focus group project, deciding who should participate is a consequential step. As a practitioner, I have followed proven principles guiding sample selection, principles that have served me well in my academic child inquiry, too.

The first principle derives from a focus group session being an act of social sharing. *A focus group is optimal when the participants are a homogeneous group, rather than drawn from dialectically opposed factions.* The *homogeneity* principle applies to focus groups within any age group, adults as well as children. For instance, in a new product project, the usual study design involves conducting *separate* groups with "trier-repeaters" (who bought the product once, and liked it well enough to repeat the act) versus "trier-rejecters" (who bought the product once, but weren't satisfied enough to repeat the act). Through homogeneous sessions, the group is more likely to excavate shared experience and assumptions, revealed through the talk of members joined in common exchange. (Trier-repeaters will tend to focus on the product's strengths and uses, while trier-rejecters will focus on the product's unappealing factors.) A decision to form a group made of opposed camps (Neocons alongside Liberals, for instance) is not recommended, for such a group, combative-by-design, likely doesn't develop the same degree of cohesion and mutual search for significance.

Academic researchers have also praised the idea of homogeneous group composition for child focus groups, although ways of carrying out the homogeneity rule vary. Caroline Heary and Ellis Hennessey (2002) have argued for homogeneity, in the sense that groups of children should be *gender-similar*; gender is aligned with distinctive interests, attitudes and viewpoints that may be left unexplored in a group that mixes boys and girls. This argument for gender-specific focus groups is consistent with applied research practice, where separate groups for each gender are the standard. In academic studies, gender homogeneity is sometimes justified as a matter of gender equity, since boys may overshadow girls in mixed groups, biasing the conversation topics that are aired (Mauthner, 1997). Male or female, the presence of the opposite gender could cause discomfort or distraction (Porcellato, Dughill, & Springett, 2002). The concern that gender-mixed groups would not work well in a focus group study seems well placed, given the greater assertiveness widely seen in boys' groups compared to girls' groups, on seemingly neutral issues such as computers (Large & Beheshti, 2001).

Girls are apt to cooperate with others in focus groups (even when they have never met before), whereas boys are more prone to personally assert themselves, to posture and position. In a set of gender-separated focus groups I once conducted about a retail play setting, I gave the kids a very large sheet of plain paper, and asked them to together draw a map of the place. Left to their own devices, girls completed the entire task in less than 10 minutes. Boys took over twice as long and still didn't finish, because of assertive disagreements about which boy would draw which part of the map. This illustrative case is not exceptional. Even in interpreting the meaning of children's comments, sociolinguistic variation by gender has to be factored in; American boys overall have a greater affinity for critiquing during focus groups, relative to girls. The base level or normative level of criticism, then, differs for boys versus girls. The complaints of each gender need to be weighed accordingly, in assigning meaning to evaluative comments. This sort of adjustment is aided by the homogeneity principle of scheduling separate focus group sessions with boys versus girls.

Nevertheless, some scholars have included mixed-gender groups in research. Joseph Tobin (2000) has combined, within a project, gender-homogeneous and mixed-gender sessions. It is possible, in some circumstances, that the topic of a group discussion may be so conducive to bonding (as in the case of kids who share the same illness) that a successful mixed gender session is feasible (Horner, 2000).

Another issue of sample composition deals with the age range of children who make up a session. The homogeneity principle implies what to do—to *keep age ranges tight*. I prefer—as do Kennedy, Kools, & Krueger (2001)—that children remain within a maximum 2-year age range. A minority of practitioners base the selection not on age, but on a child's grade in school, once again with no more than a two-grade span per session. Some scholars have suggested an even tighter age range. Large and Beheshti (2001) have favored no greater a gap in age than 12 months, because of the dramatic age-related changes in behavior and cognition. Age discrepancies can strain group exchange and dynamics, because of dissimilar abilities and social experiences. Once the span of age goes beyond 2 years, these variations become excessively hard to manage.

The research design will also need to take into account the age at which children are ready candidates for the demands of the focus group process. On the basis of American sociolinguistic behaviors, I have found that *8 years is the earliest age when children reliably exhibit the full-fledged conversational give and take* that is the method's backbone. At age 6 or 7 years, children are more appropriately interviewed in a very small group setting (such as a triad interview or individual interview). Five-year-olds are amenable to being individually interviewed, although this is a pronounced challenge relative to older kids. (There is no shame in setting 6 years as a minimum age for individual interviews, as many interviewers do.)

The issue of age intersects with the issue of interview duration. For 8- to 11-year-olds, interviewed in a group, the scheduled time for each group interview might range from an hour to 90 minutes (although cases may vary); this range is consistent with advice in the academic literature. In practice, the outer time limit is influenced by several factors—the moderator's proficiency, how involved children are in the topic, as well as age-related attention span. The older the child, the longer the span of time he will be able to remain focused. The more skilled the moderator, the greater the facility with keeping children engaged over time. As I gained experience, I found that my group interviews lasted longer, often close to 2 hours.

Another issue is whether the children interviewed should be *strangers or acquaintances*. Lewis (1992) and Hill (2006) are among the researchers who praise the "friendship" approach to interviews, in which acquainted or friend peers are invited together. Some argue that interviewing a group of friends eases moderator load, since children will be comfortable with one another, thereby posing one less challenge for the moderator (Kenyon, 2004). My own experience endorses a qualified view, one that also recognizes disadvantages to the friendship-based approach. Friends generally come with a group dynamic of their own, often with a well-entrenched, friendly but established social hierarchy (Mauthner, 1997). In interviewing pairs of friends, I have found that a dominant friend can prevail almost completely over a subordinate friend. In a group interview, friends may carve out their own space in the conversation, using "inside" humor and references no one else is familiar with, and may overlook the larger group context and its invitation to raise issues freely. After all, friendship goes on after the focus group is over, and this can have a filtering and inhibiting effect. Children who are strangers may need to strive for group cohesion, but it may turn out to be a more pliant and in some ways less inhibited social space.

In the final analysis, inviting friends for focus groups is a decision that should be compatible with the topic. If studying a game played by two people, or a social intervention based on supportive friends, conducting the research within the frame of friendship would be appropriate. In most applied studies, these circumstances don't apply; overridingly focus groups are a method in which strangers, not friends or acquaintances, come together and share ideas or thoughts.

The children invited for a focus group, besides being homogeneous in age and gender, should be qualified to speak on the subject in question. Therefore another principle: *the children invited should be screened to have prior experience with the issue or topic.* This stipulation ought to be applied to group or individual interviews. Children who have never been to a zoo cannot be expected to give rich reactions to plans for a new zoo. Children (or adults, for that matter) can be poor sources of information about nonevents, such as what they missed by not being homeschooled, or what has kept them from ever collecting baseball cards, or how they were affected by never having gone to camp. If there is a new experience that needs to be explored with children, find a way for participants to experience that new thing prior to coming to the group discussion, such as placing a product in their home for a period of time prior to the session, so that children have a basis to react. A chance to use a product can sometimes be part of the group interview itself. Even so, children need a frame of reference to use in making sense of a new entity, which is why children who are going to try a new instant hot cereal generally are screened to eat instant hot cereal. In short, screening decisions should take into account whether children have experience relative to the subject matter.

A decision to be made before inviting children to the focus group is *how many* children to include. The academic literature carries a consensus recommendation that *focus groups with children need to be smaller than adult focus groups,* and I agree. Six boys at a time, or seven girls at a time, would be the maximum I recommend prior to adolescence. Some scholars have recommended even smaller groups of children, as few as four to five (Morgan et al. 2002). Very small group formats are used quite a bit in applied research, to save on expenses or to prevent moderator fatigue in a densely scheduled project. (Crowd control is easier with a smaller group.) Triad interviews (three kids at a time) have a very good track record in applied research, creating an intimate and relatively manageable group. Seven-year-olds and some 6-year-olds, who at that young age may not be appropriate candidates for a full focus group, are many times less intimidated by the relative intimacy of a triad than by a larger group. There is less social risk, perhaps, and a chance for the group to become closer knit.

Children who agree to take part in a focus group or triad often sincerely want to join in and like to be recognized for the accomplishment. I don't endorse the practice of "over-recruiting" children, that is, recruiting more children than the moderator can handle (a common recruiting practice for adults, to allow understudies for those who may not show up). My preference is to invite as many children as the moderator plans to take into the session. This can be inconvenient if too many children

---

Date of Interview _____

Time of Interview_____

FAMILY SCREENER

CHILD'S NAME_____ PARENT'S NAME_____

ADDRESS_____

CITY_____STATE_____ZIP_____

TELEPHONE (HOME)_____(CELL)_____

RECRUITED BY_____DATE RECRUITED_____

CONFIRMED BY_____DATE CONFIRMED_____

A. Hello, this is _____ of _____. From time to time, we talk with customers like yourself to ask your opinions about various products you might use.

Today we are talking with parents who have children between the ages of 8 and 11 years living at home. Do you have any children living at home who are between the ages of 8 and 11 years?

Yes [ ] ...CONTINUE BELOW
No [ ] ... THANK AND END

B. Exactly how old are all your children? [RECORD RESPONSE BELOW.] Is your ___-year-old a boy or a girl? [CHECK SEX.]

	AGE (fill in)	SEX (check reply)
Child # 1	_____	Girl ☐ Boy ☐
Child # 2	_____	Girl ☐ Boy ☐
Child # 3	_____	Girl ☐ Boy ☐
Child # 4	_____	Girl ☐ Boy ☐

NOTE: *You will be recruiting 26 kids for four focus groups. There will be sessions with boys aged 8 to 9 years, and 10 to 11 years. (Recruit six boys per session.) There will be sessions with girls aged 8 to 9 years, and 10-11 years. (Recruit seven girls per session.)*

C. Earlier you said you have a child who is _____ years old. I'd like to ask you some questions now about the activities done by that child. Has your boy/girl who is ___ years old ever attended the following events? [READ LIST. CHECK ALL THE APPLY.]

A birthday party at McDonald's... [ ]
A trip to the circus.................. [ ]
A Chicago Cubs baseball game... [ ] *** TO QUALIFY, MUST BE CHECKED
A minor league baseball game...... [ ]

(cont'd)

D. You mentioned that your boy/girl who is _____years old has attended a Chicago Cubs baseball game. How long ago was the last time they attended? (DO NOT READ LIST. CHECK APPROPRIATE REPLY.)

More than two months ago..... .[ ] THANK & END
Two months ago or less.........[ ] CONTINUE

E. Some of the work we are doing involves asking the children themselves some questions. May I speak briefly to your ___-year-old boy/girl?

SAY TO CHILD:
Hi, my name is _____. Thank you for coming to the phone. I need to ask you a few questions. First of all, how old are you?

_____ [fill in]

I'm trying to find out about the places kids go to have fun. Do you ever go to the movies? Tell me a movie you went to. What was that movie like?
No need to record reply

Did you ever go to a Cubs baseball game? Tell me a game you went to. What happened in that game, while you watched?
No need to record reply. This question is to ensure that child recalls and is familiar with the game.

CHECK QUALIFICATIONS AND QUOTAS. ASK TO SPEAK AGAIN TO THE CHILD'S PARENT. INVITE CHILD TO INTERVIEW (IF QUALIFED AND WITHIN QUOTAS). GIVE INFORMATION ON DATE/TIME/LOCATION AND TOKEN OF APPRECIATION.

cancel because of illness (a rare occurrence), but when all the children come (a common occurrence) it avoids needing to eliminate a child and risking disappointment or rejection.

In screening respondents for one-on-one or group interviews, professional qualitative researchers employ a written screener, structured to enlist the number and type of children stipulated by the project. Parents and children both answer questions in the screening process. Children can verify parental claims and ensure their familiarity with a topic and their qualifications to take part. Here is an example of a screener (used by phone or in person), for a study of the child audience for a professional baseball team. The particular team mentioned is for illustration purposes, since the screener could be adapted to work for any team or entertainment activity.

The Setting

There is too little contact between scholars and practitioners about focus groups. Most scholars, it seems, are unacquainted with the substantial support structure for applied focus group research that exists in North America. Hundreds of focus group facilities are found in office buildings and shopping centers around the United States, each one equipped with a hostess, a waiting area, and attractively furnished interviewing rooms. Directories that list these sorts of places are not exhaustive, but listings include more than 375 such facilities in the U.S. (Greenbook, 2006) and as many as 1,000 worldwide (Quirk's Market Research Review, 2006). By usual practice, many focus group facilities also recruit participants for the sessions, based on the moderator's specifications set forth in a screening questionnaire.

At a qualitative research facility, the interviewing rooms are usually designed to accommodate adult focus groups. The furnishings of an interviewing room include: an ample table intentionally shaped for group facilitation, comfortable chairs, discrete audio (and often video) recording equipment, and a viewing room (behind a one-way mirror) where interested clients sit comfortably and observe.

The viewing room is seldom empty during a market research project, in my experience. Executives who commission a study and their associates come to have a look, even traveling extensive distances to do so. I have had the experience at many sessions when there were more observers behind the viewing mirror than informants in front of the mirror. Occasionally someone watching has been a highly ranked individual with a vested interest in the project. I once interviewed mothers and children while a major corporate CEO watched from the viewing room, and talked with me mid-session about respondents' points. Some moderators have gone to the extent of coaching viewers in how to listen, observe, and take notes (Fedder, 1985). In my experience, marketers using focus groups are highly motivated to have a closer and more humane window into human experience than quantitative data permits. Viewing group interviews often stems from this motive. A senior client once told me, when he worked at a well-known company making baby products, that he would insist that his new subordinates attend focus group after focus group conducted with mothers of infants; the mandatory attendance would only cease when he saw evidence that the junior executives could empathize deeply with the inexpressibly intense mother–baby bond. Fully disclosed as part of consent, observation contributes to building human connection and understanding, especially for viewers not of the respondents' gender, age, social class, ethnicity or other life circumstances.

The relatively business-like furnishings of a focus group facility are not always ideal for children's sessions. The usually large adult table can be too overbearing, and a smaller less formal alternative might need to be moved in; folding tables can serve well. Chairs that swivel or move on wheels tend to be distracting, so substituting other chairs is wise. The waiting room may be reminiscent of a medical or dental waiting area, children have told me after they were relieved to learn otherwise. The microphone might be mounted to hang so low from the ceiling that children target it for throwing things. Trying to conduct groups for children can involve a partial makeover of the setting, changing furnishings to make a childproofed, conducive place for young participants.

In office settings, some moderators manage overly adult furniture by eliminating tables and chairs altogether, having children sit in a circle on the floor or on mats or large pillows. This approach is reminiscent of how story time is conducted in nursery school in the United States. Generally, for American kids 8 years and older, sitting on or near furniture is an expected, age-appropriate cultural arrangement. Morgan and colleagues (2002) argue that on-the-floor seating conveys an "atmosphere of equity" because the moderator is on the same level as the participants. But in fact, the physical tallness of an adult interviewer relative to the children means that a grown-up will at least to some degree tower above kids, when everyone is seated on the floor. By contrast, if kids are seated on chairs, there are ways in which this enhances, rather than detracts, from equity and power issues. First, with furniture the adult has less chance of needing to control kids' physical movements by explicit ("bossy") directives, since chairs provide an unobtrusive means of child containment (Kennedy, Kools, & Krueger, 2001). Second, if the children are seated in chairs, the adult can lower her height by kneeling or squatting on the floor, with the effect that the seated children look down toward the adult, a stance reversal I have used often to draw out reticent kids (when positioned near them). At the same time, many tasks done in a group interview (eating or drinking, handling a product, drawing, sorting, etc.) may be easiest for school-age respondents seated at a table (rather than the floor). I find sitting in a circle on the floor to be an adult stereotype for how to operate at a child's level, but one that doesn't always work out as intended.

Attending to details can help to orchestrate a child-conducive atmosphere. If taping the interview, try to arrange the equipment so that kids can see or hear themselves by playing back the tape, a practice recommended in the methodological literature (Kenyon, 2004). It's fun for kids to hear themselves, and in the process familiarize themselves with the recorder.

Nametags worn by kids are also helpful for icebreaking. Kids can make or decorate their own nametags, and talk about their tags in introducing themselves (Hill, Laybourn & Borland, 1996). (Incidentally, name labels with good adhesive are a help, to avoid children being distracted as they fiddle with a half-adhered nametag.)

Careful troubleshooting of the materials in the room is advised to remove what might be distracting or hazardous. Keeping troublesome material out of sight can obviate the need for interdictions, heading off power issues. When the moderator uses less correction or directive intervention, this pays off in a greater sense of equity and child-centeredness.

When I began doing qualitative research in academia, I missed the services made possible by focus group facilities (recruiting subjects, making sure interviews are properly taped, and the many ways in which having a hostess is supportive of a successful project). But on the other hand, focus groups under academic auspices tend to be in naturalistic settings such as homes, summer camps, or community centers. These sorts of familiar settings can be advantageous for interviewing children, since they are less formal and less adult-oriented than focus group facilities. Having the interview in a child-friendly nonschool setting can be an antidote to the staid, adult–child power imbalance endemic to adult settings (Darbyshire, Macdougall, & Schiller, 2005; Hill, 2006; Horner, 2000), assuming that the moderator plans each session to be compelling enough to sustain attention. Even Disneyworld has held productive sessions using professional moderators, not necessarily in an office facility, but in a room right on the grounds.

The Moderator's Craft

William Wells (1974) once pointed out that, while almost anyone can learn the mechanics of survey interviewing, the sort of nondirective interviewing central to focus groups is another matter. In a survey, the questions are all spelled out beforehand and the interviewer merely needs to follow the script. In a focus group, hypotheses are a work in progress during the unfolding of the interview, such that questions may morph and shift to reflect ongoing or evolving meanings. Focus groups aren't intended as a way to fish for answers to preordained questions.

They are a way to more thoroughly comprehend a problem, understood in terms of people's shared meanings and situated behaviors. The facilitator is not only questioning the participants, but is working to discern schemas and framings that help to model actions and ideas. Thus there is a kind of elaborate learning on the part of the moderator, who seeks— as Calder (1977) once put it—to "experience the experience" of the informants, and through intersubjective discourse to form hypotheses that correspond to respondents' experience. Qualitative research, and focus groups specifically, are ways of figuring out what the parameters of a problem are, how the concepts should be parsed, what intricacies shouldn't be discounted. Rather than counting heads to assess opinions, the researcher is finding out the best way to "count to one," how to construe the elements as natives do. The goal is to figure out what counts, from informants' perspectives. The hypotheses being formed in a focus group, through the probing, listening, and synthesis of the moderator, are prefatory, foundational, prime.

Mentored to be a focus group moderator, I internalized the idea that I was there, facilitating the group, to learn. Listening was my most important job. To be sure, the moderator should speak to introduce a topic area, to redirect straying conversation, to draw out the reticent, to clarify a point and so on. But the talking should be focused on the respondents, not the moderator's concerns. (Sometimes, when groups veer off a topic, it is telling with regard to what really matters to participants.) The participants have the answers, if the moderator is willing to give herself over to their exchange. Thus the personal qualities of a successful moderator include talents of both listening and learning.

Barbara Thomas, the master moderator who trained me, once listed (in an undocumented presentation) traits that characterize people who lead groups successfully. Such people are:

- Open, honest and don't try to trick or manipulate,
- Warm and friendly, and able to establish a relaxed atmosphere,
- Excellent listeners who pick out detail, nuances (and I might add, intriguing contradictions),
- Curious and social people, who enjoy interacting with others,
- Nonadversarial or nonconfrontational in approaching people.

Regarding children's focus groups, I would say these same five qualities serve a moderator well in working with children. I would supplement the list for working with children, however, adding additional attributes for effective children's moderators. The most successful children's group interviews are led by those who:

- Play well, are inventive and facile,
- Tolerate chaos without losing focus,
- Are tenacious, willing to try as many approaches as it takes,
- Are patient, yet able to keep things moving in a fast-paced, intense process,
- Exhibit humility and acceptance of others.
- Can act responsibly, without dominating.

The qualities I've listed are needed in child-relevant interaction, and in staying on track of children's meandering but thematic points. Children are harder to interview than adults. Establishing and keeping rapport requires a reservoir of strengths, for children will at times be disorderly, playful, slow to respond, fading in interest, jumping ahead, or possibly concealing or resistant to the adult who dominates or formalizes. Children have not yet mastered their culture's social, communicative graces in entirety. Moderators must find a way to reach and activate children's powers of expression. A totally verbal or too abstract exchange is prone to slide off track, misconnecting with children's abilities or exceeding their cognitive limits.

In the academic literature, many have written about challenges and pitfalls they confronted in facilitating groups of children. These challenges trace not only to the interview, but the processes before and after. A researcher preparing to facilitate a child focus group is about to engage in a thrilling challenge, and it is prudent to be forearmed. Fortunately, inventive ways of scaffolding children through a smooth and informative group interview have been made known by academic and applied moderators.

The Moderator's Plan: A paradox of focus groups is that while the interview is a real-time activity laced with improvisation, thorough planning is still crucial. A moderator is an investigator of a problem, and must internalize the problem up front. This may be more crucial for a child focus group than an adult focus group; the compressed time period (with children's short attention spans) and complex interviewing challenges of children's group interviews conspire to detract, if a moderator is not prepared. Like a sprinter getting ready for a race, the facilitator will have a brief time in which to run the course, but will do so better if thoroughly briefed and ready in advance.

Appreciation of the research problem (whether for focus groups or individual interviews) starts with a thorough inquiry of relevant persons and sources. What was the background that led up to the problem? How has this problem been thought about or approached up until now? Are there prior studies that can be digested for approaches to the problem? As an applied researcher, I encouraged clients to weigh me down with all past research on the problem, which I read assiduously. Understanding the problem is important because, as William Wells (1974) has written, the moderator must hunt for clues and answers in the session like a hound following a scent. The facilitator needs to sense when there is a wisp of an answer, so that the most promising trail doesn't go undetected. Advanced briefing gives the moderator a better nose for the issues.

Once the moderator is steeped in the research problem, he can lay out a strategy for how to communicate with children to explore the problem. Assuming that focus groups are a legitimate approach, and that six or seven children will be attending for about an hour or so, an appropriate discussion guide can be prepared. A discussion guide differs from a questionnaire, for it is a flexible tool not fixed in final form. The order of coverage is likely to morph as the moderator adapts to children's discourse. Some unplanned items may get added, and others dropped. One moderator I know likes to put the study's main objective centered at the top of the discussion guide. This is to remind all involved that the work in the group is to pursue the objective even if that means retreading or appending the plan. Moderators are most effective when taking advantage of those times when kids broach a subject, unaided, as they are triggered by their own train of thought. Dictating exactly how or when kids talk about an issue can keep the moderator from tracking with the kids, and such impositions can throw kids off their own track. The moderator also ought to adjust vocabulary, in order to better reflect kids' terminology. I once heard a focus group moderator's story, told with a message: as a novice the moderator was busy staring down at the words on her discussion guide, figuring out what her next approach to an issue would be, completely missing the fact that one of the kids was wildly trying to get her attention to explain the very issue. Learning how to gracefully take advantage of opportunities that arise, without being rigidly tied to the discussion guide, gets easier with practice. (A young moderator once espoused that moderating is like playing handball or racquetball: the balls are flying too fast at the beginning to keep up with all the demands, but with experience it's as if the balls start to move in slower motion.) Moderators do best when they surf the contours of kids' inclinations as much as possible, rather than imposing their a priori contrivances on children.

Still, a good discussion guide can be a moderator's salvation. The guide expresses the issues or problems translated into a set of questioning areas, which in practice is excellent preparation for listening well. The discussion guide gives a set of cues for drawing out each matter of interest. The discussion guide can be a checklist for the moderator to mentally scan to be sure all the issues of interest are getting airtime. Some of the areas will be covered on the fly, at a time when one of the children mentions it and the moderator is perceptive enough to react and listen. Others may be probed through an explicit planned activity.

A general principle in a discussion guide (whether for group or individual interviews) is to start with broad, overarching issues first, and gradually get more specific. (This applies to children and adults alike.) A focus group on asthma medicine taking (conducted to explore reactions to a planned adherence intervention) might start with a discussion of asthma, then shift to what children do to take care of their asthma, then what medicines they take, as well as who remembers and initiates taking each one, how often they skip, likes and dislikes about taking each medicine, and finally, reactions to the planned intervention. By initiating the focus group with an overview of managing asthma, reactions to the intervention can be set within children's own frameworks and conceptions articulated in the initial discourse. Also, starting with a general discussion helps the facilitator to know particular children and how their unique experience or beliefs might relate to their reactions to the specific intervention. Finally, general questions can be good "starter" questions, easy for participants to manage, breaking ground for what comes later (Horner, 2000).

When preparing a discussion guide, I often have a fairly good idea of approaches that might work well, from experience. If I plan to have children gesture with a thumbs up or thumbs down after watching a particular movie segment, my discussion guide might simply say, "Thumbs up/down (Why?)." If I am showing kids several alternatives of a product, the discussion guide might read, "After all shown: Favorite/ Least Favorite (Why?)" meaning that I will ask which is the best liked, worst liked, and the basis for these judgments. The words on the discussion guide are not necessarily the literal wording I would use to ask the question. (The probe, "What part makes it your favorite?" would be a more usual and workable way of asking, "Why?" for example—it is more tractable and tangible.)

In working with children to probe reactions to a new product, I have developed a workable, engaging approach. It involves asking the children to imagine, in their minds, the inventor of the new product. I might preface a set of questions by saying, "Let's pretend there's an inventor who is making the product, and he wants to know what you think of his invention." The avatar of an "inventor" provides a ready way to probe kids about abstract features of the product, in a manner they can fathom. Children pick up on the idea, volunteering, "Tell the inventor not to change a thing." Or, "The inventor needs to try all over again." I can probe all sorts of specific issues by asking the kids how they would advise the inventor. The discussion guide might show this, only in abbreviated form:

Inventor role-play: What if the inventor of this asked you:

- Is it a good invention, or not really?
- Good parts/bad parts about the invention?
- What parts should the inventor change?
- If inventors got grades and report cards, what grade would this invention get?
  - Why that grade? How could they change it to get a better grade?
- What would you tell the inventor about:
  - The way they made the invention (color, size, how it feels)
  - The sort of kids who would/wouldn't like the invention (boys/girls, kids of what age, etc.)

During the interview, every planned question does not have to be played out literally, nor should it. If kids already thoroughly explained that they don't like the product because of its "lame" grey color, that point is already well-understood so there is no need to revisit the topic. Children, like adults, appreciate being listened to the first time they make a point; it's a sign that the interviewer cares about and values what they say. Additionally, an able children's moderator adjusts how the questions are asked so as to reflect children's particular cognitive and verbal skills. The idea is to do the probing in a manner that flows with the conversation and suits the particular group of children, using their frameworks and terms to probe the issues.

It works well to let children communicate hands-on or visually as well as verbally. I often plan for hands-on or visual materials that allow kids to see, show, or manipulate as well as tell. Coming up with props is part of preparation. Once, a major company was opening a retail store for children's clothing, and the store was expected to be full of novel features, unlike anything children would have experienced. Describing those features to kids would have been taxing and not communicative, and I anticipated we would learn very little if I merely explained the store verbally. To make the ideas more graspable, I asked the firm to make a model of the new store, in which each one of the features was included as a freestanding element that could be pulled out of the display in the same way a child pulls a toy bathtub or table out of a dollhouse. Since the model would be tactilely and visually present and interactive, I expected the model to empower children to understand and react more fully; models and replicas boost recall even in 3-year-olds (Salmon, 2001). Children indeed responded with ease to the features of the store and how these features were placed in the overall space. Making this model in advance provided a revealing and tractable tool, through which children were able to have clearer comprehension and response than if it had been a strictly verbal interview.

In group and individual interviews, I have used an assortment of props. Among the examples, consider: toys that resemble furnishings in a hospital; a toy doctor's kit; shoes that can be worn to pretend the child is a character; large illustrations that show the successive windows in a software program; pictures of characters from commercials, made into a deck of sortable cards; illustrated boards to visually represent new products; built or prepared prototypes of product ideas that resemble the finished item.

In planning a group discussion, then, the moderator must internalize the issues, prepare a discussion guide (as a flexible tool), and gather any props that will ease communication through hands-on or visual interaction. Ideas are best presented in a more concrete, graspable form.

The Respondents' Arrival: Because a focus group is a social event, it goes without saying that the action starts as soon as people get together. Young respondents may arrive one by one, as the moderator is making final preparations for the session. If the moderator can free up a bit of time to spend with the kids as they arrive, this impromptu overture can provide a head start for rapport building. Icebreaking topics to chat about should be kid-relevant: the sports teams on the child's clothing, the siblings who accompany them, a holiday coming up or just past, pets, vacations, and so on. This preliminary chitchat can set a tone of warmth and sharing. One favored practice of mine has been to introduce kids to each other and get them started on mutual riddle or joke telling, while they wait. (I may ignite this process with an age-appropriate joke of my own.) If a child who is waiting looks meek or tense, I go over in a friendly manner and introduce myself, trying to soften the youngster's misgivings with friendliness. (Some kids just need to know where the bathroom is, or need someone to take them there.) On occasion it helps before the session to remind children that their parents will be right nearby, waiting, and ready to reunite with the child when we're done, which won't be long because the time usually goes by very quickly. (It's generally not advisable to let a parent accompany the child in a focus group, mainly for the obvious reason that the group is between children.)

Now and then, American parents volunteer children for a study without their child's enthused commitment. One common scenario is that the child is extremely shy and the parent thinks the research will draw out the child's sociability. The point of parental separation can also be a trouble spot. On occasion, I've taken the step of escorting both the parent and child, together, on a preview tour of the interviewing room, which helps to reassure both generations. It can't be overemphasized that sensitivity to a child's needs before the interview, as well as during it, is an optimal practice.

William Wells (1979) described a moderator as a lovable person who seems to have no opinions of her own to express, what he called an "animate inkblot." But a good moderator is more generous than an inkblot. Having a genuine desire to make kids comfortable and able to enjoy the focus group can go far to establish a conducive atmosphere for beginning the session.

Starting the Session

Once the session starts, it remains important for the facilitator to sensitively put himself in the children's sneakers. An adult from the U.S. who is interviewed has a fairly good notion of what to expect and what is going on in an interview. But consider what a child experiences when an unfamiliar grown-up "starts asking a lot of questions, some of which are hard" (Wells, 1965). The child can struggle to think of what to say, and lack an understanding of the intent of the questions. In some respects, a partial metaphor for the child's plight is that of graduate students taking orals: the person answering can feel powerless, and tell themselves they got off on the wrong track completely. Anxiety, frustration, shyness (and boredom, perhaps) can torment the answerer. To forego such a negative experience for a child participant, the moderator begins each session with a full and clear explanation of what is about to take place. This warm-up explanation helps to set up children's understanding of what is to them a unique situation. The introduction needs to clarify and empower.

Here is a version of my usual introductory explanation, which covers the main points I try to make with children at the outset of a focus group.

I'm **so** glad you came. I'm Cindy [Point to my name tag.] Has anybody here every done this before, or maybe someone else in your family did it? Oh, your mom did this before? What did she tell you about it? [Let child describe.] You see, a focus group is really, really special. Mainly, we do this because some grown-ups have questions they don't know the answers to, so they asked me to see if you could help. That sounds funny doesn't it, that kids would know answers the grown-ups don't know? But there are lots of things that kids know all about and grown-ups don't know very much about. Who do you think knows more about video games: kids or grown-ups? [Let them answer.] Who knows more about Pokémon: kids or grown-ups? [Let them answer.] [Continue with examples until kids clearly get the idea that kids can know more than adults about some subjects.] So when I ask you a question, it's not like I'm a teacher. Have you ever noticed that teachers ask you questions, but they *already* know the answers, like, 'What's 2 + 2?' When I ask you a question, *you're* the one who knows, and I'm trying to learn. You're teaching me today. As long as you're telling me what you really think about something, that's all you have to do. By the way, I've found that different people think different things a lot of the time, and that's fine. Let's try an experiment. I'm going to count to three, and when I get to three I want everybody to *shout* out their favorite color, all at the same time. 1, 2, 3! [Let them shout—usually a variety of colors are yelled.] See how people might have different answers about what they like, and that's great. Just tell what you really, truly think, even if you're thinking something different from everybody else. [Repeat the yell-your-favorite exercise as needed, perhaps using movies, sports, or animals, to be sure kids understand that conformity is not expected.]

Sometimes you might have an idea that you think to yourself, you think, 'it's such a small idea, it might sound kind of dumb, I won't tell it.' Did that ever happen to you? Well, I've listened to a lot of kids and I found out, that the really small ideas often help me to

---

(cont'd)

understand the most. [Gesture along with speaking the words "small" and "most," using thumb, finger and hands.] So no matter what you're thinking, big and little ideas, just say it. Sometimes I might show you something and ask if you like it or not. It doesn't matter if you like it, or hate it. It won't hurt my feelings, because I'm here to find out what you really think, and it doesn't matter if you don't like it. I won't get in any trouble. Okay, there's one more thing. I want to make sure I hear all your ideas. So if everyone starts talking at the same time, like with the favorite colors, I might not be able to hear what each person said. And I want to hear everybody. Sometimes my ears need to keep up. So if I remind you to talk one at a time, that's why, it's so I can hear you.

Do you see this? [Point to tape recorder.] We're making a tape of this so I won't forget anything you said. Has anybody ever heard your voice on a tape recorder before? I can play some of the tape back in a couple minutes, if you want. The tape is so I won't forget a single thing you said. The tape is to help me remember. Nobody will get to listen to the tape, not your mom, not your aunt, no one else. [If there is an observation room, explain about some grown-ups in the room taking notes, clarifying that no other grown-ups are back there, such as parents. If kids ask to see the people in the observation room, I ask them to turn on the light so they can be seen, and let everybody wave at each other.]

OK, is there anything else I could explain some more? Any questions? Okay, well this is what we're gonna do. Everybody has a nametag. I want everybody to know each other a little better. So let's have each person tell your name, how old you are, and tell me one thing about you. The one thing about you can be anything you want, something you really like to do, when your birthday is, how you fight with your brother, I don't care what it is. But you have to think of one thing about you that you will share with everybody. I'll start. My name is Cindy, I'm 56 years old. And one thing about me is I really like to find out things from kids. Okay, who wants to be next?

My introductory prattle is designed to accomplish several things. It establishes that this is a time of active, even playful, involvement, by asking the children to participate, and by giving them a chance to yell together their favorite color. The warm-up empowers, in multiple ways: leading children to appreciate the nature of their knowledge superiority over adults, assuring them that their "little ideas" have big merit, that dissonant opinions still matter, and that they are here to tell what they already know, not to be quizzed. My entire demeanor suggests openness and respect, even in the honest admission of my age. Implied is a kind of authentic "naïve curiosity" on my part (France, Bendelow, & Williams, 2000), whereby I am ready to learn afresh, in an empathic and open way. The rule I invoke (to speak one at a time) is justified as child-empowering, to make sure I hear and understand each kid.

During children's introductions, I usually make a seating chart, a step especially helpful on days when several sessions are held and I need to keep straight kids' names. During the session, I also am prone to surreptitiously make other notations on that seating chart, such as a relevant term spoken by a particular child or some other detail I might return to in later probing.

Being a Catalyst for Discourse

When a moderator is hired in applied research, she is apt to be judged based on what happens after the introduction, during the meat of the interview when children are encouraged to talk about the project issues. The moderator is expected to be a catalyst for talk that is illuminating and relevant. Yet facilitating this sort of conversation among kids can be fraught with unexpected turns. If children don't talk, or stray to other topics, or behave in ways that converts the interview into frenzy, the moderator has to be intrepid and try his best to turn things around. Some moderators, to reduce the risk of overly quiet responses, screen young participants to be articulate to the extreme. Unfortunately, that practice makes the sample unrepresentative of children overall: children with greater verbal skills not only talk more fluently, but sometimes understand commercials when other children wouldn't, read instructions when other kids wouldn't, and so on. Rather than adjust the children to the focus group, a moderator can and should instead adjust the kind of questioning to the children. Questioning strategies can help ensure that even less articulate children are given voice, or gesture, or whatever form of expression they can manage. After seeing a commercial or product, for instance, I might initially have all the kids give a thumbs up or thumbs down (placing thumbs in an up or down position) at once, a familiar gesture to American kids. The gesture provides a reading of how each boy or girl feels, even the reticent ones, which can kick off a more inclusive discussion.

A certain amount of energetic activity is one of youth's perquisites. Playfulness and noise characterize many children's group sessions. I once conducted focus groups in a focus group facility, which was (perhaps foolishly) also hosting focus groups with adult stockbrokers in the adjacent room. My respondents were boisterous and vocal, and following a knock on the door, I was told that the stockbrokers would like my participants to be more mature and reserved. Alas, I calmly explained, they are third-grade boys, and this is how third-grade boys sound when discussing athletic shoes. The stockbrokers moved to another available room. Moderators, to achieve equity with children, need to heed children's usual sociolinguistic patterns—even when this involves excited laughter, chanting, or exaggerated poses. Sedate but chatty respondents, who have mastered rules of courtesy, are not generally under a decade in age. (In church or the classroom, children's restrained behavior is adult-enforced.)

Minimizing dictatorial discipline has been a means, both in focus groups and in participant observation, to cultivate confidence and disclosure. Being tolerant of kids' exuberance allows the moderator to be less generationally "other" and more privy to kids' sharing. Of course it isn't possible for the adult moderator to be viewed by kids as one of them; in the final analysis the moderator is still a grown-up, one with a designated responsibility. But the sort of *demeanor exhibited by a children's moderator is ideally more kid-oriented and equity-seeking than, say, a teacher would be.* The moderator's respect for the kids, and for their ways of communicating and interacting, sets a more level playing field for a free exchange.

Another goal for the moderator is to *incorporate a broad approach that can flexibly accommodate children's cognitive, verbal and other differences.* In children's classrooms, many times there is a pronounced emphasis on linguistic communication, reflecting the goal to teach literacy skills (Gardner, 1983). But not all children are above average in verbal ways of knowing things (Gardner, 1993). Since a moderator endeavors to learn from all the participants, it is prudent to use multiple modes of communicating, while avoiding abstractions that children won't grasp. Visual and nonverbal modes of representing ideas work well with children of today's cyber era. Dealing with photos or pictures, perhaps making a collage, is a possibility. (More ideas for visual approaches are in Chapter 6.) Role-play is another option, such as acting out an interaction with a parent or a physician or a pet. (As a kind of power inversion, kids enjoy pretending to be a parent and having me play the part of the child.)

Sometimes, a moderator starts out on shaky ground, since she wants to ask children about a fairly abstract issue. With creativity, there is usually a way to make the abstract topic discussable in more concrete terms. Probing reactions to a new product idea, for example, is an encounter with what Wells (1965) called the "abstraction dilemma," since sometimes no fully finished product exists for kids to evaluate. One solution is to use illustrations or mock-ups of products, which work better than verbal descriptions. Children's responses to ideas can also be turned into a visible, concrete procedure. A ledge of wood is placed along the wall to use as a ruler that "measures how good an idea is." Each product mock-up or prototype can then be placed along the "ruler" based on how good it is (with the extreme endpoints being best and worst possible.) This can be a physical act by the children—if the moderator chooses one person in the focus group to stand and move along the ruler to where the other kids indicate (by shouting, "Go" or, "Stop"), placing the prototype or illustration in that spot. This accomplishes an act, both physical and visible, in which all the kids have a part in forming a consensus about each item. Children take turns moving along the "ruler," since there are usually multiple items to be rated. Girls and boys deeply enjoy yelling out, "Go, go, go!" until the standing child has moved along to the appropriate place (when they shout, "Stop!") After all the items are all placed along the wood, it becomes visible which ideas have the most and least appeal, merely by where they have been placed. Evaluation, by this procedure, emerges through kinesthetic and visual means. As all the items are arranged along a visual scale, the moderator can readily probe what sets one idea off from another, on the ruler. (e.g., "What makes this one higher than this one?")

It is clear that moderators of child focus groups do well to employ discourse that involves seeing, touching, moving, and not just conversing. In a study for a symphony orchestra's youth concerts, I once asked children to recreate an orchestra performance through reenactment and drawing, which put into relief the involving, memorable parts of the performance. With girls' groups I have appropriated girls' playground games to fulfill the goal of hands-on involvement, such as a game of clapping and naming in which girls clap in rhythm as they recall material. (The material can be names of medicines, names of brands, names of places, or whatever relates to the project.) Pretending using a dragon or a space creature as one of the roles, has been tried with success by scholars and applied researchers (Hill, Laybourn, & Borland, 1996). I sometimes invoke make-believe by impersonating a character while asking questions. A space alien is one of my favorite impressions. Space aliens are expected to need edification about human ways, and when I ask in the emotionally flat voice of a would-be alien, it seems a superb invitation for children to explain ordinary habits about which aliens know nothing. (For the use of alien characters in a puppet-based study, see Epstein et al., 2008.)

A sense of fun, or even suspense, adds involvement. I might ask a kid in the group to close their eyes and point to a placard, which will decide what we do next. I'll ask everyone to close their eyes, until I place a prototype on the table and then ask them to look all at once. I'll pick up on something fun the kids suggest, that can help to make the process enjoyable for them. Once, when interviewing kids about flashlights, I agreed to turn out all the lights, and then participants could show me and tell me how to play with flashlights when it's dark. This turned out to be the most productive part of the interview in providing deeper understanding of how kids related to flashlights, literally shedding light on the meaning of such play.

Moderator Troubleshooting

But what is a moderator to do if things go amiss in the group process? Problems can develop quickly, since children respond to each other readily. Altercations occasionally happen. I once interviewed kids at a table made up of two smaller tables put together. Accidentally, a boy at the double-table moved his end of the table in a manner that squished another boy's fingers between the tables. Although there had been complete harmony up to that point, the hurt boy lurched to physically assault the other lad once his fingers were hurt. In situations like this, the moderator has to move to protect the children, and exert authority immediately. Occasionally, I've been known to take a disruptive, dominating child aside and ask them to modify their ways in order for everyone to be heard. Rarely, I've even asked a child to leave after extreme disruptive behavior persisted. (This is not a way to build trust among the other kids.) Generally, though, if the moderator can head off temptations and troubles in advance, by having a kid-conducive setting, and an involving and varied set of materials and activities, the need to exercise adult domination can be minimized.

It is a tricky issue for the moderator when one child talks so much that the others can't have their say. This makes other kids resent the dominator (Hill, 2006). If hints fail to sink in ("Let's let the other kids have a say") another approach that can be helpful is to ask the verbal overachiever to help the moderator ask questions, to understand the other kids better. That allows the child a special role, but in the service of getting others to talk.

When all is said and done, young interviewees in a successful focus group will feel like this is their turf, their space, and their comfort zone—both through the means of discourse and through the equity and respect with which they're treated. The boisterous boys whom I interviewed next door to the adult stockbrokers had just that sort of kid-attuned time.

The Parting

Treating kids well in a focus group doesn't end with the last comment. It is important for the children, when they reunite with parents, to do so with some support. I find that a surprising number of parents ask me after a focus group "How did she do? Did she do alright?" In these situations, it is as if the parent wants me to sit in judgment of how their child performed. Pronouncing to the parents what a pleasure it was to meet their children, and how helpful they all were, can be affirming for parents and kids alike.

In applied research, children are often given a token of appreciation for their participation, usually money. Some projects provide a gift in kind, such as gift certificates or a toy. In some academic projects, children are interviewed in school and there is no tangible reward, since the interview in principle is thought of as having educational value (Murray, 2006). Children interpret a monetary (cash) gift, in my experience, as earnings. Kids feel a sense of competence and accomplishment (what Erikson called industry) betokened by being paid cash.

After the children go home, it behooves the moderator to keep the children firmly in mind during the analytical process. For if the moderator has prepared thoroughly and remained mindful of the problem, the process of analysis is already set in motion during the interview itself. The best moderators implicitly strive to model and hypothesize, throughout the session. Some of a moderator's questions may be motivated out of a germinal insight that is yet to fully form. Inklings seeded by the interview may develop to fuller insights later, such as when driving home, listening to tapes, or working with transcripts. The moderator role and the interpretive role are ultimately indivisible or continuous. Insights and lessons surface during, after, and prompted by, children's participation in the focus group. It is not unusual for a moderator to reap, during analysis, what she sowed during the interviews. Ghostwriting, the practice when someone else writes the report who was not involved as an interviewer, is less than optimal since it breaks the seamless link between interviewing and interpretation.

Special Applications of Focus Groups

Focus groups, the flexible, child-focused form of research, have taken variant forms in the service of giving voice to children. Two variations based on focus groups are peer-led focus groups, developed by scholars and Nongovernmental Organization (NGO) workers, and ideation or brainstorming applications, utilized in marketing and applied research.

Peer-Led Focus Groups

In a focus group, children are given voice through the moderator's active listening to their conversation, without dictating the discourse. In a peer-led focus group, this stance is taken one step further, by having a young person serve as *moderator* for his age-mates. The evolution from focus groups to peer-led focus groups was influenced by the trend toward peer-led teaching, as well as participatory research (Murray, 2006). Peer-led teaching or peer-led education has been used in public health, when a young person imparts information and guidance to others, such as on sex education or substance abuse. In my teaching, I have used peer-led education with college students, by having students in my classroom develop and present materials on alcohol abuse to other students on campus.

Participatory research recognizes the fundamental rights of children to active involvement, by engaging children in research about children (Alderson, 2000). Many of the young people involved in participatory research have been adolescents (Kirby, 1999). Peer-led focus groups have been conducted with children under 12 years old also, sometimes using a moderator just slightly older than the participants. Nongovernmental organizations with programs impacting children, such as Save the Children, have been at the forefront of the participatory youth research movement (Kirby, 1999). If properly trained in the processes of research, children can make important contributions. In planning stages or for pilot interviews, children can help to plan appropriate ways of asking questions (even when adults conduct the interviews).

In a study of children's involvement in accidents, for instance, the young people had a different conception of "accident" than the adult interviewer. When consulted about what would be an appropriate way to word the opening query, the children suggested that the interviewer "ask us about our scars." This way of asking the question reaped rich responses; scars, the bodily sign of past accidents, were evocative of accident narratives (Alderson, 2001).

In a peer-led focus group, the responsibility of the child conducting the focus group is considerable. Training for the peer moderator needs to be thorough, including role-playing during practice focus groups. And as would be the case for a new trainee of any age, the very lack of experience can impede the outcome. On the one hand, young moderators have the potential to relate well to respondents their own age. Being from the same generation can break down the differential in power between moderator and informants, and can engender sharing even about taboo topics (Kirby, 1999). On the other hand, child moderators still have to deal with issues of keeping participants interested, and exerting enough authority to encourage equal participation. A youthful moderator may have barriers in achieving an interpretive vantage point, because they may take for granted the systems of meaning of their peers. Peer-led focus groups seem most promising in community-based work with adolescents, in cases where interpretation and hypothesis formation are less central, when the emphasis is on actively involving young stakeholders. Peer-led focus groups are no panacea. All things considered, training a peer to be a researcher in some ways allies the young person with the methods and goals of adults more than with teens or children. The attempt to take a glimpse at a totally youthful discourse is somewhat undone, for the peer leader is acting out an adult-affiliated role.

Playstorming

Brainstorming or ideation, as a formal technique, is usually conducted among adults who have knowledge relevant to a project. The purpose of the method is to develop new concepts or creative solutions, by inviting a group together who are familiar with the systems or domains related to a problem. A facilitator works with the group to encourage the creative process and to channel that process toward solution finding. Facilitation of ideation is a specialized skill that not all moderators develop, but which is often highly developed among specialists hired to lead ideation sessions. Leading a brainstorming session usually involves encouraging the wide-ranging, free flow of ideas, and suspending criticism of ideas during the idea-productive process (Oech, 1983).

Trying to involve children under 12 years old in brainstorming, to develop solutions for their own problems, can be difficult, for children are not trained in public health, software development, consumer marketing, or other such fields from which solutions ultimately derive. Yet the goal of engaging children more actively in the process is attractive, for it might lead to solutions that are child-relevant. An intriguing way to involve children, without the fallacy of equating youth to professional know-how, is playstorming, a method I have employed several times in my applied work. Although there are no published documents about playstorming, the technique is nevertheless documented through the "grey papers" of client reports, at least one of which reports confidentially on a project that led to massive success in market.

Playstorming involves a creative play session among children, nested within an ideation session for adults. Five or six children, all of whom enjoy creative play and imaginative activity, and also have familiarity with the topic in question (such as using an electric toothbrush, if the goal is developing a new electric toothbrush), are assembled with an experienced, mature moderator proficient with child-centered inquiry. The moderator prepares a series of playful activities that involve the subject matter of the problem. For instance, if the project involved a new way of taking insulin, the kids might role-play or act out with puppets the best possible, most wished for insulin delivery. The play might involve crafts or art, such as constructing a new pretend version of a syringe, out of art materials, that incorporated any shape, form or function the children desired. The idea is to have a play rich session; the moderator would also elicit children's comments and explanations about their play. Each play-like session might last about 2 hours, assuming that a fun, involving, and varied schedule is devised.

Throughout the play session, a group of adults (known as the gallery), screened to be creative, child-friendly, and with substantive expertise in the problem, are on hand (in another section of the same room) to watch the children. The gallery might even be part of some of the play. (If the children invent a game, the adults from the gallery might be invited to play the game.) A facilitator skilled in brainstorming methods with adults would work with these adults throughout the session and afterwards. In this brainstorming, the stimulus of watching the children catalyzes creative ideas by the gallery, in reaction to children's acts.

Playstorming can be a fertile means of developing ideas that have a good fit with children's needs. The adult witnesses to the children's play benefit from the child-relevant, topic-focused, and stimulating play. The adults engage in developing ideas, but through a method that encourages connection with children. This connection is then reflected in the developed ideas.

❚❚ Some Limits and Strengths of Focus Groups

An entire industry has developed around the focus group, so it is not surprising that at times the method seems overused, a kind of unquestioned, routinized rite. Depending on the goals of an inquiry, other methods in fact may be more appropriate. Children can't grapple with every issue well in a group interview. And in the American context, very young children (under 8 years old) may not have the proclivity for mutual give and take, as required for group exchange. Ethnic and cultural appropriateness, when considering diverse populations, also need to be assessed. Issues of privacy may be obviating. Additionally, there are projects where the goal is to understand communication, not between people, but based on *individual* exposure and interpretation such as from a film, textbook, commercial, or computer interface. This sort of information needs to be gathered person by person. Individual interviews provide a "clean" read of each individual's interpretations and reactions to communicated material, without peer influence. Focus groups would not be ideal for these sorts of concerns. In short, focus groups aren't always the route to the answers needed.

In the end, the value of focus groups with children lies in how the method enhances cross-generational understanding. The artist Henri Matisse said, "It is necessary to look at all of life with children's eyes." Focus groups can help to achieve that ambition, since children come together, and give a glance at the life they share. Adults have the option to look, listen, and to appreciate with respectful attention.

❚❚ Child Focus Groups Across Cultures

We live in a global marketplace in which marketers now appeal to consumers worldwide, and social problems in one place reflect problems elsewhere. Focus groups have been familiar tools in many countries, often initially for market research; for instance, focus groups have been conducted in Japan since the 1960s. Among diverse ethnic groups in developed countries, focus groups are now well-established. In the United States, qualitative researchers with specialized practices in their own ethnic group (African-American, Latino, etc.) have expanded the range of the method.

Focus groups with children have taken place in near and far cultural locations, often by nongovernmental organizations and others who seek to optimize services to children. From planning better care for AIDS orphans in Malawi (Cook, Ali, & Munthali, 1998), to better fulfilling the rights of children and women in Bosnia and Herzegovina (Nyroos, 2004), to enhancing the social capital of street children in Moscow (Stephenson, 2001), to uncovering children's experiences with violence and ill treatment in Cambodia (Miles & Thomas, 2007), to exploring the barriers to education within South Africa's AIDS pandemic (Van der Riet, Hough, & Kilian, 2005)—all of these programs by nongovernmental organizations and related groups have used focus groups to incorporate an understanding of children's lives. Still, there are complex issues that arise in planning focus groups across varied social groups. Wisely, local moderators are used when possible, just as focus groups for marketing research often attempt to match the ethnicity of moderator and participants. There is a double-whammy in difficulty if the moderator has to cut across generational *and* cultural barriers during a group session. The comfortable exchange of meanings implicit to a group discussion is aided by the common ground of culturally shared language and communication practices.

Although surveys attempt to achieve cross-translation (by being translated bidirectionally into and out of a language), that notion is more problematic with focus groups. Ethnographic methods tend to regard the investigator as the chief instrument of empirical engagement. Aligning a focus group to local meaning systems and social habits is the responsibility of the moderator. In participant observation, the research is often done over an extended time period, allowing for a learning curve by the researcher regarding the language and cultural ways. The need isn't necessarily immediate for a fieldworker to be quick on her feet in a culturally appropriate way. But a focus group project tends to be instant onset and quick acting. Local moderators who are from the group under study bring a real asset to ensuring a locally meaningful group exchange, not to mention a culturally valid analysis.

In line with a complex array of necessary skills, moderating focus groups (with any age group) follows a learning curve as experience accrues. A full-time practitioner will be able to amass fluency and expertise more rapidly than someone whose professional orbit includes single or occasional projects. Along the course of a career, considerations may vary with the stage of professional development.

Apprentice: A less fiery baptism to the challenges of the method may be to first try focus groups with adults or teens prior to conducting group interviews with children. Mature respondents entail less stretching across generational lines.

Unless you have a mentor who is an old hand at focus groups, a way to commence might be to avail yourself of a training program available in the private sector. Such programs have given many moderators a chance to begin the skills of facilitation while being guided and critiqued by a pro. Such a program, based in Rockville, Maryland, is the RIVA Training Institute which is staffed by respected, seasoned, full-time moderators. Another source of training is the Burke Institute in Cincinnati, Ohio, which provides training for a variety of methodological specialties used in market research, including focus groups. To my knowledge, these training programs are geared toward adult respondents, not young children. But for apprentices without focus group experience, such programs are ways to be guided in basic moderating skills—a good first step.

Journeyman: With some experience under your belt as a moderator, you might wish to have access to the network of professionals who facilitate focus groups full-time. Look into joining the Qualitative Research Consultants Association (QRCA), a group that holds annual conferences at which professionals share skills and issues with one another. Some sessions are included from time to time that deal with youth, but even the sessions about adults can be instructive and worthwhile. The annual conferences provide an opportunity to discuss fresh ideas and shared concerns, such as ethical challenges.

Another resource available in the private sector comes from the firm, Sigma Validation. Under the limits of privacy safeguards, Sigma Validation verifies a respondent's history of participating in focus groups, based on their database of studies. This can help identify "professional respondents" who have overparticipated in interviews.

Master: You know how to do focus groups with children, and have made it an important part of your career. What's next? Mentor someone or teach a class. Give presentations at the QRCA, or workshops at academic conferences. Children's voices will be best heard if there are many, rather than few, who can facilitate kids' exchanges. Help others to get started, and invest in the excellence of the field.

6 ::

Visual Methods in Interviews

*Stare. Pry. Listen. Eavesdrop. Die knowing something. You
are not here long*
— WALKER EVANS, PHOTOGRAPHER

A popular bit from the oral folklore of my childhood was the riddle
"What's black and white and red/read all over?" Two answers circulated among local kids in the mid-twentieth century: either "a sun-
burned zebra" or "the newspaper." Remarkably, both responses have
become virtually obsolete today, in our era of sunscreen and full color,
visually represented news. Newspaper readership is on the decline, and
to shore up appeal, newspapers increasingly depend on color pictures
and graphics rather than strictly "read" text. More and more, North
Americans and Europeans ingest information visually, with round-the-
clock TV and Internet newscasts providing instantly available images
for the looking. Movie directors now assume that viewers of all ages
deal with visual representations with ease; quick-changing editing
sequences, animations, inserts, pop-ups, and computer-generated
dynamic graphics are standard fare. Websites and video games play off
visual skills with provocative "eye candy" and visual special effects.
Some cell phones and computers have cameras built in so that users
(including the young) are outfitted to be makers of their own visual dis-
plays, to be shown off if desired over the World Wide Web. Literacy, in
the twenty-first century, has become a matter of visual processing and
not just verbal processing (West, 2004).

For school-age children who are learning to read, children's books
teach visual adeptness along with written literacy. Series like *Where's
Waldo* and *I Spy* entertain children, not through text narration, but
through sight games. Magic-Eye 3D pictures, holograms, and other
visual tricks proliferate in publishing. Juvenile dictionaries, kids'

encyclopedias, and children's magazines (including, perhaps ironically, the *Weekly Reader*) have all far surpassed photogravure-like printing of old in their plentiful, high quality color illustrations. Elementary school teachers in training, destined to teach children literacy skills, use approaches like video that reflect their visually influenced upbringing (Hayes & Petrie, 2006).

Anyone who seriously considers the role of visual material in post-industrial society can see that communicating with children only through words would leave out an important means by which information is now socially exchanged: visually. Scholars who, some decades ago, called for enhanced use of visual approaches in education to meet future needs, are becoming vindicated in today's social environment (Arnheim, 1969; Kellogg, 1970; Goodnow, 1970). Visual discourse is in vogue in post-modernity.

Outside of post-industrial countries, I should add, the local conventions and practices for visual expression may follow a different pattern. The Me'en in Ethiopia, or the Songe in Papua New Guinea, aren't inclined to construe and deal with pictures. Within cultures that are pictorial, children may not be inclined to be individually inventive, but rather responsive to familial adults and peers in how they regard drawing or visual expression (Braswell, 2006). Lisa Mitchell (2006) found that drawing was enjoyed by children in a Philippines village, but was openly derided and dismissed by the adults around the children. When Mitchell's research team circulated children's drawings in the community, almost no adults showed up to see them. Children in Mitchell's study regarded some drawing tasks as being highly directed by the adult researchers, as if each child was being "tested" and expected to produce a "correct" version. The use of a visual method needs to be appropriate for a cultural environment (Gil & Drewes, 2006). This applies to the task, and also how the task is carried out or put on display.

Howard Gardner (1983), the psychologist who proposed a multi-dimensional theory of intelligence in which visual-spatial abilities make up a unique, set apart component, has demonstrated that emphasis on visual processing abilities varies cross-culturally. By Gardner's account, the Gikwe Bushman residing in the Kalahari, for example, can deduce much detail merely from seeing the animal track of an antelope: its size, sex, build, and even mood. Memory for visual material is especially keen among Kenya's Kikuyu, whose children are taught to recognize the family livestock and differentiate it from others, based on color, markings, horns, and size. In such a society, children have long been expected to learn and master visual skills alongside verbal. It would seem an oversight to *not* use visual modes of inquiry in such a visually oriented environment.

This chapter concerns approaches to interviews that incorporate visual modes of communication. Included are such activities as drawing, photography, video making, and visual cues and props. Such tactics build on an expectation that an interview is, in part, about an exchange ("inter") of looking ("view"). Incorporating visual approaches can extend the modalities through which a researcher attempts to connect and see eye-to-eye with a child. Even children who are not full masters of language are possibly confident in the use of visual imagery (Westcott, Davies, & Bull, 2002). Communicating visually with the young can be a way of facilitating and honoring age-relevant modes of perceiving. Visual tactics do not eliminate the need for verbal discourse, and must be selected and implemented in a culturally anchored way. But visual approaches hold vivid potential to cast into relief children's views.

Children exhibit individual differences in visual aptitude within a society, as Gardner's (1983) theory insinuates (West, 1997). Researchers seeking to adapt their methods to fit the visual proclivities of particular children will find that visual methods are well-suited to children astute at visual processing. No single method is best for all contexts or all children, of course, but methods based on seeing add a robust capacity to reveal children's views in ways that go beyond oral communication (Driessnack, 2005; Lev-Wiesel & Liraz, 2007; Miles, 2002). Looking into visual avenues of communication can make good on the intention of embedding a study within child-conducive and culturally appropriate discourse. In turn, this empowers children, even children from disadvantaged backgrounds for whom conventional verbal or written discourse can be straining (Shams & Robinson, 2005). Robert Coles maintained that the tools used by child artists to communicate visually are enabling examples of visual communication, giving even emotionally blocked children an option to truly express themselves. As Coles (1992) articulated the virtue of nonverbal expression: "Crayons and paper can become instruments of a child's truth." Children, even when at a loss for words, often exercise visual means to point to and draw out what is on their minds.

⠶ Visual Cues and Props in Interviews

Much empirical data has been collected (within a developmental psychology experiment-based paradigm) on how visual aids and props support a child's recall in an interview. Much of this effort has been motivated by an interest in children's recall when serving as witnesses, such as in criminal investigations or court testimony. Eyewitness accounts by young children are known to be challenging to elicit and subject to suggestion. Showing the child stimuli that can be seen or touched (models, props, anatomically correct dolls, puppets, and so on) is a recommended, experimentally based practice (Meyer, 1997). As many as 68% of child protection workers say they rely on anatomically detailed dolls, in interacting with children (Steward & Steward, 1996). Physical props enhance the child's communication in two ways, Nigro and Wolpow (2004) have summarized based on past research. First, physical props provide cues for memory retrieval. Second, props help children to convey complex or emotionally difficult information, information that is beyond the child's level of verbal fluency or sophistication. Much as training wheels or swimming kickboards help novices to ride a bike or swim, props scaffold children's attempts to hold their own in an interview.

Yet props work relatively better as stimuli for accurate remembering in certain instances. A number of studies have found that very young children (age 3 years or younger) lack the skills of symbolic representation to make use of dolls as a prod to accurate remembering (Bruck, Ceci, & Francoeur, 2000; DeLoache & Marzolf, 1995). That is, 3-year-olds are helped less toward accurate recall by anatomically representative dolls than are children age 5 years or older (Goodman & Aman, 1990; Gordon et al., 1993). The use of real props, objects that were actually present during an event, increase the amount of accurate recall when looked at or used for reenactment, although they also introduce some reenactment errors. Scale models increase the amount of correct information attained from children, compared to a strictly verbal interview (Salmon, 2001). Overall, for children at or over age 5 years, the use of props and cues can enhance accurate memory, even in the case of a time delay since the event.

Of course, accuracy of memory is not the only factor a child-centered researcher might be concerned with in an interview. Many researchers, echoing the goals of play therapists or child social workers, wish to engender communication about an event or topic so that the child can express concerns, feelings and meanings, rather than just provide factual evidence. Here too, the news is suggestive that props aid children. For the use of toys and cues enhances affective expression by kids. One explanation for this catalyzing impact is that props or visual cues, like

Rorschach and Thematic Apperception Tests used with adults, are prompts well-tuned to subjective, emotional responses (Garbarino & Stott, 1989). In a cultural context where children use objects for play, playthings or art objects can serve as grist for thinking and imagining as they do in everyday play or play therapy (Webb, 1999; Gil, 1994). When children act out an emotion-laden event, as they might do with props, they communicate more descriptively (Wesson & Salmon, 2001). Nancy Close (2002) has described how toys play a privileged role in the communicative process of play therapy:

> Children really do engage in play to express feelings, resolve conflict, and assimilate a difficult experience. This kind of play can be encouraged in all young children and can serve as a springboard for discussion of difficult issues. Simple open-ended toys, which invite fantasy play, are the best materials to choose when trying to set up a play environment for a child. An attractive set-up of toys is almost like setting a stage or a table for a special meal. It is inviting to the child and communicates that the adults are interested in the child's play and the ideas and feelings connected with it.

Show and tell with toys or other props is an approach that has held value with kindergartners and other school-age kids—not only in school, therapy, and criminal justice, but also in discourse with children in medical settings, such as hospitalized or dying children (Oremland, 2000). Talk therapy by itself, on the other hand, has earned a paltry track record in clinical encounters with kids. Those who do child therapy by and large depend on play-related methods rather than direct question and-answer. Watching what children do with toys and props is regarded as an essential source of information by play therapists, who regard words as relevant but insufficient for enabling children's self-expression and self-revelation. Child-centered researchers have taken a lead from clinical social workers and play therapists, in adopting ways to interview kids in groups or individually: age-appropriate props and visual artifacts, from toys to puppets to scale models to pictures, have earned respect as serious tools.

▪▪ Drawing out Children's Ideas, through Drawing

Art integrated with talk opens up a frame in which children control what to show and discuss (Milner & Carolin, 1999). Drawing, clay use, collage, or other art forms are time-honored practices in clinical settings, bringing value as spurs for involvement. Drawings can be the main tactic in a study, or can be combined with other questioning and activities.

Drawings are not restricted to a particular society. Free-form drawings were used in a study of kids in Israel, the West Bank and Gaza, for example, giving kids in all these locales an effective means to project their identities pictorially (Elbedour, Bastien, & Center, 1997). Although children in all three locations found drawing to be a medium amenable to them, there were national differences in the *ways* kids' identities were visually rendered, such as a varying degree of identification with the Intifada. Displaying identity visually (through drawing) held cultural relevance across varied settings, but also sufficient flexibility to reflect ethnic particulars. In a study using drawing done in Puerto Rico, children drew as a means to show their impressions of (and stigma toward) AIDS sufferers, revealing the value of visual expressiveness to index social intolerance (Gonzales-Rivera & Bauermeister, 2007). In an ever smaller world, tools with any degree of cross-cultural transferability are just what researchers search out for child studies. It comes as no surprise that global, nongovernmental organizations (such as UNICEF) use drawing with children as a mainstay method.

The advantages of drawing extend to the conduct of interviews. Art therapists and researchers commonly find that asking children to draw leads to rapid, easy rapport, presuming of course that the clinician or interviewer does not judge the child's work, or exert pressure or influence on the art process. Children under 12 years old typically relax as they settle into the inherent pleasures of artwork; this is a helpful turn of events in befriending a reticent young informant. Thomas and Silk (1990) have speculated that a mélange of motivations underlie the pleasure usually taken by kids from art: aesthetic and sensorimotor satisfaction, realizing in perceivable form a topic of involvement and interest; and (as Thomas and Silk put it), "the creation of a symbolic world in which [children] can exercise the control which they lack in real life." The latter motivation, of course, is consistent with the goals of child-centered research to empower and foreground children's own frameworks. Children who draw have latitude for expression, and control over the medium in use. As Martha Driesnack (2006) has observed, a sheet of blank paper sets out the boundaries framing an activity within which the child has choices and means of expression. Children who draw are making manifest a circumstance as they choose to render it, personally controlled from their very own hand. Drawing has strengths as a multisensory activity, too. The drawing provides *visual* cues (helpful with memory), provides an outlet for *motor* activity (as the crayon or paint is applied), and may be an associative tool that triggers *auditory* memories, at least in clinical work addressing trauma (Burgess & Hartman, 1993).

Drawing is a stock in trade of child therapy, reflecting that affective (as well as cognitive) dynamics are intrinsic to children's picture forming. In emergency intervention settings, drawings serve clinicians as media of communication about children's stressful or traumatic experience (Children's Aid Society, 2002; UNICEF, 1994). Art gives traction to expressive inklings, bringing emotional nuance into tangible, viewable consideration.

This transubstantiation of feelings through art applies to everyday art from in-home environments, as much as to professional therapy. Kathy Ring (2006), in a study of everyday routines used by American children for meaning making, found that children age 3 to 5 years initiated or requested drawing in homes where parents provided resources and space to draw. Home drawings may not be scrutinized for affective meanings, as a matter of routine, in the way that therapists and researchers have scrutinized the output of children's art. But preschool-age children draw with vigor and earnestness, and regard the activity as meaning saturated. According to Ring's study, American mothers considered art a playful activity that helps children to make sense of experiences, while also supporting a visual sort of narration.

The treatment of child art has been based on split traditions (running across both therapeutic and research applications), reflecting two divergent approaches taken toward signification. These two variants can be understood through a linguistic metaphor, as a division between those who treat drawing as a *noun*, and those who treat drawing as a *verb* (Guillemin, 2004). The drawing-as-a-noun proponents have developed regimens used to analyze children's drawings by scrutinizing the drawing itself, such that the picture per se holds the epistemological footprint, the clues to significance. The drawing-as-a-verb proponents are more interested in the process by which the child makes meaning through art, as well as the child's interpretation of their own artwork. Those who favor the verb approach to drawing, regard artwork as an observable, dynamic process. This group tends to use a more child-centered approach, in that the child is consulted about the meaning of the drawing, and observed in the course of making the drawing.

Judith Rubin (1984), a prominent figure in the field of art therapy, recommends that therapists listen to children's verbalizations while working on a drawing, and treat the context of making art as inseparable from the art itself. She does not feel that the form of the drawing (such as shadings, completeness, color, smears, etc.) should be treated as formal, set indices of particular traits in the child. She asserts that the epistemological value of the drawing lies not exclusively in its particular form, but in the child's overall approach (such as whether there is care to stay within the lines, to draw with deliberation, etc.). Nurse-researcher Martha Driessnack (2006) has supported the view that children should be asked to talk about their own art (which is facilitated by the fact that drawing enhances children's verbal confidence) in order to provide child-given explanations of the picture's meaning. Driessnack documents a research trend of late toward process-oriented, child-derived interpretations of drawings. One example is a study of asthma self-management by Pradel, Hartzema, and Bush (2001), who conducted open-ended drawing interviews in which the child was asked to draw a time when they were sick, at the same time conversing with the probing interviewer: "What was happening in the picture?"; "How did you feel?"; "How did your body feel?" and so on. The children's commentary while drawing became integral to the study analysis.

Despite the recent trend away from noun-like interpretation, some adult researchers and therapists continue to interpret drawings as artifacts that speak for themselves, decoded through standardized procedures that do not involve the child. Here, the drawing is collected and later coded without the child's reflections. In one noun-like investigation of children's perceptions of their teachers and school adjustment, children were asked to "draw a picture of you and your teacher at school." Drawings were then rated according to depicted dimensions of teacher–child relationships, such as closeness or conflict (Harrison, Clarke, & Ungerer, 2006). Similar coding of drawn elements has been applied over varied subjects.

This decoding of art per se, in the "noun" approach, is continuous with a number of traditions of interpreting children's art. Psychodynamic theorists have in the recent past viewed drawings as projective tools like inkblots or dreams, and read into the details of the drawing based on, for example, where items are positioned on the page, wavering lines, inversion of figures, shadings, omissions of self from the drawing, absent family members, and myriad other particulars (DiLeo, 1983; Furth, 1988). Cognitive theorists too, have often assumed that pictures are ciphers indicative of set, patterned, and encoded meanings. In Goodenough's (1926) "Draw a Man" test, drawings have been unpacked as the basis for assessing intelligence. Kellogg (1970) viewed the shape and line formations of drawings as universally readable along developmental lines, a perspective now diminished in favor of cultural relativism. The draw and write technique, developed for research in schools but also used in health research, has been employed fairly recently as a noun-like assessment, based on graphic depictions of children's knowledge about a particular topic, such as nutrition (Backett-Milburn & McKie, 1999; Piko & Bak, 2006; Ryan-Wenger, 1998).

Not all researchers who employ the draw and tell technique pin the analysis on drawings alone (MacGregor, Currie, & Wetton, 1998). Deriving conclusions apart from an artist's felt meanings nevertheless occurs. Drawings of a child in the hospital have been coded as indicative of anxiety levels (Board, 2005). A series of studies have used drawings as a means to accurately diagnose migraine headaches (Stafstrom, Rostasy, & Minster, 2002; Stafstrom et al., 2002; Unruh, 1983; Lewis et al., 2002). Drawings of human figures have been analyzed, based on characteristics such as asymmetric limbs and crossed eyes, as signifying emotional problems in children of military parents (Ryan-Wenger, 2002). Whether or not children attribute stigma to AIDS patients has been studied through kids' drawings of people with AIDS, decoded by adult researchers based on pictured physical attributes and depicted behaviors (González-Rivera & Bauermeister, 2007). An inventory of coping strategies has been imputed, based on glossing figure drawings as emotional indicators (Carroll & Ryan-Wenger, 1999). In each of these studies, children's self-reports were not emphasized or even sought. Rather, these drawings by children have been viewed divorced from their young creators (just as might be the artifacts that belonged to deceased children in an archaeological site). The pictures are interpreted based on presumed projections or tracings left in the art, in structured and systematic ways.

Nancy Ryan-Wenger, a researcher and practitioner of the "noun" approach to interpreting child art, wrote case studies analyzing single drawings in issues of the *Journal of Pediatric Health Care*. After inviting others to submit to the journal drawings for her to analyze, she used each drawing as the basis for an interpretation, without meeting or talking to the child. In one such case, she considered a picture that was part of a book made by Hillary, a 6-year-old girl with lymphobastic leukemia. Hillary's book chronicled several days of Hillary's life. The particular picture (shown in Figure. 6.1) shows a small girl with a nurse preparing to do a finger-stick.

This is how Ryan-Wenger (2001b) assessed the developmental status of the unseen and unheard girl, Hillary:

> The Denver II developmental test indicates that 75% of 5-year-olds should include at least 6 parts ... By age 6 years, girls are expected to include the head, eyes, nose, mouth, body, legs, arms, hair, and feet in their human figure drawings ... All 9 items were present in these figures; therefore the drawing is developmentally appropriate.

Ryan-Wenger also assessed the child's emotional status, based on the drawing:

> The little girl's smile belies her anxiety, as illustrated by the figure's heavily shaded face (Hillary is white). The figure of the nurse reveals several emotional indicators: Sketchiness of the nurse figure compared with the child, no neck: impulsivity. One hand "cut off" (hidden): insecurity. No eyes shown behind the

Figure 6.1

glasses: anxiety. Arms pressed to the body: shyness, timidity. Shading of the stockings: anxiety.

As an implication, Ryan-Wenger offered that this ill child illustrator was understandably anxious and insecure. She added that writing a book or diary can be a means to help defuse anxiety. The picture Hillary drew, Ryan-Wenger implied, could provide an outlet for communicating feelings that words could not express, or that were private in nature.

In another example of a drawing unpacked by Ryan-Wenger, an 11-year-old from Sarajevo made the illustration shown in Figure 6.2. Ryan-Wenger (2001a) categorized this as a "kinetic" drawing since it depicts figures in action. This is certainly the case, in fact, like an R-rated action film, the illustration shows blood everywhere (visible in the colored original) with six children lying on the ground and another being assisted by a medic.

Consistent with her other analysis, Ryan-Wenger treats this drawing as intrinsically projective of emotions. However, this time she does not concentrate on the way people are drawn, but comments on the obvious horror in the scene itself, pointing out that the ambulance and medics are shown in "stark white" (interpreted as "good"), standing against the otherwise "evil" situation. She notes that there is an impression that no one cares about the suffering shown, since the windows are lit but empty. The picture, she suggests, is a reminder that nurses who

Figure 6.2

encounter children who have faced emotionally charged situations might be advised to suggest that children draw, and then to analyze each drawing using picture-based ("noun") content analysis methods.

In line with the fact that drawing produces a tangible product able to be considered apart from the child artist, art has often been viewed as projective, as reflecting the child's inner impulses in a manner visible and adequately assessed from the picture itself. A drawing is, after all, an object, and thus invites itself to be read objectively. Yet those who have looked at the art of dead painters in a museum, and wished they could consult the artist directly as to the meaning of the painting, also have a crucial point. Not consulting the child who produced a drawing neglects the dynamic process of meaning creation by which the child has formed the picture. The child's agency is disregarded or passed over, and the young artist is treated as interpretively irrelevant.

A number of researchers using the "noun" approach to drawing (treating children's art as self-evident objects) recognize that troubled children (judged so from a drawing) also have a need to communicate felt meaning through personal exchange and direct expression. Ryan-Wenger, for example, acknowledges that if she were caring (as a nurse) for the Sarajevo artist, she would ask questions about how the child perceives the events depicted, probing the degree to which the young artist's experiences may be risks to healthy growth. In a joint study by Carroll and Ryan-Wenger (1999), children's drawings of persons were content analyzed without child consultation about the drawings. Still, the authors recommended, based on their findings, that parents should discuss issues of fears and worries verbally, in conversations with their kids. In a sort of irony, conversing with children may be clinically advised, yet foregone in noun-like research.

In my experience there is a synergy between drawing and speaking, when engaging a child. There are many children hesitant to use words, who become more verbal once they start work on a drawing. This is borne out by research that shows that drawing enhances accurate memory and verbalization. When a child draws along with narrating an event verbally, both retrieval and communication seem to be aided by visual cues (Salmon, 2001). By providing a focus apart from an interrogating interviewer, drawing appears to put the child in greater control and reduces the errors made. Art has even been used with street children, normally wary of adults' intentions, successfully serving to overcome barriers by giving control and framing of expression to the kids (Young & Barrett, 2001). Robert Coles (1992), the psychiatrist and scholar, has described a quiet girl with fatal leukemia, under his treatment, who resisted all his attempts to strike up a conversation. Dropping his foiled efforts at verbal exchange, Coles gave the girl crayons and paper. She soon set to work making drawings, and amidst that activity, she and Coles came to talk about her feelings and illness in robust ways.

In my view, interpreting a drawing reflects a triangulation between the child's art and the child's talk, as these mutually clarify the meaning to be imputed. Following significant trauma, children experience reduced verbal skills, but drawing enriches their narrative description (Lev-Wiesel & Liraz, 2007). The component features of the drawing, in such cases, do not stand alone in a determined or exhaustive way. Rather, the compositional and technological features of a drawing are part of a larger whole, in which children's verbal and visual accounts are entwined (Guillemin, 2004). It may be the case that art involves dense, latent layers of significance that artists are not privy to, as has been taught to child therapists since Anna Freud (Coles, 1992). Yet if the goal is to give voice to children, the final word shouldn't rest on adults viewing pictures in isolation. Adults may second-guess in error when they ignore children's stated meanings about drawings. Thus, I wouldn't treat drawing as a default form of data collection that can be used to gain surreptitious entry into a child's emotional or cognitive life, without also inquiring, in a sensitive and empathic way, about a child's sense of her own art. If research is to give voice to children, a good place to start is with a young artist's prerogative to give her own account of the meanings contained in her newest masterwork.

Art has other uses than to indicate emotion or cognition. For one thing, a picture can simply represent how something looks, as rendered from a child's perspective. It can be a way of materially portraying an imagined place (utopic or dystopic), an imaginary friend, a mythic figure (God, Santa, the Easter Bunny), or a wish come true. It can allow a child to show how they imagine the unseen empirical world, such as the makeup of their inner body (Mitchell, 2006). Art makes substantive form out of matters inchoate, dim, or unfamiliar, allowing the child power to better express unformed ideas and viewpoints. In a world once described by novelist Gabriel Garcia Marquez (1998), many things lacked names, and in order to indicate those things, it was necessary to point. Art can be a way of pointing to the things a child is still coming to terms with, or has no terms for.

The job of the qualitative researcher is no different with drawing than in other research: to listen and watch (Clark, 1996). Watching a child create, and at the same time listening as the child opens up to explain what is being shown in a drawing, gives the adult researcher access to juvenile intentions and meanings. It would be remiss for a child-centered researcher to disregard what children have to say, just when children are empowered (by art) to explain.

Lessons Learned about Drawing-Aided Interviews

Not all children possess equivalent skill or attraction for creating visual art. Research shows that young artists themselves make social comparisons from child to child, mentally noting which classmates' drawings are singled out for display by a teacher. Social comparisons can instill doubts about personal ability, particularly in middle childhood when peers shape ideas of what makes a good or bad drawing (Boyatzis & Albertini, 2000). A lack of confidence about drawing can inhibit, as other researchers have confirmed (Bales, 2005). In fact, some children may not like to draw at all. It goes without saying that nothing can be gained by coercing a child into artwork if they hesitate. Using multiple methods in informant interviews, I have learned to simply ask every child being interviewed: "Do you like to draw? It doesn't matter if you're a good drawer or not. But would you like to make a picture?" Children who don't want to draw are spared that part of the interview.

Much has been made of the developmental progression in children's art. As mentioned previously, children up to age 3 years do not use symbolic representation in a mature way, so drawing should be considered carefully as applied to preschoolers before age 4 years (Boyatzis, 2000). My own use of drawing has been with children age 5 years and over. At age 5 years, some children still produce scribble-like pictures, but nonetheless enjoy the process of showing someone how they picture things, at their own level of artistic rendering. As children get older, their drawings tend to become increasingly well-formed and detailed, and may take longer to complete. As American children reach age 11 years or so, drawing tends to become a specialized interest of those known to be "artistic," even as the popularity of art declines in other kids.

When I use drawing in a child-centered interview, I usually provide children with an ordinary white sheet of typing paper, and a standard box of washable Crayola markers with eight colors (red, brown, blue, green, purple, orange, yellow, and black). Generally, I have found that it is best to keep drawing tasks and tools straightforward and basic, so that a child can get to the artistry at hand without distraction.

Markers, in my post-1970s experience, hold an advantage over crayons among young Americans, perhaps because markers give more precise control. In the rare case where children have complained that my supply of eight markers lacked the proper colors (such as when children volunteered that they would like to have pastel shades to draw the ethereal, feminine Tooth Fairy), I have purchased and added those colors to the choices. In a study of Halloween, I found that the orange and black markers had to be replaced frequently, in order to give each child a fresh set of all the colors to use.

Drawing, as a tool of child-centered inquiry, entails no accurate or legitimate way to depict a subject, and shouldn't lead to any sort of value judgment placed on a child's artistry. As the child lets her "hand do the thinking" (words used by a child) (Coles, 1992), I take a receptive rather than judgmental stance, attempting with curiosity to follow the artist's train of thought and meaning. I inquire what the drawing depicts, in terms of the child's sense making. The child's art is in no way a performance or display for my aesthetic gratification or evaluation; rather it is an expression that can manifest the child's ideas, feelings, and experiences, in ways that supercede words. An interview is not an art lesson, during which the adult is empowered to judge or coach, but rather a learning session for the adult researcher, in which the child's drawing and commentary mutually inform.

As cases in point, a few specific examples of drawing used in child-centered qualitative studies that I have conducted are described (and illustrated) in the next sections.

Chronic Illness

In a study of children's experiences with asthma or diabetes, I asked 5- to 8-year-olds to do drawings during two successive interviews. In the initial interview with each child, after a brief discussion of what asthma/diabetes meant (to the child) and what he did and experienced about asthma/diabetes, I asked: "Would you draw me a picture of the *worst time ever* with your asthma (or diabetes)?" The drawings helped to initiate narratives of illness (Kleinman, 1988), narratives that often were punctuated with pangs of emotion. Sometimes, a drawing and its explication extended to aspects of coping. In visually carrying out my request, many children seemed to use the drawing process to offer up a display of suffering, for my witnessing. Drawing accompanied by conversing constituted a satisfactory or even therapeutic experience for the children.

(An observant mother of a diabetic son wrote in her journal, days after observing the interview, that she thought she would also invite her son to draw as a form of support, the next time diabetes upset him.) Rapport between the child and the interviewer (me) benefited, as I was invited in to hear about a highly significant time. The child appreciated, too, that as an interviewer, I saw the value of the story and listened fully (with eyes and ears). A sense of security and support came from making difficult events approachable and graspable. It was as if the artistry provided a way to look even the most painful moments in the eye, with a companion witness (the researcher). This was invaluable for setting a tone of openness and sharing.

To illustrate (with a drawing—originally in color—by a 7-year-old with asthma), the bed in Figure 6.3 was rendered when Peter was asked to draw "the worst time ever, with your asthma." The interview was conducted in the boy's bedroom, as he and I sat, in privacy, on the floor. Without much coaxing, Peter spoke aloud and answered questions as he worked on his picture. When Peter set about to draw himself prone in bed, he initially drew a frown on the face depicting himself. The scene was of a night when he was alone in his room having an asthma attack, while the rest of the family slept. On the pictured occasion, he was vulnerable and in a desperate state of breathlessness. The concerned frown

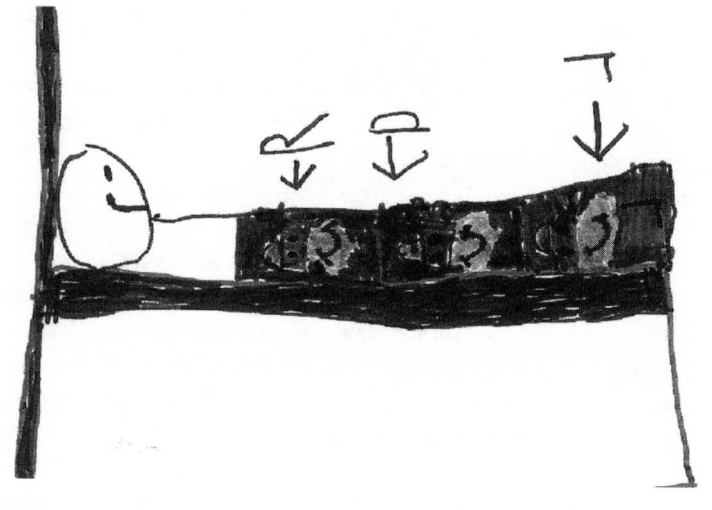

Figure 6.3

depicted on his face (drawn at first) conveyed his distress. When Peter added to the drawing the sheets on his bed (a representation of the same bed sheets covering the actual bed in his room), he changed the facial expression to a distinct smile, as shown. His bed sheets were adorned with the TV characters, the Teenage Mutant Ninja Turtles, three of whom were drawn with alphabetic initials pointing to each character. At the thought of the Turtles, Peter's mood brightened. The Ninja Turtles cheered him because they were heroic imaginary companions, akin to the Velveteen Rabbit or another transitional object, but on two-dimensional sheets rather than as a plush toy. When the young man felt sick or anxious from asthma, he felt reassured that the trusted bed-top Turtles would manifest to rescue him from suffocating symptoms: "I think about, like, they'd be real. And they, like, help me try to get rid of ... stop being sick and everything. They come up and help me." Pointing to one of the Turtles, he went on, "he would disguise himself and go to the doctor's office and tell him what's the problem. And he'd say, 'I've got a real sick person at the house, and he needs your help because his mom doesn't know what to do, and we need your help." (Clark, 2003). Peter coped with the fearful breathlessness of nocturnal asthma through super-heroes that compensated for his fragility. An as-if rescue was shared through a drawing; pictures can give form to even ethereal conjurings of imagination.

In a second interview 3 months later, children suffering from asthma or diabetes (in the study just invoked) were interviewed again. At the end of this second and final interview, I invited each child to "Draw me a picture to show me what would happen if asthma (or diabetes) was cured. What would happen the day after there wasn't any more asthma (or diabetes)?" There were two bases for this fanciful query. First, I expected the exercise to give a reverse indication of illness-related hardships. That is, through drawing what was a happy possibility upon elimination of the illness, the artwork would indicate troublesome aspects of illness that children would gladly miss. Second, I also hoped this optimistic fantasy would provide children with a positive note on which to close our relationship. Both expectations came to pass. The fantasized post-cure world was indeed gleefully uplifting as an exercise. And indeed, the act of imagining a world without the child's illness did provide evidence, in inverse form, of what disabilities or limitations were wished away.

The drawing shown in Figure 6.4 is the work of 10-year-old Sarah with asthma. Sarah eagerly wielded the markers to draw multiple scenes

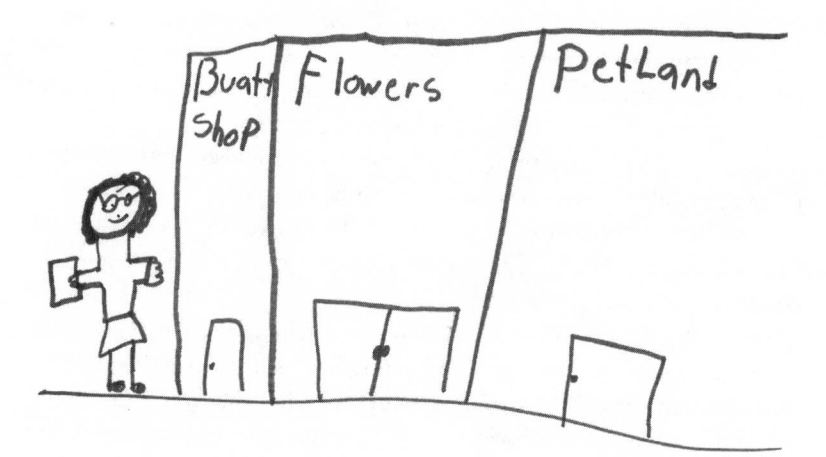

Figure 6.4

of her life envisioned after the fantasized cure. In one picture (not shown) she depicted herself playing basketball without wheezing, playing so well that she outscored her opponent, Michael Jordan. In the drawing shown here, Sarah visualized how post-cure, she would be able to visit locations that housed lung-irritating asthma triggers: a florist, a pet shop, and a hair salon. As she drew all these settings, I was taken aback at how much was off-limits to her, in real life. Sarah's actual world was sorely attenuated, excluding the chance to smell and wear perfumes, to buy a bouquet of flowers, to pet and watch the puppies in a pet shop, or to go with her mom to the beauty parlor. Those were all activities that triggered asthma symptoms. By portraying a world without asthma, the constraints could be emphatically acknowledged, and eliminated, at least in the mind's eye. Sarah and I could mutually appreciate her envisioned better time, even if insinuating, implicitly, the strictures of Sarah's current life.

American Children's Myths

In a study of contemporary American mythic figures—Santa Claus, the Easter Bunny, and the Tooth Fairy—I asked children to show me what the character looked like, by drawing the character. ("Could you show me _____, by making a picture?") Usually my request for a portrait was made close to the beginning of each interview focusing on that one character, as a means to break the ice. As each child began to use the markers,

I asked if it was okay to ask some questions while the child worked, things about the character that I wished I knew. Most children readily talked as they represented the character, via image. Children are usually receptive to this talk-and-draw process.

Once children have produced a drawing it can also serve as a playful prop. Children would hold up a character's picture as if it were a puppet (held to the side) or a mask (held in front of a child's face); the drawing could thus be put to work as a means of role-playing, as the child ventriloquized. Such play was revealing, on many levels. In the most straightforward way, drawings exhibited salient aspects of the figure discussed: for instance, by looking across drawings, it was clear that children assumed that Santa wore red, that the Tooth Fairy was feminine and somewhat spirit-like, and that the Easter Bunny was like a natural rabbit, rather than anthropomorphized (Clark, 1995). These details could enrich and triangulate the verbal descriptions from the interview.

To recap, the drawings did yeoman's duty in a study of mythic entities. Art helped to establish rapport, made the interview enjoyable and involving for children, gave fodder for additional play, and literally showed prominent, widely held features of the characters under study.

Halloween

As the autumn chill descended during the years 1999, 2000, and 2001, I interviewed children following Halloween, keen to learn about the child-related meanings of the festival (Clark, 2005). Many of the symbols of Halloween carry dark or frightening meanings, and to reduce the risk of anxiety I wanted children to retain some control throughout the interview. To let kids start out our exchange in a way that set an unthreatening agenda, I decided to ask the kids to show, visually, topics that we might discuss, as a way of empowering them to broach the salient aspects of Halloween. I asked each child to "draw me some Halloweeny things." (This wording worked very well with children, even if it sounds odd to the adult ear.) The request elicited the child's visual sharing (on paper) of things associated with Halloween. Children drew varied combinations of pumpkins, witches, ghosts, bats, spider webs and other icons, and these pictures served as our toehold into a wider discussion of Halloween. As might be expected, the drawings sometimes revealed emotional associations, especially fear or suspense, as the sketch in Figure 6.5 exemplifies.

Figure 6.5

As the child took control of making a drawing, sources of anxiety could be cast out in the open. Although the symbols were not innocent, drawing at least made them fathomable, and tractable rather than indiscernible or hidden.

Another drawing process used for the Halloween research involved as-if pretense. I asked the children to think about what it would be like if there was an entire planet or world like Halloween. Children were invited to draw that world. I suggested that the planet picture could show things that grew there or lived there, the weather, things that happened there, whatever a young artist wanted. By having children imagine Halloween as imbuing a world apart, the topic was removed to a distanced and safer context. Concurrently, a window was indirectly opened to the imagery, mood, and impressions of Halloween, all in the guise of the "world" metaphor. (The "world apart" metaphor is a commonly used device in applied qualitative research, especially to explore brand image in consumer research.) Some children declined to draw the Halloween planet, and preferred to talk orally about the world of Halloween. Giving kids the option to draw a Halloween world if they wanted, however, was a way to glimpse aspects of the festival's landscape.

Applied Research

Art with children can fulfill many a research aim. It's possible that art is just as broadly useful for child-centered inquiry as is conversation, given the many ways applied researchers (myself included) have made use of art. For example: children who visited a particular playground (in an evaluation study) drew a map of that playground, a way of representing their take on the place. Another commonly used form of art is collage (such as cutting out pictures of animals or people from magazines based on which are most reminiscent of a topic). When studying lunch food for a manufacturer, I provided each child in a focus group with play-dough and a paper plate, and asked them to sculpt the best lunch they could imagine eating (served in as-if fashion on the paper plate).

A puppet-making exercise, which I used in an applied focus group, explored children's admired role models, and the connection of such esteemed figures to kids' eating. Poster board, precut into basic human shapes (in multicultural flesh tones), was given to kids to make puppet figures of "someone you admire the most." (Markers and other crafts materials, such as yarn, feathers, and felt were available to embellish or add detail to the figures.) Some kids made representations of sports heroes, some rendered as-if members of their own families, and some made puppets of pop stars or singers. These "heroes" (represented by the puppets) became would-be participants in a pretend puppet "press conference" at which questions were asked (using a fake microphone) about the character and their food likes and eating practices. This was an enjoyable way (for children and interviewer alike) to learn about children's role models, and what eating preferences or habits were associated with admired persons by kids.

Drawing: Observations

Generally, my invitations to children to visually create (drawings, puppets, making patterns on blank jigsaw puzzles, etc.) have been done in conjunction with verbal interviewing. Combining art with verbal tasks can extend kids' attention spans and sustain their involvement.

Art making can be a catalyst for story telling. Pictures can help to open communication, even about subjects intensely sensitive or negative. Such subjects include trauma and suffering, illness, Halloween frights, and the perceived stigma and taboo of AIDS (González-Rivera & Bauermeister, 2007). Artistic portrayal has a way of unlocking access to what is usually unspoken, a challenge familiar to therapists dealing with child victims of war or crisis, for whom art provides safe expression (Garbarino et al., 1992; Monahon, 1993; Raynor, 2002; Webb, 1999). Art has a way of finessing delicate or aversive subject matter, as if children can use artwork to let things come into better focus, to reify what has been troubling them, and thereby to make the entailed feelings more approachable and mentionable. Art, since it is on view for both interviewer and child, invites sharing. Therefore, art can build trust and intersubjective connection within an interview, as the interviewer and child together watch the child's creation unfold (Banister & Booth, 2005).

The reifying value of art gives it the power to make the unseen, seen. With markers at hand, mythic entities are rendered visible to the naked eye. Such is the case with Halloween ghosts, the ethereal Tooth Fairy, or in a study of Japanese kids, the afterlife (Sagara-Rosemeyer & Davies, 2007). The uncanny can be visualized and coaxed to deliver clues about felt experience and perceptions.

Art has meaning-sharing power through its visual form. A picture is a seeable "screen," making manifest what is in the mind's eye of the child, and can be worth many words from a child's limited vocabulary. It is not surprising that art can foster rapport and involvement by reducing the strain to explain, for it expands what can be communicated.

Drawings, incorporated into reports of findings after a study is completed, can be attention-getters. I have found that the right drawings selected for display along with an oral presentation can be worth more than a thousand of my carefully chosen words, for the purposes of clarifying to adults, exactly what children wanted us to understand. The audience for the research, like the researcher who collected the drawing, has a sense of witnessing the child's view intimately from a picture.

This sense of communicative intersubjectivity has precedents, especially in the field of art therapy. Anna Freud, an innovative user of art in child psychotherapy, wrote (quoted in Coles, 1992) that children drawing pictures "are telling us what they see, what they want to see, what they hope someday to see, what they hope we don't see [yet but] they dare hope we do, after all, see!" Children's art invites compassionate connection. What children include in a picture, drawn to share with an adult, can link us to profound meanings, if we are open to what the young are showing and saying, and able to shift our own understanding into that framing.

∷ Photoelicitation (PEI)

Many years ago, I interviewed 11-year-old Sheila, who prior to the interview, was asked to bring with her an item that could be photographed to be put in a time capsule, as a way to "show people in the future what life was like for kids like you now." As her contribution for the time capsule, Sheila brought her baby album, a book of photos of herself as an infant. Sitting down with me, she flipped over each page of the photo album, picture by picture, discussing each situation, and also reflecting on the feeling that she had toward those years. Here are some of her comments:

> Here's one. The first mother's day where I didn't…make anything in my diaper … This is me taking a bath in Florida. This is me and my boyfriends … That's my grandma. And my grandpa, he died. [I asked how it made her feel to look back at this time.] It makes me feel, sometimes I wish I was that little 'cause when I was little everyone paid more attention to me. Like, 'Oh you're so cute.' And then [now] they look at me and say, 'oh' [imitating a bored tone of voice].

The effortless way photos could allow an 11-year-old to share her knowledge about occasions removed in time and space (even being toilet trained with nothing "in my diaper"), and to reflect broadly about feelings associated with those events, would come as no surprise to those who have used photoelicitation. Photoelicitation, a method in which informants tell about experience by showing and discussing snapshots or video, is a research strategy that directly capitalizes on the familiar social discourse of sharing photographs. Photoelicitation is becoming rapidly accepted among child-centered qualitative researchers as a technique usable to very good effect.

Perhaps photoelicitation, in which informants speak about photos first hand, has ridden the coat tails of post-modern fascination with subjective explanation. Or perhaps the source of interest is simply that photographic technology has become convenient and affordable in settings from Chicago to Ethiopia (Ewald, 2002) through single-use cameras or digital videography. Possibly the use of photographs in published ethnographies triggered an appreciation of records taken with a camera. Or, it may just be the recognition that photos (like drawings) cause conversational pathways to open. We live in a world where people of varied walks of life take, show, and tell about many millions of photos per day (Vronay, Farnham, & Davis, 2001).

For whatever reason or reasons, a Kodak moment ripe for photoelicitation seems to have arrived among qualitative researchers, especially those wanting child-centered portraits of experience. Giving cameras to the young and asking them to photograph or shoot video, and later to narrate or comment on the scenes they produce, is not a novelty. There has been an enlargement of interest in photoelicitation, implemented as a child-centered method in applied and academic inquiry (Harper, 2002). The method's favorable prospects derive from: its relevance and derivation from ordinary social activity (sharing snapshots), its widely demonstrated feasibility, the capacity for revealing children's (and others') salient experiences in contexts and ways that would not otherwise be transparent, and its pronounced evidential value for research. If present trends continue, photoelicitation promises to establish itself as a valued part of a qualitative researcher's tool kit, alongside currently recognized methods such as participant observation or focus groups.

Nonetheless, you would not be alone if you have not heard the term photoelicitation. The method has gone by a number of names. The dispersion of names points to the likelihood that photoelicitation diffused from multiple points of innovation. As Caroline Wang has expressed it, the method is the "daughter of many mothers" or many influences. (Wang & Burris, 1994). Among the divergent labels applied to photoelicitation have been PEI (for "photoelicitation interview"), autodrive, stimulated recall, visual narratives, photostory, photo-voice, photo novella, reflexive photography, hermeneutic photography, photo diaries, photographic interviewing and photo-evaluation. Under this Babel of labels, the method has been written about in sociology, anthropology, geography, marketing, health care, education and more. Across these diverse fields, the method itself has been consistent: introduce photographs or videos into an interview setting, for the interviewee (or focus group) to consider, comment upon, and explain (Clark, 1999; Harper, 2002).

The photographs or videos shown in an interview can come from two possible sources. First, photos can be made by the participating informant(s); the developed snapshots are then described or narrated by the photo-taker(s). This is a hermeneutic process of framing, constructing (photographically) and then explicating aspects of experience. This first possible approach is the one I have used most often in child-centered inquiry.

A second possibility is for the researcher to take or gather the photographs, inviting the child to comment on pictures taken by someone else. I have used this second method on occasion, also, such as having a professional photographer shoot pictures of features at a playground, pictures used by children in a focus group; the children sorted the pictures to show "which stuff on the playground was good stuff" and which wasn't. Although children didn't photograph their own shots, the pictures provided were a visual aid in discussing aspects of the playground. The pictures also served as cues that led to recounting memories about interacting with the playground features. In a study of a camp for children with cancer, Epstein, Stevens, McKeever and Baruchel (2006) likewise employed photographs taken by an adult, not the children in the study. (Epstein's team had to forego letting children be the photographers, after the camp directors raised ethical and practical concerns about attaining consent for campers to take pictures during camp.) Instead of having campers take photos, the researchers garnered a selection of shots to show the children in post-camp interviews. In these interviews, an intriguing pattern emerged. The child participants often fetched their own photos of camp (taken as personal souvenirs) and added these to the "study" photos, indicating that the children actively used the photos as a forum to collaborate with the interviewer. This volunteering of personal photos underscores how photo viewing is an authentic discursive routine. Photos, in ordinary use, put personal meanings on display to be shared with others, exemplified by Epstein and colleagues' sessions that evolved into a quasi-travelogue about cancer camp, with photos mutually exchanged.

Before elaborating on the benefits of photoelicitation, let me first illustrate in photos and words with a brief, specific example.

Photoelicitation: A Case

The Brent family had two boys with diabetes, 8-year-old Richard Brent (who took part in my study) and his big brother (Clark, 1999). Although younger, Richard had been diagnosed with diabetes prior to his brother, at age 13 months. The diabetes regimen was a familiar routine to him, and by his mother's account, he did not speak of diabetes much on a day-to-day basis. Richard talked with me about his diabetes during two individual interviews, each session an hour in length and using varied methods including drawing and photoelicitation. In our first session together, I offered young Richard a single-use camera, explaining that he should take pictures (or if he wanted to be in the picture, to appoint a cameraperson) to show me "what it was like to have diabetes." Written directions (Clark, 1999) were given to Richard's parents, and explained that "since pictures can be worth as much as (or more than) words, we are providing … a single-use camera to take pictures of your child's daily life with their illness and its treatment." In the study of 5- to 8-year-old children, parents were asked to take the pictures their child requested. To some extent, parents also exercised initiative to take pictures of their own choosing. The Brents, like the other families in the study, were asked to return the camera in a postage-paid envelope, provided to them with the camera. The Brents sent me back their camera in plenty of time for developing prints. When I returned to their home, I brought along two copies of the prints (one set to use in the interview, and one set for the family to keep).

During our ensuing meet-up at Richard's dining room table, Richard fingered through the pile of pictures and decided which ones to show me, sometimes putting aside a photo for "later." He eagerly placed before both of us photos of himself doing his insulin injection, a skill he had recently mastered, and which gave him evident pride. Richard also noticed some pictures that had slipped his mind, so the photos (consistent with Barker & Weller, 2003) served as a jog to memory. One forgotten photo showed him at an All Star baseball game he was invited to play in, an honor. Coming across the room to look at the picture, Richard's mother reminded him that he was testing his blood sugar level during the game (with a lancet he called a "pricker"), for he was scheduled to have his test and insulin shot mid-game. As I asked about each of Richard's photos, I wondered aloud whether that was a good time or a bad time. A "bad time," came Richard's immediate reply about the All Star game. The blood test, he explained, meant that he "didn't get to play baseball."

Figure 6.6 shows photos taken of Richard doing his injection and blood test, which were originally in color.

Another sequence of snapshots drew the attention of Richard's brother, who came over to stand behind us and look on as Richard flipped through the shots one by one. In these photos, Richard was

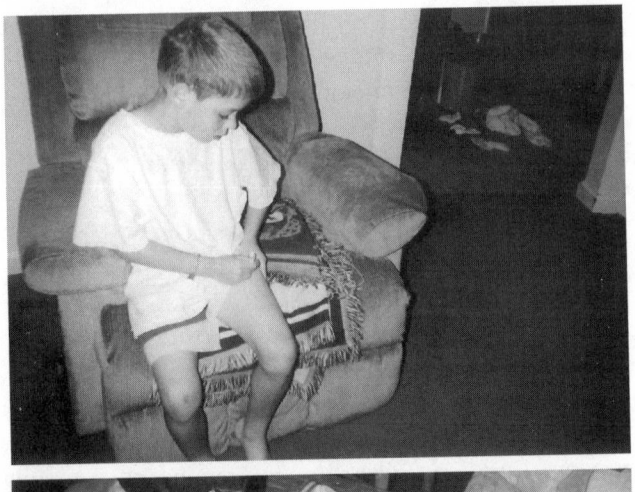

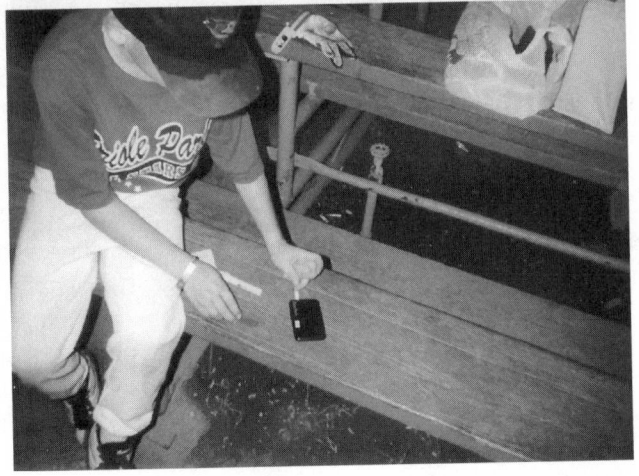

Figure 6.6

shown in line for refreshments at the school Halloween party. Before the words formed in my mouth to ask, "good or bad time?" Richard volunteered that this was a "bad time." As Richard explained, "This is the part I don't like. Do you know why? 'Cause I can't have the chocolate bars, cupcakes, the frosting on the cupcakes, the banana crunch thing which is on 'em, the cupcakes, cupcakes, cupcakes." I asked Richard how he felt in the picture, while he was standing at the buffet of treats. He said he was sad but that he just put aside his feelings. Richard's brother, who had been quiet up until Halloween was mentioned, then joined in with Richard. Both boys spoke passionately, with evident anger and resentment about being deprived of treats at Halloween. Their passion built when Richard presented a picture of himself, sorting through the Halloween treats he collected door-to-door Halloween night; the sorting process was to eliminate items forbidden in his sugar-free diet. Commenting on this picture, Richard reflected, "I am mad because this candy's here and I can't have it.".

Figure 6.7

Richard, like the other kids I interviewed, used the photos as a means to revisit his feelings and experiences through records that visually caught illness-related events "in the act." Many instances elicited reflection: self-injection, exclusion from All Star game play during treatment, forgone Halloween feasting, a doctor's visit, a blood test, recording blood test readings, and eating a meal at McDonald's. The snapshots provided Richard with a relevant vantage point and visual cues mostly of his own choosing through which to recall and consider events. This bestowed on Richard a ready opportunity to articulate associated meanings, rather than ignore or dismiss the habitual, familiar tribulations of his illness. As he disclosed his thoughts and feelings, Richard was in control, choosing which pictures to discuss at which time, pacing his own rate of disclosure, and having me as a ready audience for his willing recollections. His brother and his mother were allied with him as he narrated, and these family members occasionally weighed in to prompt Richard's memory or to support his stirred feelings.

Photoelicitation was advantageous for Richard, empowering him to disclose significant experiences, good or bad. Across the children in the study, photoelicitation supported sharing about children's experiences with chronic illness, since it equipped kids to revisit, in close-up representation, events they had a hand in selecting for attention. Yet looking over the photos also enabled some distance from events, helpful to interpreting those events from a meaningful vantage point. The boys and girls I gave cameras to took part with me in a photo safari about the fears, frustrations, and triumphs of the illness experience, all vividly captured over the course of daily happenings.

Photoelicitation: Strengths as a Child-Centered Method

Photoelicitation has had broad application across the life span, including youth from early childhood to adolescence. Kids as young as 4 to 5 years old have employed cameras to make visual records of their classroom (Clark & Moss, 2001; Cook & Hess, 2007) or have photographed during a visit to a museum (Fasoli, 2003). Minors under 12 years old have been studied through photoelicitation, literally across continents—including in North America, Australia, Europe, Asia and Africa. Homeless children, street children, poor urban kids, child monks, and children with learning problems have all taken part in photoelicitation research, and their participation has been forthcoming and actively engaged. Photoelicitation has been used with video, such as video-based studies of youth with chronic illness, made by the kids themselves (Chalfen, 1981; Rich & Chalfen, 1999; Rich, Lamola, Amory et al., 2000; Rich, Lamola, Gordon et al., 2000).

Such videos made by children have had proven, practical application. The videos have been commandeered for training physicians through riveting, patient-centered depictions.

With its broad age and cultural reach, photoelicitation can be compared to a virtual passport for entry into the world of the informant. In a typical study, photoelicitation empowers a child to call the shots, taking active control over the photographic record. The child becomes, in effect, a research collaborator, shaping the selection and consideration of evidence. In turn, the researcher is given privileged access to the child's world, as the child frames it. Often the photos taken by children cause the adult researcher to rethink prior notions (Samuels, 2004). Fourth and fifth graders living in urban Los Angeles made photographic images of their neighborhood, including not only the scenes of urban blight that the researcher expected, but also places such as malls, which were zones of pleasure and comfort to kids (Buss, 1995). In my own work, I was surprised at the extent to which chronically ill children showed, in photos, how they used play and comforting toys (transitional objects) as active means of coping with diabetes and asthma (Clark, 2003). Photos that might have seemed off-topic to adults become indications of how children parse and interpret experience from an emic perspective. In a photoelicitation study by Irish researchers, children made photographs of well-being ("feeling good, being happy and able to live your life to the full"); the Irish kids included images of pets and nature, categories not included in clinical theories of mental health (Gabhainn & Sixsmith, 2006). When inner city Midwestern American children were asked to photograph "hope," the constructs that underlay their camera choices were more immediate to their lives than researchers expected; children located hope within accessible scenes, such as cleaned up yards amidst a neighborhood's deterioration (Kelly et al., 2006).

Some photos give adults access, indirectly, to child-only turf. Street children in Kampala, Uganda, who are excluded by virtue of age from certain places and banished elsewhere based on presumed deviancy, live in hidden spaces (Young & Barret, 2001). In their recorded scenes for a photoelicitation study, street children captured views of their sleeping spots, their pick-pocketing activities, and similar contexts where others (including adult researchers) cannot enter. In a photo-based study of a German school, young students were uninhibited enough to take their cameras to taboo locations such as bathrooms or the principal's office (Shratz & Steiner-Loffler, 1998). In a Danish study, children photographed places that were their own special locations for retreat and play, places sought out despite the scolding they received from adults if they scaled a forbidden fence along the route (Rasmussen, 2004).

In short, expectations by researchers of what children think, and what is "for children," are apt to expand in unpredicted ways, through photoelicitation. The empowerment of child informants leads to a shifted frame of understanding, an adjustment of the grown-up researcher's line of vision.

The capacity of photoelicitation to empower kids is multifaceted. The empowerment comes with wielding the camera but also with the way photos shift control to the child during the interview discourse. Similar to drawings, photographic pictures seem to catalyze conversation, creating a synergy between visual and verbal communication. Children often feel confident in having taken photos, conveying an association of fun and mastery within the interview. In turn, they participate readily, including verbally. Looking at pictures brings about a kind of interviewer–child collaboration, and readily defines an informal and egalitarian social context in contrast to school-like or test-like settings in which adults are the interrogators. The researcher's role is to listen, to clarify as needed, and to move along with the conversational momentum. The photos energize the discourse with a kind of perpetuating driving force, giving rise to one name given to photoelicitation: "autodrive" (in Heisley & Levy, 1991). Less awkward than conversation alone, talking about the photos involves visual props in which the child has a stake. The shared attention to each picture automatically directs the focus of talk to the visual information at hand. As things go, it is easier to keep young informants on task, even those who are less cognitively or linguistically developed (Clark-Ibánez, 2004).

The taking and making sense of photos is well suited for exploring a child's orientation toward the world. It is as if a photographic tracking device, under the control of the child, can pass through the child's environment proceeding where the child proceeds and recording in photo form those things that the child deems worth capturing. Although it is true that the photos are selective and do not duplicate exactly the child's path in the world, they do make a kind of tracing of what the child judges, in a sense, to be worthy of apprehension. For researchers interested in the meaning construction of children amidst social or physical environments, photoelicitation is apt. Each photo is a framed bit, positioned for comment, which facilitates parsing out aspects of experience in manageable memes, each prepartitioned by the child. The photos reveal much about the angle at which children see things, and children's stance within the environment.

Researchers, a group not usually given to gush about a methodological innovation, have repeatedly done so when declaring photoelicitation to be an ideal method for child-centered research. This child-empowering tool has important lessons for researchers, about children's perspectives and lives. "Images, it seems, can help elicit memories, feelings, and conflicts forgotten or perhaps never acknowledged," wrote Mahruf, Shohei, & Howes (2007) about photoelicitation. Children's selective photographing, and the chance to tell about what the photos depict, ensure that children's accounts are cued to what kids find salient. Catalyzed by the pictures, young people more readily describe their affective experiences, aided by seeing vivid events and settings in snapshot form (just as Richard did with regard to diabetes).

Marjorie Faulstick Orellana (1999) has noted that photoelicitation calls for adult researchers committed to noticing, hearing, and appreciating the landscapes and meaning of children's lives, without intruding. Although this does not mean abandoning the researcher's adult frameworks, it does call forth a second way of seeing that is child-aligned. The researcher must calibrate and coordinate between her own prior schemas and the possibly very different parameters of the child's showcased account. The photos (or videos) at the heart of the project call for enhanced capacity to see, a kind of double vision, quite in line with the aims of child-centered research.

Photoelicitation: What's the Catch?

Every method of research has disadvantages. Photoelicitation, despite its remarkable promise and child-centered suitability, is no exception. Many of the drawbacks are minor, when weighed against the ample advantages. First, there are costs involved (buying cameras and developing or printing pictures). Further, problems can arise with the cameras or developing (Butler, 1994). Such issues include occasional operation problems with a camera, or technical problems with computer downloading for digital cameras. Mis-shots or blank film sometimes occur. Collecting all the cameras for developing can be a challenge when some children don't follow through to return them. In some social contexts, there have been scattered problems with theft of the cameras.

By and large, however, these sorts of problems are neither focused nor widespread.

An issue that poses more of a persistent challenge involves privacy and ethical issues, especially as these issues are mediated by Institutional Review Boards with strict guidelines on visual material. Child photographers can and do shoot pictures of persons without written permission or releases. At the very least, this can stand in the way of publishing the photos. Occasionally, someone depicted in a photo may be shown in a problematic way. Becky Herr-Stephenson (Ito et al., 2009a; Ito et al., 2009b) has told of a boy informant who reportedly shot a picture of his sister, naked. His mother punished the misdeed by destroying the camera. Matters of privacy must be carefully weighed, especially if the researchers plan to display the photos in the community or in publications.

Photoelicitation: Observations

Challenges aside, photoelicitation takes research in a direction away from top-down arrangements and toward child-empowerment. Children not only obtain a voice, but also a lens, through which to convey what matters about their lives and experiences. They are able to show their worlds close up, to recapture feelings related to circumstances, and to ponder their world from a bracketed or distanced vantage point that invites reflection about meaning. The camera triggers a path to ready narration, of events drawn from children's own spheres of living.

If photoelicitation was a movie, its rating for child-centered inquiry would be thumbs up.

∷ Metaphor Sort Technique (MST)

The final visual method to be discussed in this chapter is known as a Metaphor Sort. A Metaphor Sort uses pictures, chosen by the researcher or research team, which are shown to a child (usually in an individual depth interview). The child sorts the pictures to show and explain which are the best metaphors for an experience or topic. This method builds on metaphor-aided questioning derived from applied consumer research, widely used by focus group consultants (Zaltman & Higle, 1993). Consultants Bystedt, Lynn, and Potts (2003) tell of a range of metaphorical approaches used with adults and teens, including picture sorts as well as collages. (Collage work is a method used, additionally, by researchers in action and community research.) Whether sorting pictures or using them to make a collage, the respondent is typically asked to choose visual images that relate to, correspond to, or symbolically stand for the topic at hand. An array of pictures of various animals might be used as tropes for rental car companies. A set of pictures of chairs in diverse styles might be compared to television brands. The picture-metaphors are intended to expand the basis for thought, bringing about creative connection making (Bystedt, Lynn, & Potts, 2003).

In psychological and anthropological work, metaphor has been credited with the capacity for "naming the nameless." Metaphors signify ideas, even those with dense or ambiguous meanings, through making connections from one domain to another (Becker, 1997; Fernandez, 1986; Lakoff & Turner, 1989). That which is inchoate or unexpressed, can often be grasped and explained by metaphor—a principle behind team mascots, festival symbols, or poetry. Metaphors are part of children's meaning making in everyday use (Verbrugge, 1979; Winner 1988).

Bystedt, Lynn, and Potts (2003) provide guidelines for planning studies employing metaphor with adults, that suggest: selecting the pictures from a separate domain than the issue under consideration; representing a wide span of choices in the pictures; choosing pictures that are evocative, rather than bland; presenting all the pictures in the same way (such as laminated to the same size card); placing numbers on the back of the pictures, so that the interviewer can make reference to the numerical label rather than descriptive (and potentially leading) terms. These guidelines, in my experience, are also good ones when doing an MST study with children.

Upon deciding to use the MST approach in my study with 5- to 8-year-old chronically ill children, I hoped the method had potential to help delve into children's emotional reactions to illness. Visual metaphor, as part of play, is a common way for clinicians to explore children's feelings in therapy (Frey, 1993). Metaphor helps children to concretize inchoate notions and feelings from situations, even traumatic situations. Children use play metaphorically in spontaneous play, too, such as pouring gravy over broccoli as a way to reenact a flood, or using a spinning top as a trope for vertigo. Metaphor empowers children to express what matters to them, by virtue of being a nonliteral, creative act that allows wide latitude in meaning expression. Metaphor enables kids to creatively derive common ties or attributes between domains, with scope to make the linkages they choose.

In an interview when pictures are sorted, metaphor potentially brings about a process in which the child and the interviewer are mutually engaged in signification, since both are there to "get" the child's imputed connection of meaning, as the child links a picture to a well-known object or experience. In other words, a common ground can be established through the insights being actively worked out with the pictures, intimating the interviewer as an active witness to the child's meaning making. Of course, this sort of mutuality depends upon shared membership within a common culture, enabling shared symbols and culturally derived denotations between the researcher and child.

Metaphor Sort: A Case

Using the MST with chronically ill children proved more advantageous than I expected. Following Arthur Kleinman's (1988) principle that illness is not restricted to physical symptoms, but also extends to cultural, social, and personal implications, my goal was to prompt children to richly express the significance of the illness in their lives. I gathered pictures (Clark, 2004) that, based on previous ethnographic work with American kids, would cover a range of child-comprehensible material. The pictures were all pilot tested by children, and some were eliminated based on being redundant or unclear. Another adaptation I made was to the apparatus used for sorting. I used two plain open boxes into which the pictures would be placed in two, separately boxed categories. The boxes were meant to be a cue to children that the items sorted together belonged to a given category—all contained in common, based on the child's attribution.

I used two variations of the MST in the study. In one variation of the MST, children were asked to sort through 25 laminated pictures of places (ranging from a dark cave to a sunny playground to a burned-down forest) and to place the scenes in one of the two plain, unmarked boxes. The children could choose pictures of places that conveyed the same mood or feeling as their illness and place those pictures together in a box known as the "asthma box" or the "diabetes box" (depending on the child's particular illness). Conversely, pictures with a mood or feeling different from the illness were to be placed together in a separate box. The same depicted places were sorted regardless of whether a child had diabetes or asthma; the illness asked about was of course the child's own condition. The pictures included: (1) a girl gleefully descending a curving water slide; (2) a vaguely seen city skyline, with a bridge in the foreground covered in fog; (3) an empty hallway with a series of closed doors and a pair of empty boots; (4) a porch with unoccupied rocking chairs, looking out on a sunny, green wooded scene; (5) a flooded plain, in which the top of a building could be seen above the floodwater; (6) a snow-covered home, lit by outdoor and indoor lights, with a vehicle's snow tracks in the driveway; (7) a vivid island sunset over a tranquil sea; (8) a large, dense crowd of people assembled in a city park; (9) a dark and dingy gothic mansion set atop a hill amid dark, colorless clouds; (10) two human figures, one with a fishing pole, sitting on a floating raft surrounded by water, with rich green vegetation reflected in the water; (11) a girl swinging on a rope-and-board swing hung from a tree, against a background of a blue sky, rolling green hills, with a rabbit nearby hopping along a wall; (12) sparkling blue water, with the dark tails of sharks visible above the surface; (13) an interior scene, with a neatly made bed and an empty chair, looking out a window toward a day-lit swimming pool and the surrounding lush, wooded landscape; (14) two adult swans, swimming in water next to emerald green trees; (15) a colorless scene of trees, without much light, and evidence that some of the trees have been destroyed by fire; (16) six people in a room full of artifacts, including books, games and sports equipment, with some items scattered about the room; (17) a flooded area lit up by the hot colors of the fire burning in the background; (18) a cabin set in a rocky mountain location, with colorful blooming flowers in the foreground; (19) a dark cave, in which one person can be seen deep in its dark recesses; (20) trees that have been completely devastated by fire, with one stump of a trunk and some branches visible but lacking any remaining color of life; (21) an unpaved road leading deep into woods that become darker and less green as the road progresses; (22) a lush, green landscape, complete with a waterfall and healthy greenery, and water in the foreground; (23) a densely wooded scene, with two fishermen in a boat on a body of water; (24) a playground with children at play, lit up bright yellow by the sun; (25) a child and an elderly man in a boat with fishing equipment, both smiling as the child proudly holds up a fish on a line, before a background of blue sky, a green-covered landscape and a calm, blue body of water. NOTE: These pictures were not assumed to hold meaning in and of themselves, but rather, the pictures were to be actively used by the child to make selective metaphorical connections.

In the second MST variation, children were asked to sort through 30 depictions of objects, shown in laminated picture cutouts that were shaped to conform to the outline of the object. The items to be sorted were chosen to include familiar (though not necessarily literally real) objects, selected to encourage a range of responses. The cutout pictures included: an open jack-in-the-box, a closed jack-in-the-box, a witch, a handheld remote control, boxing gloves, a spider, a treasure chest, bubbles, a lightning bolt, a magic wand, a blanket, an ice skate, an airplane, a school bus, birthday candles, a bumblebee, a train, a baseball helmet, a rainbow, a life jacket, red shoes (like those worn by Dorothy in the film *The Wizard of Oz*), a toothbrush, a car, a magic carpet, a teddy bear, an open umbrella, a kite, a butterfly, a Christmas stocking, and a bomb. The instructions with these cutouts were for the child to place in one box the pictures of objects with the same mood or feeling as a specific medical treatment (such as insulin shots, a metered dose inhaler, etc.). Most children had more than one salient treatment in their illness regimen, and were prompted to sort the set of objects repeatedly for each salient treatment. Children referred to this visual sorting of pictures as a "game" and became playfully involved in expressing how they felt about their treatments through their chosen visual metaphors.

As mentioned, the use of plain white boxes (for both the "place-as-illness" metaphor and the "object-as-treatment" metaphor) had a purpose: to vividly show (via what was boxed together) that the pictures in the box were all of one group or category along with the illness or treatment. The pictures in that box were literally shown to be separate and distinct from the pictures in the other box, which were not in the same group or category as the illness or treatment. This underscored in a tractable way the intended meaning of the sorting task.

In explaining the MST task to children, I used large, obvious gestures as I explained how the pictures would be put in the appropriate box, showing that pictures would be attracted or repelled based on similarity. (An instructional wording that worked well was to explain, "The pictures that are like asthma (or diabetes) will be attracted to that box like a magnet, and the other pictures will get away and get into the other box.") Children caught on to the task well. They readily explained in words why they chose a particular visual metaphor. For example, the following child treated the picture sorting as a form of play, as many children did, and became involved in expressing her ideas through the visual metaphor.

[Girl, age 6 years, with asthma. Holding a picture of a baseball helmet above her head in a pretend gesture.]

Cindy: The helmet's on your head, and it feels like your nebulizer [a machine used to treat asthma]; how come?

Girl: The nebulizer is so boring, and a helmet is not very exciting.
Cindy: Okay [points to helmet], boring, boring, boring.
Girl: [Showing next picture] An umbrella.
Cindy: What does an umbrella do?
Girl: So you won't get wet.
Cindy: Does a nebulizer do anything like that?
Girl: Yeah. It gives you air so you won't die.

Through the use of the MST, children were able to explain their concerns, many of which had been unknown and unmentioned by parents. Children expressed anger at particular interventions, anxiety over death, appreciation of trustworthy treatments, and so on. Children maintained control over whether and when to bring up an issue. I therefore avoided the ethical quandary of unintentionally "teaching" a child about a hazard or problem of which he was unaware, since I was not the one who broached the subject. Through the sorting task and talk about it, children raised and framed issues on their own terms, while I listened and tried to understand. The MST proved, in this sense, to be a highly child-centered approach, one that enabled children to express abstract or inchoate ideas through concrete, familiar objects and scenes. Those children with limited vocabularies and incomplete language development took advantage of the visual metaphors as a way to convey feelings through linked images, rather than rely on only language-based communication.

Children often interpreted pictures in ways I did not anticipate, and when this happened, I went along with their version. Some ignored the sharks swimming in an aquatic scene, presupposing the scene to be a cheerful ocean, devoid of creatures, or perhaps with friendly whales present. The boxing gloves, included in the cutout pictures, were discussed by some kids as if they were warm mittens. A life jacket was perceived to be a bulletproof vest by one child. Children with asthma repeatedly imputed danger to pictures that seemed harmless to diabetic children; many of the scenes of flowers and trees (4, 10, 14, 18, 21, 23, 25) triggered concerns by asthmatic children that these were dangerous places, because of allergic reactions to flora and fauna. Indeed, children expressed pronounced dread about asthma, by pointing to the dangers lurking in the pictures: [Of a tranquil pond] "It looks like it has mold in the pond, I'd be sick," or [about a demolished house] "When I feel the house is blowing up, is when I'm coughing." The scenes linked to illness proved to be illuminating about children's illness experiences. To express the anxious, life-threatening meanings of asthma, for example, children linked the illness to lifeless scenes of fire damage, lightless caves, or flood. Scenes associated with diabetes were generally more benign, and included living plants and other signs of life.

Insulin injections, disliked by diabetic children, were compared to negative and hurtful entities such as the "sting" of a bee, the "bite" of a spider, the "scary" feeling of lightning, the "boom" of a bomb, or a "mean," "bad" witch who does harm. Through metaphors, children interpreted insulin shots as intrusive, painful violations. The same children were more positive in the tropes they constructed for blood tests, for which the "prick" was less onerous and violating, partly because it was more often self-administered than an injection. Blood testing was repeatedly compared in the MST to protective, safe objects such as a "snuggly" teddy bear, a protective umbrella, a bicycle helmet or a life jacket. Sometimes the metaphors employed had multiple layers of meaning. To show how a blood test kept him protected like an umbrella, a boy gestured by holding the umbrella over his head—but in addition, he explained that a blood test made it easier to balance his insulin level, much as an umbrella aids a circus performer walking a tightrope.

An unanticipated incident had to do with the cartoon-style bomb, included in the cutout pictures. Shaped like a sphere with a fuse at the end, this picture was removed at the time the 1997 Oklahoma City bombing occurred, to ensure that no children were unnecessarily frightened. The bombing is a reminder that the meanings of visual stimuli are fluid, and reflect events in the social world, as well as reflecting the individual knowledge base and subjectivity of the child.

Metaphor Sort: Observations

Like drawing and photoelicitation, the MST is also a visual medium that serves to catalyze, complement, and support children's verbal utterances. Although there is less documented use of the metaphor sort, particularly across cultural contexts, than for photoelicitation, all the same the MST seems to be a tool with great potential. Graphic representations give both the child and the interviewer something to "hang on" in the midst of negotiating shared discourse. The pictures give the child points of reference, symbols to manipulate, and manageable ways to fulfill metaphor's mission of organizing and expressing meaning. The nonverbal use of pictures places the child on equal footing with a talking, mature interviewer, extending the child's modes of expression in an age-appropriate way.

Of course, the way the metaphor sort is used will depend on having culturally relevant, as well as child-relevant, stimuli.

The Metaphor Sort truly brings about a sharing interplay of the interviewer and the informant, in a collaboration rather than a hierarchy. For metaphor is partaken together: an active signifying process of the child, shared when the interviewer also grasps the meaning. It has been said of Wendy Ewald (2002), who does joint photo work with children, that she achieves intersubjectivity in her art, which is at once the children's and hers (Hyde, 2005). Metaphor, like a joke, plays at issues of meaning and bonds people together when both "get" the connection that is implied. Metaphor, actively and playfully constructed by children for the benefit of an adult inquirer, makes the adult the beneficiary of the child's play. In this, of course, the MST shares the remarkable potential of children's drawing or photoelicitation: All these methods help see to it that we do not lose sight of the child, no matter what our grown-up predilections.

7 ::

Scissors and Kaleidoscope:
Child-Centered Analysis

Get in the habit of analysis. Analysis will in time enable
synthesis to become your habit of mind
—FRANK LLOYD WRIGHT

Conducting inquiry in America to find out children's meanings involves making way for poetic turns: protection through superheroes, explanation through object-metaphors, humor or song as a release from what is literal, photos to envision unspoken aches, drawings to envision possibilities, and the list could go on. Whither goes all the poetry, some might inquire, when a reasoned analysis begins? One might expect all the poetic flexing and imaginal gymnastics to fade in the light of analytic singularity, once the adult analyst applies reason to sort through the semiotic elements. But there is a catch. If interpretations are to be child-centered, children's poetics and imaginal thought should be elements considered in the analytic process, too.

The interpretive challenge of dealing with children's nimble poetics calls for extrapolating thick meanings amidst ambiguity. Children near and far tend to have memes that are complex, not flat. Interpreters must synthesize, not merely boil down, taking full advantage of densely meaningful narrations, recitations, and enactments. The cacophony of multiple voices, across individuals and between generations, may threaten pat analysis at first. The symbolism children use—from Ninja Turtles to First Communion—is packed with socially fluctuating, juxtaposed, and oppositional references. Our reports must complexify (to use a coined term I once heard from a child), not just simplify, to appreciate fully even while being systematic.

The tendency for kids' meanings to embody paradox, tangle, and flux can be stunning. A hypothetical illustration (using a commercial symbol) may be informative. Suppose that you are an applied researcher, about to do a child-centered assessment of the character who currently represents a contemporary line of children's hair salons, Sharkey's. The personifying symbol of the salon chain is a shark. On the logo and signs, the shark icon smiles through sharp teeth, while wearing a white barber's coat, with a comb in its fin and its scissors pocketed. How might youngsters getting a haircut react to the prominently displayed shark? Does the creature seem like a friend or a threat? Does he lend protection or concern to kids? Certainly symbolism linked to haircutting is involved, as the shark is dressed like a barber and has sharp teeth likely suggestive of cutting. A haircut, particularly a first haircut, is not necessarily a neutral experience to a child, as most hair stylists to the young can attest to the associated anxiety. Sharks in American culture also tend to have threatening associations (the movie *Jaws*, the song "Mac the Knife," etc.). Would a child be keen to have their first haircut in the hair salon of a Great White? Yet a contrary possibility arises from my past observations while studying children eating shark-shaped snacks. When gobbling a snack shaped like a miniature shark, children I've witnessed have shown their glee at getting the best of a would-be shark, a kind of enacted power inversion. Jonah swallows the whale, one could say. Nothing conveys personal ascendancy as much as devouring what threatens, in essence cutting it down to size, as children do when taking vitamins shaped like dinosaurs, or as dogs are imagined to do when eating biscuits shaped like dog catchers. If through participant observation, an anthropologist watched children refer to the shark in Sharkey's hair salon, it is possible that a mélange of meanings might emerge. A clothed shark out of water possibly may seem tamed and therefore unthreatening, at least for the meantime. Symbols are prone to parody, bending, contradiction, and opposition. Power was tamed in Samson's cut hair, so it could be that shark power cancels cutting anxiety at Sharkey's salon.

Humans, children included, tend to traffic in wholesale contradictions and oppositions, when it comes to semiotic matters. Witness the cowardly lion, the ugly duckling-swan, the friendly giant, the airsick eagle, the dufus detective, the train that leaves the tracks, the friendly ghost, the mutant outcaste-hero. I once did a qualitative study of the widely known clown Ronald McDonald, a character so richly faceted with ins and outs that nearly 2 hours transpired in my oral presentation of the intricacies of his appeal to children. Santa, the Easter Bunny, and other spirit-like entities are mystifying if richly ambiguous (Clark, 1995). Play itself is replete with enigmatic meanings, as Sutton-Smith (2001) concluded from a career as a folklorist of play.

If children deal in ambiguity, child-centered inquiry can't help but do so. Child-centered inquiry accesses social settings, activities, experiences, and self-reports and dips into it all to retain a fully variegated, humane understanding. Both latent and blatant fantasia are found in children's lives. A qualitative methodological approach, although it may be out of step with reductionism, befits the ambidextrous, pliant meanings that children consciously or unconsciously bring to bear.

In my own child-centered inquiry I have often looked for inspiration to clinical play therapy, a field of facile knowledge about child interplay and nuanced interpretation (Clark, 2007). Quite some time before the new sociology of childhood came into vogue, play therapists grappled with intricate balances of child concerns, placed in the context of thick rather than thin descriptions. The brilliant therapist Donald Winnicott (1971) believed that therapeutic, symbolic play was both a sign of a child's core issues and the means of coming to terms with those concerns. Intriguingly, Winnicott held that play therapy itself gave the interpreting analyst an opportunity to try out hypotheses about children's meanings, through making overtures and getting feedback from the child. Child-centered researchers, too, indirectly try out particular interpretations when engaging children in playful give and take in the field. Confirmation (or disconfirmation) of initial hypotheses get woven into the discourse of play or talk, through adult–child exchange that brings children's parameters to the fore.

The ample published literature on how to interpret qualitative material generally deals with adults, not kids. But children aren't miniature adults. Past the age of 15 years or so, mature, verbal, reflective American informants can be counted on to be self-analysts of their own behaviors and assumptions, to an extent. That is, interviewers of adults can, with consistent effort, ask adult informants to reflect and volunteer second order insights about their beliefs or actions. "Now that I think of it," a man might say, "I think we have a Christmas tree because it connects today with our past. It's like we can enjoy memories of the years of our family's life when we put the collection of ornaments on the tree." Such second order reflections on symbolic behaviors constitute a kind of do-it-yourself unpacking, a commentary to help the researcher build up verbatim evidence on what natives interpret for themselves. By comparison, second order explanation isn't very forthcoming from kids under 10 years old. Children sort, draw, and narrate when you ask them—but interpretive self-reflections that integrate and explain are rare. The analyst of kids' material must work harder to find interpretive paydirt; the analyst must read between the lines, and painstakingly reflect analytically on social exchanges and patterned behaviors. Children's poetic and narrative accounts serve semiotic missions, but the blueprints to these missions are unlikely to be handed over by children, ready-made. Like a play therapist, an analyst needs to be assiduous and symbolically astute. Cobbling together hints, bits, odds and ends (to bring interpretive sense out of the bricolage) calls for creative synthesizing on the part of the adult analyst. Insight necessarily goes beyond what's literally stated by children (Slade & Wolf, 1994).

The order of the day in analysis, then, is a need to reap a broader, more complete, translation out of patches and patterns. Take, for instance, the study I did of the Tooth Fairy as reported by children. Children framed the fairy as "she" and drew pictures of her with pastel colors. They often spoke of her or drew her as living "up there," "in heaven," or "with God." Some kids asserted that God and the Tooth Fairy were acquainted, or that God initiated the Tooth Fairy in the work of coin–tooth exchange. The Tooth Fairy was perceived to be effervescent, not solid or grounded like a usual mortal. Although children did not blatantly state that the Tooth Fairy is a spiritual rather than material being, the assumption could be read between the lines by the pattern of their explanations. Kids didn't directly state why the Tooth Fairy was feminine, either, but references that were made pointed to a sort of gentle, "let nature take its course" attitude toward healing associated with (female) nurses and mothers—not a (male) dentist's harsher drilling or a father's aggressive intervention in pulling out a tooth. The Tooth Fairy did not condone pain and harsh intervention. She was a girl, in part because she gently and preventatively healed like a female healer would.

As a rule, the hard work of child-centered inquiry is perhaps most felt in the analysis. Going beyond a superficial or piecemeal reading, and drawing out synthetic, emergent patterns from children's words and visuals is an analytic imperative. Child-centered analysts need to deftly make the most of fragments of semiotic material that operate as an emergent patchwork.

I would not attribute to the analyst such leeway that he can conclude whatever he wants to, but rather that the interpreter be a sensitive seeker and collector of tracings, indirect reference, and parallels. The emotional intelligence and social intelligence that make for a good participant observer or interviewer remain invaluable at the analytical stage. The astute inquirer can sense when children give clues about meaning, yet deftly handle the implied significance without overstepping.

There is no need to be baffled or put off by the challenges of the analytical process. Although children leave trails that are not paved with patent explanation, nevertheless the tools available to qualitative researchers are robust. The tools of coding, organizing, or generating grounded theory through systematic categorization can corral and tame abundant evidence. Routinized sorting of field notes and transcripts can neatly assemble material and help to underscore sustained themes.

Beyond the mechanics of lending order to evidence, the able detective work of the analyst is essential. Analysts need to be discerning scouts, detecting holistic patterns from Holmes-like traces and finding encompassing accounts to explicate the patterns and their likely significance. Working as an applied researcher, this is central to my qualifications and professionalism.

⠃⠃ Data Management: Scissors

Glesne and Peshkin (1992) have written that qualitative analysis is a recipe with "equal parts drudgery and intuition." Under such a formula, a consensus might be that the drudgery is comparable to the *data management* process, the systematic organizing, categorizing, and coding of field materials. Data management is the big job of taking voluminous records from a study and assembling them in order. Such a step allows for systematic and efficient reference and comparison. Since the volume of data in a qualitative inquiry is typically cumbersome and can take many forms (field notes, interview transcripts, artifacts, drawings, photos, videos, etc.) organizing it is essential and helpful. The data management process enables the analyst to become systematically acquainted with, as well as to readily access, the range of collected evidence. A colleague once observed that the best qualitative researchers seek to, "take a bath in their data," to seep in and saturate themselves with their problem and what bears on it. But my colleague wasn't endorsing taking a "data bath" amid chaotic, disorganized verbiage. Immersion that can happen amidst an orderly arrangement of data leaves room for the analyst to reflect and delve as he sees fit. Boys can be sorted from girls, age groups can be compared, playground versus classroom behaviors can be contrasted, positive and negative reactions can be tallied, and the like.

The procedure of data management can be readily described, perhaps, by explaining the process as a manual exercise or procedure, as it might have been done decades ago before computers. Explaining how to do data management by hand was a topic of an article put forth by the late market research scholar and practitioner, William Wells (1974). The method he explicated was known as the "Scissors and Sort" or the "Long Couch, Short Hallway" technique. (Today computer software can do the same steps electronically.)

First, Wells said, all the interviews and field notes should be transcribed. In the case of children, the transcriber will need to have an ear for child language and pronunciation, which I have found to be essential. It is a good idea that a transcript be annotated for inflections of language, pauses, tones of voice, and nonverbal embellishments (such as singing, mimicry, etc.) Was the child's tone incredulous, gleeful, bored, teasing, ingratiating, confused, and so on? The sentence, "It was good," has a broad range of possible meanings, for example, which can be better discerned if the child's tone and embellishments are noted.

Using paper copies of typed transcripts (since Wells had no computer), he directed that text be manually coded and bracketed to mark units representing a thematic subject. The next step in Wells' procedure would be to cut each interview apart into bracketed portions (stapling multiple pages if needed); then, sort the parts by topic, using a long couch, a short hallway, or some other physically suited site. When the analyst goes on to write a report, providing connective tissue between the cut apart topics, the sorted piles (stacked into relevant themes) could readily be tapped for illustrative material or evidence, set along with insights derived inductively. These insights are more than snapshot descriptions, but seek to account for dynamic patterns (Catterall & Maclaran, 1997).

The technology available to categorize and sort qualitative data has advanced, from paper sheets to index cards, and in recent decades to laptop computers. Many years ago, I manually marked up transcripts with color-coded markers, and then indexed (using corresponding colored sheets) the categorized pieces. (This eliminated the need for a hallway or couch, since the colors did the sorting in a visually stimulating way.) By adding tabs to the sheets that were marked with topic areas, a large body of qualitative data could be accessed with relative ease.

Computer programs now allow for paper-free sorting of electronic transcripts, and programs continually add new helpful functions to their capabilities. The trend is that coding, sorting, and indexing of pieces of data can be done with ever more effortlessness, with the analyst at the computer keyboard. Software products today are evolving and changing quickly, with innovative additions too burgeoning to predict. Qualitative research software is sometimes referred to as CAQDA, which stands for Computer-Assisted Qualitative Data Analysis (Dohan, 1998). Among the score or more of programs currently available, some prominent versions now offered are: Atlas.ti, Ethnograph, N6, NVivo, Qualrus, and Hyperresearch. Hyperresearch, at the present time, is available for use with either Windows or Macintosh systems, whereas the others are for Windows. Proponents of grounded theory (Strauss & Corbin, 1998), a paradigm which builds theory from observations, have praised the way CAQDA provides them with an amenable electronic interface.

Among contemporary qualitative analysts, a not uncommon view is that current computer software is best suited to aid the "drudgery" aspect of interpretive research, rather than augmenting the humanly produced intuitive and inductive insights so often thought to be the method's hallmark.

∷ Holistic Insights: Kaleidoscope

Winston Churchill once said that statistics (tools closely associated with the credibility of numbers-based analysis) can be likened to a drunk's lamppost, used more for support than illumination. The sort of illumined enlightenment that Einstein called a "leap in consciousness" is often closely associated with qualitative analysis, in that qualitative inquiry is thought to bring about deep, clear, seeing perceptions about intricate human phenomena (Giacomini, 2001). The idea that inductive holism can lead to considering anew, or at least with increased insight, is closely associated with qualitative inquiry. Insight is involved when, as anthropologists say, the familiar is made strange, or the strange is made familiar. Insights of good qualitative researchers, like the jokes of great comedians, give ways of seeing into phenomena more richly, that is, raising a new vantage point on everyday events—or of making the unfamiliar (such as a child's subjectivity) more graspable. Parsed deduction may have a role in preparing the analyst, in laying the groundwork for illumination. In many cases, an insight comes in a flash after a problem has incubated at length, and after the analyst has steeped himself in evidence. Other times, a particular facet of the evidence is mulled over extensively and turns out to have a central role in seeing the problem in a new way.

Children's poetic allusions and indirect references may yield to an overall understanding, through inductive sifting through the clues. The process takes dedication and openness toward an embracing explanation. No shred of evidence is disregarded, as the overall pattern is sought.

The inherently synthetic process that lies behind inductive insight bears comparison to a kaleidoscope. I choose this metaphor not because a kaleidoscope is a child's possession, but because of how the workings of a kaleidoscope can sift, then show, alternative arrangements of all the bits and pieces. In contrast to the "scissors and sort" procedures of data management, there is a greater element of play, artfulness, and rearrangement in inductive insight, reminiscent of a kaleidoscope. The small pieces of glass and colored materials in the toy, peered at with intensity, are *flexibly* adjusted and looked at in different lights and with different arrangements of the pieces on view. Qualitative researchers also regard their research material flexibly, trying out varied conceptual approaches and frameworks as potential explanatory structures. The forms seen through a kaleiodoscope have a pleasing symmetry, and are appreciated as an overriding pattern. In the same way, the qualitative researcher seeks patterns with encompassing symmetry or order. The name kaleidoscope, I have been told, comes from the Greek expression for "beautiful form to see," a premise compatible with the sense of pleasure or aesthetic satisfaction of gazing at an encompassing pattern. Researchers, no less than skilled diagnosticians, have pleasure and fulfillment when the clues fall into place and a unified explanation fits well and renders the evidence with satisfaction.

Moments of summative insight are appreciated by humans, even vicariously, judging from the longstanding media appeal of Sherlock Holmes or other case-solving detectives or physicians in the popular media. Creativity is associated with the capacity to give rise to these sorts of insights—what amounts to a new and revealing angle of sight. Such insights can inspire, or can bring a sense of elegance, wonder, or excitement (Hunter et al., 2002).

Although scant direction has been given in the past about how best to give rise to insights, it's not clear whether this ability exists widely but is taken for granted, or on the other hand is uncommon and needs to be fostered. Inductive insight is not easily harnessed by intention or explicit control. A qualitative analyst can and should prepare painstakingly by absorbing all the evidence (as Edison did with his 99% perspiration and

1% inspiration). But as Einstein perceived, insight can be elusive: "The solution just comes to you and you don't know from where or why." Like other incubative processes, creative inspiration—even though preceded by a long arduous preparation—yields the solution at a moment somewhat beyond intent or calculation. Exclamations ("aha!" or "eureka!") show a kind of delight or surprise or release when the insight comes. Trying to overscrutinize such a creative process can undo rather than trigger it, some maintain (Hunter et al., 2002).

Yet there are ways for analysts to know if they are apt candidates for the kaleidoscopic inductive task. Those known to produce insights regularly tend to combine these traits: systematic, attentive to details, absorbed with what is puzzling, unnerved by risk, persevering, and easygoing amidst ambiguity. Their interests in social theories are likely to be broad and discipline-crossing. They are likely to be playful and not bent on reaching closure prematurely. They embrace a familiarity with data, contradictions included. Importantly, the insightful child-centered researcher tends to be gifted in imagining children's experiences, mentally walking in a child's sneakers based on what the child has shared.

Reminiscent of a play therapist's exploration, the inquiring analyst may try out (sometimes unconsciously) anticipated hypotheses when interacting with children in the field. They might say, "The part I don't understand about what kids tell me is ..." to elicit help with their incomplete modeling. Children's responses to such overtures may give help in reaching, guiding or rejecting interpretations. The continuity between fieldwork and interpretation makes it an advantage to have the same person engage young informants in the field, and then also follow through with the analysis. In essence, insights are often seeded in the field, during creative probing done with a child. Upon analysis, the inquirer finds dropped seeds of ideas in transcribed discourse, recognizing and recovering what the exchange brought to light. It is as if a squirrel (the researcher) buries or stores nuts (in the exchange with the child) that can be harvested when the cache is returned to, upon analysis. "Ghost writers" who analyze data they did not have a hand in collecting may be at a disadvantage, in that they are plowing a field of ideas they did not seed, going after nuts of hypotheses they had no hand in squirreling away. They may overlook an important kernel. By contrast, the continuously involved fieldworker can appreciate and build on an idea that started in the field.

Different analysts may have different approaches for appreciating and representing data (Hunter et al., 2002). Some analysts use graphic ways to visualize patterns in data or across coded themes. Some triangulate with known research frameworks. Some stoke the fires of creativity with artistic projects, such as writing a play from the data, or making visual art while in the analytical stage of work. Some rely on grounded theory techniques.

Another possibility is that children themselves are the inspiration that galvanizes an analyst to persistently refocus and explore. Children are nimble, flexible, exemplars of seeking understanding. The painter Henri Matisse (1953) once crafted an essay about how artists could and should "look at life with the eyes of a child." He encouraged artists, by this, to conceptualize without rigidity. Matisse gave artists a pointer that might apply to child-centered researchers, as well. Dropping fixed constraints around how one sees a problem, and kaleidoscopically trying out new ways of seeing, adds to the potential for intuitive rethinking. This does not imply, I don't think, that insights come about in a willed vacuum. The rich raw material of prior conceptual models, metaphors, or theoretical lenses, remains a resource for perceiving patterns, an advantage of the researcher with broad training and interests.

Anthropologists, a group closely allied to qualitative methods, judge good ethnography as largely reflecting the accumulated talent and skill of the researcher who did the fieldwork and interpretation. They regard an ethnographer as the instrument. It is the ethnographer who calibrates to a social context and is sensitive to native ways. Ethnographers build up reputations, denoting their status as credible interpreters of particular cultural contexts. When a top name ethnographer (e.g., Margaret Mead) is called into public question, it's something of a crisis for the discipline, reflecting how name-associated fieldwork is at the heart of the profession. Individuals who enter the field and later do the analysis themselves are the essence of the anthropological craft.

Child-centered researchers are relied upon as instruments, too. They earn respect when they interact compatibly with children's conditions and sensitivities, and do analyses that bring out children's own ways as occurring in particular social settings. Those renowned at studying the young (such as Bill Corsaro, called "Big Bill" by some of his preschooler informants) have done work that tries on a child's subjective stance. Bill Corsaro is fluent at interpreting children as children, not as adjuncts to adult domains. His insights reset prevailing assumptions, by taking a child-centered, dynamic perspective. Corsaro (2003) showed that preschoolers are motivated to sustain their social exchanges of play, even if this leads to excluding those who interrupt. Telling children to "play nice" (in adult terms, suspending a play activity to include an interrupting newcomer) loses sight of children's drive to sustain interaction. Such insights have challenged the orthodoxy by which adults conceive their actions as aiding and shaping social development.

Vigilant, kaleidoscopic analysis can lead to interpretations laced with impact, at least potentially. But careful checks are in order. After an interpretation is formed, evidence-based checks to see if the explanation stands up to challenge ensures that the analysis isn't pitched too far or misdirected. In the checking process, children's meanderings and tangents should not be disregarded or routinely discarded as dross, for they may be associational clues or indicators of attitude (Irwin & Johnson, 2005). I like to outline my analytical reasoning, and then go through the outline step by step, with the evidence at hand, to argue against my own conclusions. Refinements follow. In instances when children will be consulted during an analysis, their thoughts wisely would be sought out at this stage, for a relevant second opinion.

:: A Case Study in Interpretation

As a rare example of published reflection, Randi Nilsen (2005) has written about her interpretive process, disclosing her process of analysis in a child-centered study. Revealed was the combination of heedfulness and agile thinking involved.

Nilsen described a dialectical undertaking, with the analyst's attention moving between empirical data and known theoretical models. This restless, comparative way of considering concepts and data took two forms in her account. First is the "top-down" approach, which deductively applies theory to data. Second is the "bottom-up" tactic, which inductively births conceptual schemes out of data.

The topic of Nilsen's study was the construction of social relations among children in two different day care environments in Norway. She observed a "powerful dynamic" by which children repeatedly co-constructed social relationships, not as fixed friendships between individuals, but rather as dynamic, shared ways of common being, which Nilsen labeled "we-ness" (in Norwegian, "vi-fellesskap"). We-ness, as she observed it, was marked by shared use of toys, by sharing of knowledge and interests, by sitting in close proximity, through joint play, shared talk, rhyme-making, secret-sharing, quarreling, and common breaking of rules set by adults. We-ness is not calculated toward a rigidly sustained friendship, but rather is fluid and shifting: at one time the status of three boys might be that "we are friends" and at another time that "we are not friends." The communal sharing within a close social space brought an apparent joy of being together to children, a pleasure at shared relatedness in the moment, for its own sake.

Nilsen's analysis of these themes (which were substantiated from a coding and sorting of field notes) led her to undertake a top-down analysis, drawing on established concepts from social sciences, but with an eye of critical caution. Nilsen's top-down analysis was dialectical in nature, moving back and forth, reflecting, in turn, theory then data, and back. This contrasts somewhat with the notion of grounded theory (Glaser & Strauss, 1967), which uses a more directionally bottom-up approach to form concepts out of evidence. In her analysis, Nilsen passed over some concepts in circulation among scholars (such as in-groups theory) and instead concentrated on the dynamism of children's social relations. One concept she considered was territoriality, a concept (studied by Sacks and others) she found useful, even though it is has been traditionally applied to adult interaction. (She pointed out, too, that an *adult* associated approach can draw serious respect from social researchers in ways that child-originated theories cannot.)

Out of Nilsen's choice came we-ness as a concept. Nilsen recognized that other analysts with other fieldwork using the bottom-up approach might differ in what aspects of fieldwork would be highlighted.

Part of the critical thinking that led to Nilsen's we-ness concept came from other scholars' work. Bill Corsaro's ideas had influence on Nilsen, for example. Corsaro's critique of prior research on friendships and his highlighting of the dynamic aspects of playful relating were influential.

Fluidity fueled by reflection, then, characterized Nilsen's analytical process. Concepts came from data, or from application of established theory, or both, amidst an ongoing attempt to mentally dovetail the observations with emergent explanations. Critical assessment had its part too, in the form of judging the fit between the evidence as a whole and the emerging explanation.

‼ Making an Impact

Results from child-centered inquiry now proliferate, thanks to the cross-national surge in interest over recent decades. In child-centered literature one can find studies of children's experiences in divorce, foster care, illness, dying, street life, immigration, consumption, festival, religion, and a host of other dimensions of living. Even many archeologists have come to appreciate children's significant impact on culture, by drawing upon the artifacts the young leave behind (Baxter, 2005; Kamp, 2001). Yet in much of America, social policies and academic power structures have yet to take account of the new knowledge about children's social participation. Specialized academic journals that publish work related to the new sociology and anthropology of childhood are effectively unfamiliar and uncited by core scholars in American developmental psychology. In the study of pediatric illnesses, qualitative studies that explore children's perspectives have been few and far between; Roberta Woodgate (2001) estimates only 20 such child-centered studies of children's cancer experience from 1980 to 1999. Lawrence Hirshfeld's (2002) essay "Why Don't Anthropologists Like Children?" strikes a related theme, with regard to mainstream anthropologists' sustained neglect and marginalization of studies about children as cultural actors. Hirshfeld asserted that children continue to be underestimated, relative to adults, as contributors to overall cultural production. He maintained that the extent and impact of children in culture largely goes underrecognized, failing to reflect the actual cultural impact of children's lore and practices. Although child-centered inquiry has made its way into many corners, in the United States it is an approach of the periphery more than the center of the social sciences. As a result, children's dynamic place in shaping society is relatively unrecognized as a central premise (Schwartzman, 2005). The adult-down model of socialization has by and large stood firm, despite optimistic projections made about child-centered scholarship (Ruark, 2000).

Child-centered inquiry, much as the field of women's studies that predates it, can open new vistas into overall social processes. The reminder that children have agency, and that socialization is no one-way, top-down black box but an interplay of persons in dynamic, multidirectional exchange, challenges prior views about the reduplication of culture. Listening to the implications of children's voices for general theories of culture sets out a mandate for social theorists. Unrealized potential also lies in the consideration of children's views in forming policy and shaping programs.

In the United States, it is the pragmatic version of qualitative child inquiry that has made inroads. Long before the UN Convention on the Rights of the Child, consumer-based research in America employed a child-centered model. Mainly out of the public or scholarly eye, applied researchers have for decades paid children's views serious heed in consumer studies. So successful has been the impact of child-centered research on consumption, that children's lives are often now deemed by many to be "overly" commercial (Schor, 2004; Steinberg & Kincheloe, 1997). Marketers capitalized on the fact that treating children as persons in their own right provides invaluable input for understanding the dynamics of purchase or product use. Child-centered research can, as demonstrated for better or worse in marketing, change lives. A case can be made that policy makers with socially desirable purposes should act on this larger truth, that children's voices can inform projects of all kinds, and make a pragmatic difference to all sorts of nurturing goals.

Worldwide, the findings of child-centered inquiry already have shaped many a youth-serving policy purpose. UNICEF and Save the Children, among many other organizations, have become respected users of child-centered research. Nurse-researchers in diverse countries have begun to use child-centered qualitative inquiry to study children's hospital experiences (Forsner, Jansson, & Soerlie, 2005; Lindeke, Nakai, & Johnson, 2006; Schmidt et al., 2007). Other nurse researchers have solicited children's accounts of chronic illness.

In my own work, I have seen up close how educational entities like a nonprofit magazine, a classical concert series for children, museums, or zoos get guiding insights through child-centered inquiry. In the marketing research publication Quirk's, an editorial piece discussed how the Boy Scouts of America paid heed to findings from focus groups among drop-outs of scouting. Boy Scout officials rethought approaches for activities and member recruiting after having a chance to hear the boys' views (Rydholm, 1989). Ongoing tracking of boys' reactions was implemented, acknowledging the value of staying abreast of boys' perspectives. To direct effective programs, or to enhance children's lives, it is clearly an impediment to let children be invisible to our gaze, when taking action.

But conveying children's viewpoints to the appropriate adult listeners and decision makers can be challenging. Curtis et al. (2004) discovered how tricky communication can be, in a study in various sites of a London health authority (clinics, nurseries, schools, and other sites). Many of the participants in the study were exceptional: children with special needs, young refugees, leavers of foster care, or youth influenced by the criminal justice system. The children's response to health services, as articulated in the study, called attention to an unmet essential: good relations with health professionals (such as having a trusting relationship with a doctor, or being treated age-appropriately by staff). Children emphasized that good communication mattered to them, including being fully listened to or being told accurately and clearly about how a treatment would feel.

Upon hearing Curtis' findings, the British National Health Service reacted in a rather lackluster way, indicating that there was nothing new in the study results. Curtis sincerely wondered why, if such knowledge were so familiar, it had not yet been acted upon in children's care. Three factors, she reasoned, contributed to the lack of action. First, children are powerless in the hierarchy of influence, and when given the chance to suggest improvements have trouble pressing their case. Second, a reorganization of the health authority was underway (occurring as the report was under preparation); attention was on quick-fix local solutions, whereas children's reactions were part of a larger, more general agenda. Third, the system offered no disincentives for treating children in ways counter to their preferences.

Hanne Warming (2003), in a study of a Danish day care institution, also found barriers to incorporating children's accounts of their life quality into institutional practices. Warming explored what quality of life meant to children attending day care. Quality of life, to the children, was not so much a trait of individual personality as it was an issue of the social space of the child, within the social setting of day care or within a family. Problems within social settings occurred among those who were culturally different, poor, or from marginalized families. These children reported problems with social sharing or exchange. Warming also found that pedagogical approaches heavily weighted toward formal learning tended to impede adults' comprehension of children and children's quality of life. Despite the fact that Warming's study was disseminated in Denmark, a country that accepts the provisions of the UN Convention on the Rights of the Child, children's views didn't find a ready hearing within the day care institution. Adults in charge thought in terms of practices *on* children, rather than practices *with* children; in turn, elders were assumed to know best. Learning from children's own interests and experiences did not hit a resonant chord.

If those in charge of children's care are sometimes deaf to children's voices, it underscores that excellent fieldwork and analysis are not enough. Communication of findings is also essential to effective child-centered research, especially in an applied setting.

:: Getting Adults to Listen

An added step of child-centered research, in sum, is the task of getting adults to listen and regard children's voices as worth hearing. Accomplishing this, in my experience, involves understanding adults, too, including the frameworks and hidden assumptions by which adults operate with respect to kids. Many possibilities could be at issue. Adults may complacently hold to the idea that actions *upon* children are preferred to actions *with* children. A shift in consciousness, a paradigm shift among adults, may be needed to establish the advantages of acting *with* children.

How can consciousness be shifted? Although there are certainly other ways, I have had good outcomes when approaching adult audiences through symbolism, and subtle expressive communication. I was once hired by a client to give a presentation about young kids (under 7 years old) to an audience of hard-edged managers of a cool, trendy, chic (and very "adult") advertising agency. I decided to ask all the managers who attended the meeting to put a teddy bear in their lap, as I gave the presentation, asking them to listen with preschoolers in mind. This was a symbolic way to signal that coolness or perhaps cynicism should not override hearing about children's views. Although one or two of these executives squirmed throughout the meeting, others settled in and were open to hear what I presented about children's experience. The most attentive, fortunately, was the senior ranked and most powerful executive in the room.

Another time, I was asked by a prominent athletic shoe company to do a study of girls' fashion and athletic shoes. The problem was, I was worried if the business executives coming to a meeting to hear about my findings would consider my findings potent and conclusive. The firm had a culture that evoked a hard-driving, masculine ethos, not girlish, frilly fashion. I decided to begin my presentation with introductory remarks that would remind the audience of the relevance of femininity to the company. I began the meeting by showing a 1,000-year-old engraving of the female goddess for whom the company was named. This reframed how my presentation was viewed by staff; female themes were more than incidental to the corporate identity, but rather were part of the essential corporate essence. My presentation had more impact than I ever expected.

In judging how well your child-friendly findings might be accepted by decision-making adults, it helps to be preemptive. Like a diplomat undertaking shuttle diplomacy, anticipate in advance what resistance might occur. Make sure the report you provide speaks to the concerns of the adults who might be hesitant gatekeepers for your study. In a presentation consider using symbolic, expressive communication that can reframe the presentation content for the listening audience. Another possibility is to stage a preparatory event designed to increase the familiarity and empathy of the adults in the organization, with regard to children. I have invited executives, in a meeting to learn about children, to read aloud a significant children's book, as I showed the illustrations. Or, adults might spend time reflecting on their own childhood (perhaps by bringing pictures of themselves as children), which can sometimes break the ice and lower guards. Having adults attend children's focus groups can also be helpful.

In discussing findings, comparisons can be drawn between adult life and children's lives, to enhance understanding by adults. Using metaphors that compare a facet of adult life (such as having a special, always worn possession such as a watch or ring) with experiences of children (being attached to a plush toy, with which a child sleeps each night). In a society where children seldom go to workplaces or adult taverns, sometimes adults need to be reminded that they share a great deal of common human experience with kids, though it may take different forms.

If you are lucky enough to be reporting an applied study that airs children's voices, following are some added guidelines to keep in mind:

1. *Cling to high standards of quality through the research.* Those who speak for children need to gain credibility, since childhood has been ghettoized and discounted in many institutions. Show solid professionalism. Have clear records. Don't overstretch. Think through the limits of your study design: the site, the sample, the cultural parameters, and the data collection process. Own up to those limits. Go beyond superficially summarizing, to discern what seems to be happening as a whole. Provide conceptual models that explain what's happening. Give every step of the process your best effort.
2. *Come to relevant, impactful conclusions.* Although academic reports often conclude with the familiar statement that more research is necessary, more research is not a priority in applied circles. The payoff should come from the research you're doing.

Understand uses to which data might be put, and acknowledge those uses. Much credibility comes when suggestions bear fruit. Having practical foresight and on-target advice are ways to be listened to in the future.

3. *In applied research, remember that the intellectual groundings for your insights will be assessed on a pragmatic basis.* The evocative argument that can grab attention or stimulate debate at an academic conference may not carry much clout in an organization tasked with solving problems. Keep sight of the organization's mission, and show how your child-centered findings can help in a practical way.

4. *Insist that children are taken seriously.* This advisory is offered because children tend to bring out a kind of top-down response in adults, by virtue of adults' focus on children's diminutive size and untrained actions. Empathy for kids' human experience is furthered when adults share a sense of common humanity and respect, rather than condescension.

5. *Don't be so solemn as to abandon light-hearted communication.* Touches such as using riddles or jokes can work toward an audience atmosphere that is less staid, less rigid, and more flexible. Humor and playfulness can lower tensions and drop people's guard. Just don't use humor that laughs *at* children, but rather the sort that laughs *with* children.

It is important that, as inquirers who represent what children say and do, child-centered researchers gain an attentive and responsive audience for children's accounts. Invest in planning how to carry children's voices to influential adults in resonant ways. Fieldwork that has been meticulously mined, leading to inspiring insights and thick understandings of children's vantage points, is a prelude to persuasive communication.

Audiences confer credibility upon researchers with keen discernment, who use credible evidence to draw penetrating, relevant revelations. In child-centered inquiry, the insights can have a worthy end: to coax adults to "think young" about matters of theory, policy, or program.

8 ▦

Conclusion

*A child ... would understand this. Send someone
to fetch a child.*
　—GROUCHO MARX

If you have been reading this book from front toward back, the bread
crumbs I've scattered along the way have marked out a trail toward this
premise: It is critical to do fieldwork that opens the way to know young
persons, on their own terms, in the here and now. Such an approach lets
adults bear witness to the full humanity of children, not just their trajectory toward maturity.

If research was theater, child-centered research might borrow the
actor's motto, "There are no small parts." Though small, children influence the very plot of ongoing social events, as they construct meaning
and act upon others. Immigrant children serve as cultural go-betweens
for parents, exerting pivotal influence when they interpret language and
mores for elders. (Suarez-Orozco, Qin-Hilliard, & Qin, 2005). In many
contexts, children resist adults' intended socialization, as when a
Minneapolis father for 3 years spoke only the fictional *Star Trek* language
Klingon to his son; the boy learned English (his mother's tongue), but
failed to learn Klingon. (Minneapolis/St. Paul City Pages, 11/18/09).
Children have a stake in ongoing social dynamics, giving rise to multi-
vocality and acts of inversion and resistance. Adults are mistaken when
presuming that conscious socializing necessarily has the intended
impact.

So again, as actors say about the theater, there are no small parts.
Researchers' angle of vision needs to be broad and unobstructed, to see
all the players old and young and to appreciate the dialogue and interactions in full. The sort of inquiry discussed in prior chapters allows for
entry into kids' views and habitats—an important step for informing

theories or policy decisions about multi-generational, multi-cultural worlds. Child-centered research highlights how the young actively participate in and make a mark on social discourse, in settings such as family, school, youth group, hospital, or church. At times, children's interpretations may be at counterpoint or in tension with what adults presume to "teach." On such occasions, research centered on children can help us to understand the social processes with more clarity and less adultism.

As an exercise to work out the applicability of child-centered research more vividly, a case study is sketched out below, dealing with adolescents (13 to 17 years old). Earlier chapters of this book have focused on younger children, but youth-centered research conducted during the teen years is viable and relatively facile. Tools for studying adolescents' vantage points can be readily adapted from adult qualitative and ethnographic approaches, using participant observation, interviewing and other tools. Teens are more adept than younger kids at explanation and verbalization, and amenable for either questioning or observing.

▪▪ A Case Study: High School's Unfinished Business

Perhaps because the U.S. is not yet a signatory to the UN Convention on the Rights of the Child, there are crucial enclaves of American policy where child-centered inquiry hasn't made deep inroads. An example is in the hemorrhage of school dropouts streaming out of U.S. junior and senior high schools. Research emphasizing the insider view of school defectors (as well as those who have not yet left school) could hold germane guidance for policy. In principle, young people are the ones best suited to report on why they turned away from school. Although it would be unrealistic to expect teen students to provide the missing link to rectify the stubborn problem of dropping out, teens can, through qualitative inquiry, shed light on pertinent and important ways of looking at school leaving.

U.S. school leaving rates are climbing and seemingly intractable. Almost one-third of high school students don't graduate with their class. This includes a substantial portion (at least nearly half) of minorities (Milliken, 2007). Individuals predictably encounter a host of ensuing woes after severing the tie with secondary school. Finding employment is difficult. Dropouts exhibit less than half the employment level of college graduates (Bridgeland, Dilulio, and Morison, 2006). Employment sinks to 31% for African-American school leavers (Sum et al., 2009). When employed, dropouts generally become stuck in low-wage jobs and are less likely to advance (Stearns & Glennie, 2006). In addition to these ill fortunes, dropouts more frequently have the added responsibilities of parenting children prior to marriage. Among female high school leavers, 22.6% are single mothers, compared to 2.6% of women with college degrees (Sum et al., 2009).

Especially concerning is that dropouts are without question more often imprisoned. Over half of the incarcerated have been reported not to have finished high school (Hale, 1998). American prisons are in effect fed by a pipeline of school leavers, some of whom ironically complete a G.E.D. degree (high school equivalency degree) while behind bars.

The school leaving crisis is often framed as an economic matter, since society absorbs the expense of providing a safety net or prison cell to dropouts. Substantial tax revenue is lost when students don't reach high school graduation (Stearns & Glennie, 2006). High school, from this perspective, is requisite to viable employment and citizenship. When school is stopped short of completion, paths to a secure occupation become impassable.

Quantitative studies, such as surveys, have identified issues tied to dropping out. The correlating factors have been said to comprise two dimensions: "pull-out" factors and "push-out" factors (Stearns & Glennie, 2006). Pull-out factors are factors drawing from the nonschool life of an adolescent—family, peers, church, community, and job. These involvements outside of school can raise issues that lead to a pull out of school: for instance, earning money or caring for ailing relatives. Push-out factors are internal issues located within school. Often these are factors that weaken an adolescent's bond with school or that make school seem unwelcoming. Disciplinary measures (suspensions, expulsions), academic struggles, or the lack of relational bonds (including with teachers) could "push out" a boy or girl.

The social damage from high levels of U.S. dropouts is not fully appreciated among the American population as a whole. When two-thirds of prison inmates are dropouts, and majorities of non-high school graduating African-American men do not hold steady paying jobs (Orfield, 2004), the wave of school leaving would seem to be a problem that should merit ongoing attention, including in the press. In fact, more attention has been paid to improving student test scores than to the rate of graduation. Even though graduation rate was a consideration included in the No Child Left Behind Act, there has been little public protest or accountability for the epidemic of students resigning school.

Analyses of the factors responsible for school leaving have tended to pinpoint something about the dropout or the dropout's life context: Dropouts have learning problems, dropouts have discipline problems, dropouts have economic distress at home, and so on. Dropping out is a matter of person-linked traits, by this paradigm, traits that act as fatal flaws for a boy or girl in a school environment. The very term "dropout" insinuates that the educational site of school is a sort of fixed, static backdrop, while the student choosing to leave (drop from) that fixed domain is the implicated trigger point. In other words, the emphasis is on the student who leaves school but not the instructional context she chooses to leave. It is as if a departing student was a force unto himself, like a weed that didn't fit in a prearranged garden and therefore had to take its leave. Interventions often are viewed as applicable to students, more so than to the encompassing system of a classroom or school. To name examples: New York City has paid students to go to school. Adult advocates have been beckoned to mediate between "at risk" students and school authorities, or to serve as role models for "better" behaviors that avoid disruptive, punitive measures. Skills of academic success (test-taking, study skills, etc.) are tutored. (Dynarski et al., 2008) A plethora of interventions treat the student as needing to change to fit the educational context, rather than vice versa.

To be sure, there are alternative ways of conceptualizing breaks between individuals and institutions, as some advocates have reminded. Insights can be gained by examining analogous institutional separations. When teens choose to break with the church they were raised in, the decision has come to be regarded not as a personal flaw, but as interactive with the religious institution's values or a teen's unpleasant experiences (Dudley, 1999). Another analogous problem is the employee who leaves a job—which in the management literature is viewed with an emphasis on the employment context, not primarily or exclusively the traits of a job leaver (Cangelosi, Markham, & Bounds, 1998; Horn & Kinicki, 2001; Ongori, 2007). Job turnover specialists generally don't give a free pass to institutional practices that "push out." Managers make changes to fortify employee retention, such as modified work schedules, rotation of responsibilities, recognition programs, compensation adjustments, reworking of tasks, and so on.

Both work and school embody hierarchical power arrangements, no doubt a factor entailed in issues of leaving. This book has shown how child-centered research, by foregrounding youthful views, can turn power upside down, bringing a platform for a young person to speak with greater force. Youth-centered research periscopes to a student's or ex-student's level. The vantage point could better articulate how schools could be more retentive. A richer set of generational views is relevant when trying to solve a problem involving young and old alike.

How might the student at risk for dropout (perhaps studied in contrast to a group likely to be retained) be investigated in an age-relevant way? First, *ethnographic observation* is a proven method, a method already established in education scholarship. Observation through participation lets the ethnographer grasp experience in context, from the classroom, to the principal's office, to hanging out, to skipping school, to dropping out and its repercussions. Working out the ethical and logistical challenges would seem to be worth the effort involved for the insights gained into how teens at risk for dropout perceive the process. Given schools where students (particularly minority students) exit school in large numbers, ethnography in the school habitat would be apt. (See Chapter 3.)

Another way to get a students' view of day to day experiences is *photoelicitation*. Allowing at risk students to use cameras in and out of school, in order to show, through snapshots, what school attendance and nonattendance is like in their eyes, is a workable method used successfully across cultural contexts. Photoelicitation can invite the researcher to see school as the at risk student does, using youthful filters and explanations. Since photoelicitation involves visual records, privacy considerations would need to be negotiated with the school and Institutional Review Board—not out of the question, if the photos are held in confidence by the photographer and researcher. (See Chapter 6.)

Video journals, using a video camera as a means of recording what school is like for disengaged students, are a variation on photoelicitation (employing video instead of still photographs). This has been a very productive method for teens in the past to share a personal story about a larger experience. (Rich et al., 2000). One idea would be to set up a "personal recording booth," a private place with a video camera where students can sequester themselves to tell about their day at school, each day (located in a student-friendly part of school or a nearby site). Privacy considerations in using videos for research, such as ruling out public showings or internet publication, would need to be adopted.

The Experiential Sampling Method (ESM) uses a beeper or pager to contact each student in real time and real ecology (Csikszentmihalyi, Larson, & Prescott, 1977), a way to get an up close and personal view of experience, good and bad. *Scrapbooking* as well as preparing representative contents for a *time capsule* are two other approaches that would invite reporting of the full range of positive and negative school experiences. *Focus groups* or *depth interviews* (Chapter 4 and 5) are worthwhile forums for teens to reflect upon videos taken, photos taken, scrapbooks kept, or time capsule contents. These interview approaches could be considered separately or in combination to invite reflection on experience. As part of individual interviews or focus groups, teens could be invited to grade the school for an imagined *"reverse report card"* (in which the authorities who grade student performance are themselves graded by students). Teens might also be queried about what an ideal school would be like, if it earned an A+ on the "reverse report card."

This brief illustration involves how one area of policy research (the dropout crisis) brings to mind ways to obtain youth-relevant knowledge. Such knowing is needed not because prior, adult-authored information should be disregarded for policy, but because adult-structured inquiry is not a very full prism for considering a youth-relevant issue.

There are other policy challenges and crises for which a similar work-up would be advantageous. Health education is ripe with the need to know younger perspectives—from issues of smoking, to exercise, to sexual matters, to drug use, to eating issues. Optimal medical treatment, entailing active involvement by a young patient, benefits from having input by youngsters. So does library use, literacy, drivers' education, or self-protection on the internet, to mention a few. Adults in the U.S. have had a near monopoly on decisions for the young, but haven't had a handle on what moves young people about many an issue, what reverberates with their inclinations. When it comes to youthful experience, no part is indeed too small to be respectfully explored by child-centered inquiry, whether for practical policies or viable theories.

Perhaps especially when the public image of a group of children (dropouts, or street kids, or poor minorities) has a negative taint, research needs to be open-minded—allowing for receptiveness or shared participation with kids. Children marginalized from the mainstream tend to be the ones who slip outside the tight control of adults. Adult ascendancy is not unscarred by the rift. Perhaps this invites defensiveness of adult decisions and systems.

Middle-class children in modern American society are well in hand by elders during childhood, much of the time. As Connolly and Ennew (1996) have put it:

> In modern cities children may use city centers to travel between home and school, at specific times of day on public transport. Otherwise they are accompanied by adults who increasingly hold them tightly by the hand, strap them into car seats, and provide only brief spaces for personal recreation.

Recess is on the demise in American schools in favor of adult-led instruction time. After-school time for middle-class students tends to be loaded with adult supervised activities, not games organized by kids on their own. Middle-class children spend much of their lives, in short, supervised by grown-ups in classes or adult-offered activities. (Lareau, 2003) Just when children's autonomy is being squeezed within the middle class, children in other sectors seem to slip from the grip of adult expectations—dropouts being an example.

But adults can hardly stem the tide of schools' lost youth by defending the current adult turf, by grasping at how to make the hierarchy more intractable. Adultism likely dampens, rather than boosts, the solving of society's pressing youth problems. If child-centered research is unleashed, adults will be better able to step into the shoes of the young, and to take steps that resonate with children's felt problems and needs.

REFERENCES ⠶

Chapter 1

Bearison, D. (1991). *They never want to tell you: Children talk about cancer.* Cambridge, MA: Harvard University Press.

Benporath, S. (2003). Autonomy and vulnerability: On just relations between adults and children. *Journal of the Philosophy of Education, 37*(1), 127–145.

Blerkom, L. M. (1995). Clown doctors: Shaman healers of western medicine. *Medical Anthropological Quarterly, 9*(4), 462–475.

Bluebond-Langner, M., DeCicco, A., & Belasco, J. (2005). Involving children with life-shortening illnesses in decisions about participation in clinical research: A proposal for shuttle diplomacy and negotiation. In E. Kodish (Ed.), *Ethics and research with children* (pp. 323–343). Oxford: Oxford University Press.

Christensen, P., & James, A. (2000). *Research with children: Perspectives and practices.* London: Routledge.

Clark, C. D. (1995). *Flights of fancy, leaps of faith: Children's myths in America.* Chicago: University of Chicago Press.

Clark, C. D. (2003). *In sickness and in play: Children coping with chronic illness.* New Brunswick, NJ: Rutgers University Press.

Clark, C. D. (2005). Tricks of festival: Children, enculturation and American Halloween. *Ethos, 33*(2), 180–205.

Clark, C. D., Paramo, M. C. D., & Rosen, D. (2007). Public policy statement: The rights of children. *Medical Anthropological Quarterly, 21*(2), 234–238.

Corsaro, W. (1997, 2005). *The sociology of childhood.* Thousand Oaks, CA: Pine Forge Press.

Corsaro, W., & Miller, P. J. (1992). *Interpretive approaches to children's socialization.* San Francisco: Jossey-Bass.

Denzin, N. (1973). *Children and their caretakers.* New Brunswick, NJ: Transaction.

Ebberling, C., Pawlak, D., & Ludwig, D. (2002). Childhood obesity: Public health crisis, common sense cure. *Lancet, 360,* 473–482.

Factor, J. (2009). It's only play if you get to choose: Children's perceptions of play and adult interventions. In C. D. Clark (Ed.), *Transactions at play* (pp. 129–146). Lanham, MD: University Press of America.

Frankenberg, R., Robinson, I., and Delahooke, A. (2000). Countering essentialism in behavioural social science: The example of the 'vulnerable child' ethnographically examined. *The Sociological Review, 48*(4), 586–611.

James, A., & Prout, A. (1997). *Constructing and reconstructing childhood.* London: Falmer Press.

Jarrett, O., Maxwell, D., Dickerson, C., et al. (1998). Impact of recess on classroom behavior: Group effects and individual differences. *The Journal of Educational Research, 92*(2), 121–126.

Knowlton, L. G. (Producer). (2006). *The world according to Sesame Street* [DVD]. United States: Sony BMG.

Kortesluoma, R., & Nikkonen, M. (2004). 'I had this horrible pain': The sources and causes of pain experiences in 4- to 11-year old children. *Journal of Child Health Care, 8*(3), 210–231.

Kortesluoma, R., & Nikkonen, M. (2006). 'The most disgusting ever': Children's pain descriptions and views of the purpose of pain. *Journal of Child Health Care, 10*(3), 213–117.

Kortesluoma, R., Nikkonen, M., & Serlo, W. (2008). "You just have to make the pain go away"—children's experiences of pain management. *Pain Management Nursing, 9*(4), 143–149.

Laroche, H., Hofer, T., & Davis, M. (2007). Adult fat intake associated with the presence of children in households: Findings from NHANES III. *Journal of the American Board of Family Medicine, 20,* 9–15.

Leavitt, R. (1991). Power and resistance in infant-toddler day care centers. *Sociological Studies of Child Development, 4,* 91–112.

Lee, N. (1998). Towards an immature sociology. *The Sociological Review, 46*(3), 458–482.

Leonard, M. (2005). Involving children in social policy: A case study from Northern Ireland. *Sociological Studies of Children and Youth, 10,* 153–167.

Linkletter, A. (Host). (2005). The best of Art Linkletter's 'Kids say the darndest things' [DVD]. United States: Time-Life.

Linn, S. (2005). *Consuming kids.* New York: Anchor.

Males, M. (2007, January 7). This is your brain on drugs, Dad. *New York Times.*

Malkki, L., & Martin, E. (2007). Children and the gendered politics of globalization: In remembrance of Sharon Stephens. *American Ethnologist, 30*(2), 216–224.

Miller, D., & Ginsburg, M. (1989). Social reproduction and resistance in four infant/toddler daycare settings: An ethnographic study of social relations and sociolinguistic codes. *Journal of Education, 171*(3), 31–50.

Morrow, V. (1996). Rethinking childhood dependency: Children's contributions to the domestic economy. *Sociological Review, 44,* 58–77.

Orellana, M. F. (2001). The work kids do: Mexican and Central American immigrant children's contributions to households and schools in California. *Harvard Educational Review, 71*(3), 272–291.

Polkki, T., Pietila, A.M., & Rissanen, L. (1999). Pain in children: Qualitative research of Finnish school-aged children's experiences of pain in hospital. *International Journal of Nursing Practice, 5,* 21–28.

Polkki, T., Pietila, A., & Vehvilainen-Julkunen, K. (2003). Hospitalized children's descriptions of their experiences with postsurgical pain relieving methods. *International Journal of Nursing Studies, 40,* 33–44.

Qvortrup, J. (1987). Introduction: The sociology of childhood. *International Journal of Sociology, 17,* 3–37.

Ridge, T. (2003). Listening to children: Developing a child-centered approach to childhood poverty in the UK. *Family Matters, 65,* 4–9.

Rosen, D. (2005). *Armies of the young: Child soldiers in war and terrorism.* New Brunswick, NJ: Rutgers University Press.

Smoller, J. W. (1988). The etiology and treatment of childhood. *SRCD Newsletter,* 7–9.

Sutterby, J. (2005). "I wish we could do whatever we want!" Children subverting scaffolding in the preschool classroom. *Journal of Early Childhood Teacher Education, 25,* 349–357.

Waksler, F. C. (1991). *Studying the social worlds of children.* London: Falmer Press.

Woodgate, R., & Krisjanson, L. J. (1996). "Getting better from my hurts": Toward a model of the young child's pain experience. *Journal of Pediatric Nursing, 11*(4), 233–242.

Chapter 2

Adler, P. A., & Adler, P. (1996). Parent-as-researcher: The politics of researching in the personal life. *Qualitative Sociology, 19*(1), 35–58.

Alderson, P. (2001). Research by children. *International Journal of Social Research Methodology, Theory and Practice, 4*(2), 139–153.

Aries, P. (1962). *Centuries of childhood.* New York: Vintage Books.

Balen, R., Blyth, E., Calabretto, H., et al. (2006). Involving children in health and social research: 'Human becomings' or 'active beings'? *Childhood, 13*(1), 29–48.

Barker, J., & Weller, S. (2003). "Never work with children": The geography of methodological issues in research with children. *Qualitative Research, 3*(2), 207–228.

Belanger, N., & Connelly, C. (2007). Methodological considerations in child-centered research about social difference and children experiencing difficulties at school. *Ethnography and Education, 2*(1), 21–38.

Bluebond-Langner, M., DeCicco, A., & Belasco, J. (2005). Involving children with life shortening illnesses in decisions about participation in clinical research: A proposal for shuttle diplomacy and negotiation. In E. Kodish

(Ed.), *Ethics and research with children* (pp. 323–343). Oxford, England: Oxford University Press.

Christensen, P., & Prout, A. (2002). Working with ethical symmetry in social research with children. *Childhood, 9*(4), 477–497.

Clark, C. D. (1999). Youth, advertising and symbolic meaning. In M. C. Macklin & L. Carlson (Eds.), *Advertising to children: Concepts and categories* (pp. 77–93). Thousand Oaks, CA: Sage.

Cocks, A. (2006). The ethical maze: Finding an inclusive path toward gaining children's agreement to research participation. *Childhood, 3*(2), 247–266.

Denzin, N. (1977). *Children and their caretakers.* New Brunswick, NJ: Transaction Books.

Duque-Páramo, M.C., & Clark, C.D. (2007, April). Beyond regulation: Ethical questions for research with children. *Anthropology News, 48*(2), 5.

Edwards, R., & Alldred, P. (1999). Children and young people's views of social research: The case of research on home-school relations. *Childhood, 6*(2), 261–281.

Eisen, G. (1988). *Children and play in the holocaust.* Amherst, MA: University of Massachusetts Press.

Epstein, D. (1998). "Are you a girl or are you a teacher?" The 'Least Adult' role in research about gender and sexuality in a primary school. In G. Walford (Ed.), *In doing research about education.* London, England: Falmer.

Ewing, K. P. (2006). Revealing and concealing: Interpersonal dynamics and the negotiation of identity in the interview. *Ethos, 34,* 89–122.

Fine, G. A., & Sandstrom, K. (1988). *Knowing children: Participant observation with minors.* Newbury Park, CA: Sage.

Francis, M., & Lorenzo, R. (2005). Children and city design: Proactive process and the 'renewal' of childhood. In C. Spencer and M. Blades (Eds.), *Children and their environments: Learning, using and designing spaces.* Cambridge, MA: Cambridge University Press.

Frankenberg, R., Robinson, I., & Delahooke, A. (2000). Countering essentialism in behavioural social science: The example of the 'vulnerable child' ethnographically examined. *The Sociological Review, 48*(4), 586–611.

Goncu, A. (1999). *Children's engagement in the world: Sociocultural perspectives.* Cambridge, MA: Cambridge University Press.

Goncu, A., & Becker, J. (2000). The problematic relation between development research and educational practice. *Human Development, 43,* 266–272.

Goodenough, T., Kent, J., & Ashcroft, R. (2003). "What did you think about that?" Researching children's perceptions of participation in a longitudinal genetic epidemiological study. *Children and Society, 7,* 113–125.

Greenbaum, T. (1998). *The handbook for focus group research (2nd ed.).* Thousand Oaks, CA: Sage.

Grodin, M., & Glantz, L. (1994). *Children as research subjects: Science ethics and the law.* New York: Oxford University Press.

Hart, R. (2002). *Children's participation: The theory and practice of involving young citizens in community development and environmental care.* London, England: Earthscan Publications.

Hill, M. (1997). Participatory research with children. *Child and Family Social Work, 2,* 171–183.

Hill, M., Davis, J., Prout, A., et al. (2004). Moving the participation agenda forward. *Children and Society, 18*(2), 77–96.

Hood, S., Kelley, P., & Mayall, B. (1996). Children as research subjects: A risky enterprise. *Children and Society, 10*(2), 117–128.

Hughes, D., & DuMont, K. (1993). Using focus groups to facilitate culturally anchored research. *American Journal of Community Psychology, 21*(6), 775–780.

Hughes, D., Seldman, E., & Williams, N. (1993). Cultural phenomena and the research enterprise: Toward a culturally anchored methodology. *American Journal of Community Psychology, 21*(6), 687–703.

Issitt, M., & Spence, J. (2005). Practitioner knowledge and evidence-based research, policy and practice. *Youth and Policy, 88,* 63–82.

James, A. (2007). Giving voice to children's voices: Practices and problems, pitfalls and potentials. *American Anthropologist, 9*(2), 226–272.

Lave, J., & Wenger, E. (1991). *Situated learning: Legitimate peripheral participation.* Cambridge, MA: Cambridge University Press.

Lutkehaus, N. C. (2008). Putting 'culture' into cultural psychology: Anthropology's role in Bruner's cultural psychology. *Ethos, 36,* 46–59.

Mandell, N. (1991). The least-adult role in studying children. In F. C. Waksler (Ed.), *Studying the social worlds of children: Sociological readings.* London, England: Routledge.

Mariampolski, H. (2006). *Ethnography for marketers.* Thousand Oaks, CA: Sage.

Mihesuah, D. A. (1998). *Natives and academics: Researching and writing about American Indians.* Lincoln, NE: University of Nebraska Press.

Mihesuah, D. A., & Wilson, A. (2004). *Indigenizing the academy: Transforming scholarship and empowering communities.* Lincoln, NE: University of Nebraska Press.

Mishna, F., Antle, B., & Regehr, C. (2004). Tapping the perspectives of children: Emerging ethical issues in qualitative research. *Qualitative Social Work, 3*(4), 449–468.

Pinkerton, J. (2004). Children's participation in the policy process: Some thoughts on policy evaluation based on the Irish national children's strategy. *Children and Society, 18,* 119–130.

Poole, C., Mizen, P., & Bolton, A. (1999). Realising children's agency in research: Partners and participants? *International Journal of Social Research Methodology, 2*(1), 39–54.

Rabinow, P. (1977). *Reflections on fieldwork in Morocco.* Berkeley, CA: University of California Press.

Reason, P., & Bradbury, H. (2001). *Handbook of action research.* London, England: Sage.

Rice, M., & Broome, M. (2004). Incentives for children in research. *Journal of Nursing Scholarship, 2*(36), 167–172.

Rosaldo, R. (1989). *Culture and truth: The remaking of social analysis.* Boston, MA: Beacon Press.

Ross, L. F. (2006). *Children in medical research: Access versus protection*. New York: Oxford University Press.

Samuels, J. (2004). Breaking the ethnographer's frames: Reflections on the use of photo elicitation in understanding Sri Lankan monastic culture. *American Behavioral Scientist, 47*(12), 1528–1550.

Shier, H. (2001). Pathways to participation: Openings, opportunities and obligations. A new model for enhancing children's participation in decision-making, in line with Article 2 of the United Nations Convention on the Rights of the Child. *Children and Society, 15*, 107–117.

Simonds, C. (1999). Clowning in hospitals is no joke. *British Medical Journal, 319*(7212), 792.

Sinclair, R. (2004). Participation in practice: Making it meaningful, effective and sustainable. *Children and Society, 18*, 106–118.

Smith, L. T. (1999). *Decolonizing methodologies: Research and indigenous peoples*. London, England: Zed Books.

Smith-Jackson, T. (2002). Child-centered safety research issues. *The Proceedings of the XVI Annual International Occupational Ergonomics and Safety Conference*, Toronto, Ontario, Canada.

Thorne, B. (2004). "You still takin' notes?" Fieldwork and problems of informed consent. In S. N. Hesse-Biber & P. Leavy (Eds.), *Approaches to qualitative research*. Oxford, England: Oxford University Press.

Tisdall, E., & Davis, J. (2004). Making a difference? Bringing children's and young people's views into policy-making. *Children and Society, 18*(2), 131–142.

Wengler, D., Rackoff, J., Emanuel, E., et al. (2002). The ethics of paying for children's participation in research. *Journal of Pediatrics, 141*, 166–171.

West, A. (2007). Power relationships and adult resistance to children's participation. *Children, Youth and Environments, 17*(1), 123–135.

Wiles, R., Charles, V., Crow, G., & Heath, S. (2006). Researching researchers: Lessons for research ethics. *Qualitative Research, 6*(3), 283–299.

Woodhead, M. (2008). Childhood studies past, present and future. In M. J. Kehily (Ed.), *An introduction to childhood studies* (pp. 17–34). London, England: Open University Press.

Chapter 3

Adler, P., & Adler, P. (1996). Parent-as-researcher: The politics of researcher in the personal life. *Qualitative Sociology, 19*(1), 35–58.

Anderson, D., Lorch, E. P., Field, D. E., et al. (1986). Television viewing at home: Age trends in visual attention and time with TV. *Child Development, 57*(4), 1024–1033.

Aries, P. (1962). *Centuries of childhood*. New York: Vintage.

Barker, J., & Weller, S. (2003). Never work with children: The geography of methodological issues in research with children. *Qualitative Research, 3*(2), 207–228.

Barker, R., & Wright, H. (1951). *One boy's day: A specimen record of behavior.* New York: Harper.

Bernheimer, L. (1986). The use of qualitative methodology in child health research. *Children's Health Care, 14*(4), 224–232.

Bluebond-Langner, M. (1978). *The private worlds of dying children.* Princeton, NJ: Princeton University Press.

Boocock, S. S., & Scott, K. A. (2005). *Kids in context: The sociological study of children and childhoods.* Oxford: Rowman & Littlefield.

Briggs, C. (1986). *Learning how to ask: A sociolinguistic appraisal of the role of the interview in social science research.* Cambridge, MA: Cambridge University Press.

Briggs, J. (2008). Daughter and pawn: One ethnographer's routes to understanding children. *Ethos, 36*(4), 449–456.

Briggs, J. L. (1998). *Inuit morality play.* New Haven, CT: Yale University Press.

Bronner, S. J. (1988). *American children's folklore.* Little Rock, AR: August House.

Christensen, P. (2004). Children's participation in ethnographic research: Issues of power and representation. *Children and Society, 18*(2), 165–176.

Clark, C. D. (1995). *Flights of fancy, leaps of faith: Children's myths in America.* Chicago, IL: University of Chicago Press.

Clark, C. D. (2003). *In sickness and in play: Children coping with chronic illness.* New Brunswick, NJ: Rutgers University Press.

Corsaro, W. (2003). *We're friends right? Inside kids' culture.* Washington, DC: Joseph Henry Press.

Corsaro, W., & Molinari, L. (2000). Entering and observing in children's worlds: A reflection on a longitudinal ethnography of early education in Italy. In P. Christensen & A. James (Eds.), *Research with children: Perspectives and practices* (pp. 179–200). London, England: Falmer Press.

Davis, J. (1998). Understanding the meanings of children: A reflexive process. *Children and Society, 12,* 325–335.

Davis, J., Watson, N., & Cunningham-Burley, S. (2000). Learning the lives of disabled children: Developing a reflexive approach. In P. Christensen & A. James (Eds.), *Research with children: Perspectives and practices* (pp. 201–224). London, England: Falmer Press.

Edwards, R., & Alldred, P. (1999). Children and young people's views of social research: The case of research on home-school relations. *Childhood, 6*(2), 261–281.

Epstein, D. (1998). "Are you a girl or are you a teacher?"' The "least adult" role in research about gender and sexuality in a primary school. In G. Walford (Ed.), *Doing research about education* (pp. 27–41). London, England: Falmer Press.

Fine, G. A. (1987). *With the boys: Little League baseball and preadolescent culture.* Chicago, IL: University of Chicago Press.

Fine, G. A., & Sandstrom, K. (1988). *Knowing children: Participant observation with minors.* Newbury Park, CA: Sage.

Goodwin, M. H. (1990). *He-said-she-said: Talk as social organization among black children.* Bloomington, IN: Indiana University Press.

Goodwin, M. H. (2006). *The hidden life of girls: Games of stance, status, and exclusion*. Oxford, England: Blackwell Publishing.

Goodwin, W., & Goodwin, L. (1996). *Understanding quantitative and qualitative research in early childhood education*. New York: Teachers College Press.

Hart, R. (1979). *Children's experience of place*. New York: Irvington.

Heath, S. B. (1983). *Ways with words*. Cambridge, MA: Cambridge University Press.

Holmes, R. (1998). *Fieldwork with children*. Thousand Oaks, CA: Sage Publications.

James, A. (2001). Ethnography in the study of children and childhood. In P. Atkinson, A. Coffey, S. Delamont, et al. (Eds.), *Handbook of ethnography* (pp. 246–257). London, England: Sage.

Kamei, N. (2005). Play among Baka children in Cameroon. In B. Hewlett & M. Lamb (Eds.), *Hunter-gatherer childhoods* (pp. 343–359). New Brunswick, NJ: Transaction Publishers.

Kidd, D. (1906). *Savage childhood*. London, England: Adam & Charles Black.

Lanclos, D. (2003). *At play in Belfast*. New Brunswick, NJ: Rutgers University Press.

Lancy, D. (1993). *Qualitative research in education*. New York: Longman.

Larson, R. (1989). Beeping children and adolescents: A method for studying time use and daily experience. *Journal of Youth and Adolescence, 18*(6), 511–530.

Lewis, A. (2003). *Race in the schoolyard*. New Brunswick, NJ: Rutgers University Press.

Mandell, N. (1988). The least-adult role in studying children. *Journal of Contemporary Ethnography, 16*, 433–467.

Maynard, A., & Greenfield, P. (2005). An ethnomodel of teaching and learning: Apprenticeship of Zinacantec Maya women's tasks. In A. Maynard & M. Martini (Eds.), *Learning in cultural context: Family, peers and school* (pp. 75–103). New York: Kluwer Academic.

McCall, G. J., & Simmons, J. L. (1969). *Issues in participant observation: A text and reader*. New York: Random House.

McGee, T. (1997). Getting inside kids' heads. *American Demographics, 19*(1), 52–57.

Mead, M. (1928/1961). *Coming of age in Samoa*. Middlesex, England: Penguin.

Mead, M. (1930/1966). *Growing up in New Guinea*. Middlesex, England: Penguin.

Miller, P. J. (1996). Instantiating culture through discourse practices: Some personal reflections on socialization and how to study it. In R. Jessor, A. Colby & R. A. Shweder (Eds.), *Ethnography and human development* (pp. 183–204). Chicago, IL: University of Chicago Press.

Mishler, E. (1986). *Research interviewing: Context and narrative*. Cambridge, MA: Harvard University Press.

Ochs, E., & Shohet, M. (2006). The cultural structuring of mealtime socialization. In R. Larson, A. Wiley & K. Banscomb (Eds.), *Family mealtime as a context of development and socialization* (pp. 35–49). San Francisco, CA: Jossey Bass.

Ochs, E., & Taylor, C. (1992). Family narrative as political activity. *Discourse and Society, 3*(3), 301–340.

Opie, I., & Opie, P. (1959). *The lore and language of schoolchildren.* Oxford, England: Oxford University Press.

Paley, V. (1990). *The boy who would be a helicopter.* Cambridge, MA: Harvard University Press.

Paley, V. (1993). *You can't say you can't play.* Cambridge, MA: Harvard University Press.

Powdermaker, H. (1966). *Stranger and friend: The way of an anthropologist.* New York: Norton Press.

Rich, M., Lamola, S., Avory, C., et al. (2000). Asthma in life context: Video intervention/prevention assessment. *Pediatrics, 105*(3), 469–477.

Schieffelin, B., & Ochs, E. (1986). *Language socialization across cultures.* Cambridge, MA: Cambridge University Press.

Solomon, D., & Peters, J. (2005). Resolving issues in children's research. *Young Consumers, 7*(1), 68–74.

Spencer, C., & Wooley, H. (1998). Children and the city: A summary of recent environmental psychology research. *Child: Care, Health and Development, 26*(3), 181–198.

Spradley, J. P. (1979). *Participant observation.* New York: Holt, Rinehart and Winston.

Thorne, B. (1994). *Gender play: Girls and boys in school.* New Brunswick, NJ: Rutgers University Press.

Ting, H. (1998). Getting into the peer social worlds of young children. In M. E. Graue & D. J. Walsh (Eds.), *Studying children in context: Theories, methods, and ethics* (pp. 146–157). Thousand Oaks, CA: Sage.

Webb, E., Campbell, D. T., Schwartz, R., et al. (1966). *Unobtrusive measures: Nonreactive research in the social sciences.* Chicago, IL: Rand McNally.

Wells, W. (1965). Communicating with children. *Journal of Advertising Research, 5*(2), 2–14.

Wheeler, L., & Reis, H. (1991). Self-recording of everyday life events: Origins, types and uses. *Journal of Personality, 59*(3), 339–354.

Whiting, J., Child, I., & Lambert, W. (1966). *Field guide for a study of socialization.* New York: John Wiley.

Woodgate, R. (2001). Adopting the qualitative paradigm to understanding children's perspectives on illness: Barrier or facilitator? *Journal of Pediatric Nursing, 16*(3), 149–161.

Chapter 4

Bales, S. R. (2005). *When I was a child: Children's interpretations of First Communion.* Chapel Hill, NC: University of North Carolina Press.

Benporath, S. (2003). Autonomy and vulnerability: On just relations between adults and children. *Journal of Philosophy of Education, 37*(1), 563–568.

Branch, J. (2000). Investigating the information-seeking processes of adolescents: The value of using think alouds and think afters. *Library & Information Science Research, 22*(4), 371–392.

Clark, C. D. (1995). *Flights of fancy, leaps of faith: Children's myths in contemporary America*. Chicago, IL: University of Chicago Press.

Collins, R. (2004). *Interaction ritual chains*. Princeton, NJ: Princeton University Press.

Devereux, G. (1967). *From anxiety to method in the behavioral sciences*. New York: Humanities Press Inc.

Dockett, S., & Perry, B. (2007). Trusting children's accounts in research. *Journal of Early Childhood Research, 5*, 47–60.

Elbers, E. (2004). Conversational asymmetry and the child's perspective in developmental and educational research. *International Journal of Disability, Development and Education, 51*(2), 201–215.

Epstein, I., Stevens, B., McKeever, P., et al. (2008). Using puppetry to elicit children's talk for research. *Nursing Inquiry, 15*(1), 49–56.

Forsner, M., Jansson, L., & Sorlie, V. (2005). The experience of being ill as narrated by hospitalized children aged 7–10 years with short term illness. *Journal of Child Health Care, 9*, 153.

Ginsberg, H. (1997). *Entering the child's mind: The clinical interview in psychological research and practice*. New York: Cambridge University Press.

Greenspan, S., & Greenspan, N. T. (1991). *The clinical interview of the child*. Washington, DC: American Psychiatric Press, Inc.

Heary, C., & Hennessy, E. (2006). Focus groups versus individual interviews: A comparison of data. *The Irish journal of psychology, 27*(1–2), 58–68.

Hollan, D. (2008). Being there: On the imaginative aspects of understanding others and being understood. *Ethos, 36*(4), 475–489.

Huffaker, D. (2004). Spinning yarns around the digital fire: Storytelling and dialogue among youth on the Internet. *Information Technology in Childhood Education Annual, 2004*(1), 63–75.

Lahman, M. (2008). Always othered: Ethical research with children. *Journal of Early Childhood Research, 6*, 281–300.

Lamb, M., & Brown., D. (2006). Conversational apprentices: Helping children become confident informants about their own experiences. *The British Journal of Developmental Psychology, 24*, 215–234.

Leonard, M. (2005). Involving children in social policy: A case study in Northern Ireland. *Sociological Studies of Children and Youth, 10*, 153–167.

MacDonald, K., & Greggans, A. (2008). Dealing with chaos and complexity: The reality of interviewing children and families in their own homes. *Journal of Clinical Nursing, 17*, 3123–3130.

McCabe, A., & Horsley, K. (2008). *The evaluator's cookbook: Exercises for participatory evaluation with children and young people*. London, England: Routledge.

McGee, J. (1999). *Writing and designing print materials for beneficiaries: A guide for state Medicaid agencies*. Baltimore, MD: Center for Medicaid and State Operations.

Nespor, J. (1998). The meanings of research: Kids as subjects and kids as inquirers. *Qualitative Inquiry, 4*(3), 369–388.

Newman, M., Woodcock, A., & Dunham, P. (2006). Playtime in the borderlands: Children's representations of school, gender and bullying through photographs and interviews. *Children's Geographies, 4*(3), 289–302.

Richards, H., & Emslie, C. (2000). The 'doctor' or the 'girl from the university'? Considering the influence of professional roles on qualitative interviewing. *Family Practice, 17*(1), 71–75.

Seidman, I. (1998). *Interviewing as qualitative research: A guide for researchers in education and the social sciences.* New York: Teacher's College Press.

Shweder, R. A., & Haidt, J. (2000). The cultural psychology of emotions: Ancient and new. In M. Lewis & J. M. Javiland-Jones (Eds.), *Handbook of emotions* (pp. 397–414). New York: Guilford Press.

Tanggaard, L. (2007). The research interview as discourses crossing swords: The researcher and apprentice on crossing roads. *Qualitative Inquiry, 13*(1), 160–176.

Tobin, J. (2000). *"Good guys don't wear hats": Children's talk about the media.* New York: Teachers College Press.

van Dulmen, A. (1998). Children's contributions to pediatric outpatient encounters. *Pediatrics, 102*(3), 563–568.

Wells, W. (1965). Communicating with children. *Journal of Advertising Research, 5,* 138–145.

Wilson, C., & Powell, M. (2001). *A guide to interviewing children.* Crows Nest, Australia: Allen and Unwin.

Woodgate, R. (2001). Adopting the qualitative paradigm to understanding children's perspectives on illness: Barrier or facilitator? *Journal of Pediatric Nursing, 16*(3), 149–161.

Chapter 5

_____ (2006). *Greenbook: The guide for buyers of market research services.* New York: New York American Marketing Association.

_____ (2006). *Quirk's market research review.* Eagan, MN: Quirk's.

Alderson, P. (2000). Children as researchers: The effects of participation rights on research methodology. In P. Christenson and A. James (Ed.), *Research with children.* London, England: Falmer Press.

Alderson, P. (2001). Research by children. *International Journal of Social Research Methodology, 4*(2), 139–153.

Briggs, C. (1986). *Learning how to ask: A sociolinguistic appraisal of the role of the interview in social science research.* Cambridge, MA: Cambridge University Press.

Bystedt, J., Lynn, S., & Potts, D. (2003). *Moderating to the max.* Ithaca, NY: Paramount Market Publishing.

Calder, B. J. (1977). Focus groups and the nature of qualitative research. *Journal of Marketing Research, 14*(3), 353–364.

Clark, C. D. (2003). *In sickness and in play: Children coping with chronic illness.* New Brunswick, NJ: Rutgers University Press.

Cook, P., Ali, S., & Munthali, A. (1998). *Starting from strengths: Community care for orphaned children in Malawi.* Ottawa, Ontario: International Development Research Center.

Corsaro, W. (2003). *We're friends right? Inside kids' culture.* Washington, DC: Joseph Henry Press.

Darbyshire, P., Macdougall, C., & Schiller, W. (2005). Multiple methods in qualitative research with children: More insight or just more? *Qualitative Research, 5*(4), 417–436.

Dockett, S., & Cusack, M. (2003). Young children's views of Australia and Australians. *Childhood Education, 79*(6), 364.

Elbers, E. (2004). Conversational asymmetry and the child's perspective in developmental and educational research. *International Journal of Disability, Development and Education, 51*(2), 201–215.

Epstein, I., Stevens, B., McKeever, P., et al. (2008). Using puppetry to elicit children's talk for research. *Nursing Inquiry, 15*(1), 49–56.

Erikson, E. (1950). *Childhood and society.* New York: W. W. Norton.

Fedder, C. J. (1985). Listening to qualitative research. *Journal of Advertising Research, 25*(6), 57–59.

Fine, G. A., & Sandstrom, K. (1988). *Knowing children: Participant observation with minors.* Newbury Park, CA: Sage.

France, A., Bendelow, G., & Williams, S. (2000). A "risky" business: Researching the health beliefs of children and young people. In A. Lewis & G. Lindsay (Eds.), *Researching children's perspectives* (pp. 150–162). Buckingham, England: Open University Press.

Garbarino, J., & Stott, F. (1989). *What children can tell us.* San Francisco, CA: Jossey-Bass.

Gardner, H. (1983). *Frames of mind: The theory of multiple intelligences.* New York: Basic Books.

Gardner, H. (1993). *Multiple intelligences: The theory in practice.* New York: Basic Books.

Goldman, L., & Glantz, S. (1998). Evaluation of antismoking advertising campaigns. *Journal of the American Medical Association, 279,* 772–77.

Greenbaum, T. (1999). *Moderating focus groups: A practical guide for group facilitation.* Thousand Oaks, CA: Sage.

Heary, C., & Hennessy, E. (2002). The use of focus group interviews in pediatric health care research. *Journal of Pediatric Psychology, 27*(1), 47–57.

Hennessy, E., & Heary, C. (2005). Exploring children's views through focus groups. In S. Greene & D. Hogan (Eds.), *Researching children's experience* (pp. 236–252). London, England: Sage.

Hill, M. (2006). Children's voices on ways of having a voice. *Childhood Education, 13*(1), 69–89.

Hill, M., Laybourn, A., & Borland, M. (1996). Engaging with primary-aged children about their emotions and well-being: Methodological considerations. *Children and Society, 10,* 129–144.

Horner, S. (2000). Using focus groups with middle school children. *Research in Nursing and Health, 23,* 510–517.

Kennedy, C., Kools, S., & Krueger, R. (2001). Methodological considerations in children's focus groups. *Nursing Research, 50*(3), 184–187.

Kenyon, A. (2004). Exploring phenomenological research: Pretesting focus group technique with young people. *International Journal of Market Research, 46*(4), 427–441.

Kirby, P. (1999). *Involving young researchers.* York, England: Joseph Rowntree Foundation/Save the Children.

Krueger, R. (1988). *Focus groups: A practical guide for applied research.* Newbury Park, CA: Sage.

Langer, J. (2001). *The mirrored window: Focus groups from a moderator's point of view.* Ithaca, NY: Paramount Market Publishing.

Large, A., & Beheshti, J. (2001). Focus groups with children: Do they work? *Canadian Journal of Information and Library Science, 26*(2/3), 77–89.

Large, A., Beheshti, J., & Rahman, T. (2002). Design criteria for children's web portals: The users speak out. *Journal of the American Society for Information Science and Technology, 53*(2), 79–93.

Lewis, A. (1992). Group child interviews as a research tool. *British Educational Research Journal, 18*(4), 413–421.

MacMullin, C., & Odeh, J. (1999). What is worrying children in the Gaza Strip? *Child Psychiatry and Human Development, 30*(1), 55–70.

Mandell, N. (1988). The least-adult role in studying children. *Journal of Contemporary Ethnography, 16,* 433–467.

Mauthner, M. (1997). Methodological aspects of collecting data from children: Lessons from three research projects. *Children and Society, 11,* 16–28.

McDonald, W. J., & Topper, G. (1988). Focus-group research with children: A structural approach. *Applied Marketing Research, 28*(2), 3–11.

Merton, R. K. (1987). The focused interview and focus groups: Continuities and discontinuities. *Public Opinion Quarterly, 51,* 550–566.

Merton, R. K., Fiske, M., & Kendall, P. (1956/1990). *The focused interview: A manual of problems and procedures.* New York: Free Press.

Miles, G., & Thomas, N. (2007). 'Don't grind an egg against a stone': Children's rights and violence in Cambodian history and culture. *Child Abuse Review, 16*(6), 383–400.

Mishler, E. (1986). *Research interviewing: Context and narrative.* Cambridge, MA: Harvard University Press.

Morgan, M., Gibbs, S., Maxwell, K., et al. (2002). Hearing children's voices: Methodological issues in conducting focus groups with children aged 7–11 years. *Qualitative Research, 2*(1), 5–20.

Murray, C. (2006). Peer led focus groups and young people. *Children and Society, 20*(4), 273–286.

Nyroos, V. (2004). *Evaluation of UNICEF's capacity development strategy in Bosnia & Herzegovina, 2002–2004.* New York: UNICEF.

Oech, R. V. (1983). *A whack in the side of the head.* New York: Warner Business.

Penza-Clyve, S., Mansell, C., & McQuaid, E. (2004). Why don't children take their asthma medications? A qualitative analysis of children's perspectives on adherence. *Journal of Asthma, 41*(2), 189–197.

Porcellato, L., Dughill, L., & Springett, J. (2002). Using focus groups to explore children's perceptions of smoking: Reflections on practice. *Health Education, 102*(6), 310–320.

Ronen, G. (2001). Health-related quality of life in childhood disorders: A modified focus group technique to involve children. *Quality of Life Research, 10*, 71–79.

Salmon, K. (2001). Remembering and reporting by children: The influence of cues and props. *Clinical Psychology Review, 21*(2), 267–300.

Schindler, R. M. (1992). The real lesson of new Coke: The value of focus groups for predicting the effects of social influence. *Marketing Research, 4*(4), 22–27.

Stephenson, S. (2001). Street children in Moscow: Using and creating social capital. *The Sociological Review, 49*(4), 530–547.

Tobin, J. (2000). *"Good guys don't wear hats": Children's talk about the media.* New York: Teachers College Press.

Van der Riet, M., Hough, A., & Kilian, B. (2005). Mapping HIV/AIDS as a barrier to education: A reflection on the methodological and ethical challenges to child participation. *Journal of Education, 35,* 75–98.

Waiters, E., Treno, A., & Grube, J. (2001). Alcohol advertising and youth: A focus-group analysis of what young people find appealing in alcohol advertising. *Contemporary Drug Problems, 28,* 695–718.

Waters, M. (1996). A children's focus group discussion in a public library. *Public Library Quarterly, 15*(2), 5–7.

Wee, H. L., Chua, H., & Liu, S. (2006). Meaning of health-related quality of life among children and adolescents in an Asian country: A focus group approach. *Quality of Life Research, 15,* 821–831.

Wells, W. (1965). Communicating with children. *Journal of Advertising Research, 5,* 138–145.

Wells, W. (1974). Group interviewing. In R. Ferber (Ed.), *The handbook of marketing research* (pp. 2–133 through 2–146). New York: McGraw Hill.

Wells, W. (1979). Group interviewing. In J. Higginbotham & K. Cox (Eds.), *Focus group interviews: A reader* (pp. 2–12). Chicago, IL: American Marketing Association.

Chapter 6

Arnheim, R. (1969). *Visual thinking.* London, England: Faber and Faber.

Backett-Milburn, K., & McKie, L. (1999). A critical appraisal of the draw and write technique. *Health Education Research, 14*(3), 387–398.

Bales, S. R. (2005). *When I was a child: Children's interpretations of First Communion.* Chapel Hill, NC: University of North Carolina Press.

Banister, E., & Booth, G. (2005). Exploring innovative methodologies for child-centric consumer research. *Qualitative Market Research, 8*(2), 157–175.

Barker, J., & Weller, S. (2003). 'Never work with children': The geography of methodological issues in research with children. *Qualitative Research, 3*(2), 207–228.

Becker, G. (1997). *Disrupted lives: How people create meaning in a chaotic world.* Berkeley, CA: University of California Press.

Board, R. (2005). School-age children's perceptions of their PICU hospitalization. *Pediatric Nursing, 31*(3), 166–175.

Boyatzis, C. J. (2000). The artistic evolution of mommy. In C. J. Boyatzis & M. W. Watson (Eds.), *Symbolic and social constraints on the development of children's artistic style* (pp. 5–29). San Francisco, CA: Jossey-Bass.

Boyatzis, C. J., & Albertini, G. (2000). A naturalistic observation of children drawing: Peer collaboration processes and influences in children's art. In C. J. Boyatzis & M. W. Watson (Eds.), *Symbolic and social constraints on the development of children's artistic style* (pp. 31–48). San Francisco, CA: Jossey-Bass.

Braswell, G. (2006). Sociocultural contexts for the early development of semiotic production. *Psychological Bulletin, 132*(6), 877–894.

Bruck, M., Ceci, S., & Francoeur, E. (2000). Children's use of anatomically detailed dolls to report genital touching in a medical examination: Developmental and gender comparisons. *Journal of Experimental Psychology: Applied, 6*(1), 74–83.

Burgess, A. W., & Hartman, C. R. (1993). Children's drawings. *Child Abuse and Neglect, 17*(1), 161–168.

Buss, S. (1995). Urban Los Angeles from young people's angle of vision. *Children's Environments, 12*(3), 93–113.

Butler, L. (1994). Autodrive in qualitative research: Cracking the ice with young respondents. *Canadian Journal of Marketing Research, 13*, 71–74.

Bystedt, J., Lynn, S., & Potts, D. (2003). *Moderating to the max.* Ithaca, NY: Paramount Market Publishing.

Carroll, M., & Ryan-Wenger, N. (1999). School-age children's fears, anxiety and human figure drawings. *Journal of Pediatric Health Care, 13*, 24–31.

Chalfen, R. (1981). A sociovidistic approach to children's filmmaking: The Philadelphia project. *Studies in Visual Communication, 7*(1), 2–32.

Children's Aid Society (2002). *Do not be sad: A chronicle of healing.* New York: Welcome Books.

Clark, A., & Moss, P. (2001). *Listening to young people: The mosaic approach.* York, England: National Children's Bureau and Joseph Rowntree Foundation.

Clark, C. D. (1995). *Flights of fancy, leaps of faith: Children's myths in America.* Chicago, IL: University of Chicago Press.

Clark, C. D. (1996). Interviewing children in qualitative research: A show and tell. *Canadian Journal of Marketing Research, 15*, 74–79.

Clark, C. D. (1999). The autodriven interview: A photographic viewfinder into children's experience. *Visual Sociology, 14*, 39–50.

Clark, C. D. (2003). *In sickness and in play: Children coping with chronic illness.* New Brunswick, NJ: Rutgers University Press.

Clark, C. D. (2004). Visual metaphor as method in interviews with children. *Journal of Linguistic Anthropology, 14*(2), 171–185.

Clark, C. D. (2005). Tricks of festival: Children, enculturation and American Halloween. *Ethos, 33*(2), 180–205.

Clark-Ibáñez, M. (2004). Framing the social world with photoelicitation interviews. *American Behavioral Scientist, 47*(12), 1507–1527.

Close, N. (2002). *Listening to children: Talking with children about difficult issues.* Boston, MA: Allyn and Bacon.

Coles, R. (1992). *Their eyes meeting the world: The drawings and paintings of children*. Boston, MA: Houghton Mifflin.

Cook, T., & Hess, E. (2007). What the camera sees and from whose perspective: Fun methodologies for engaging children in enlightening adults. *Childhood*, 14(1), 29–45.

Corsaro, W. (2003). *We're friends right? Inside kids' culture*. Washington, DC: Joseph Henry Press.

DeLoache, J., & Marzolf, D. (1995). The use of dolls to interview young children: Issues of symbolic representation. *Journal of Experimental Child Psychology*, 60, 155–173.

DiLeo, J. (1983). *Interpreting children's drawings*. Florence, KY: Brunner/Mazel.

Driessnack, M. (2005). Children's drawings as facilitators of communication: A meta-analysis. *Journal of Pediatric Nursing*, 20(6), 415–423.

Driessnack, M. (2006). Draw-and-tell conversations with children about fear. *Qualitative Health Research*, 16, 1414–1435.

Elbedour, S., Bastien, D., & Center, B. (1997). Identity formation in the shadow of conflict: Projective drawings by Palestinian and Israeli Arab children from the West Bank and Gaza. *Journal of Peace Research*, 34(2), 217–231.

Epstein, I., Stevens, B., McKeever, P., et al. (2006). Photo elicitation interview (PEI): Using photos to elicit children's perspectives. *International Journal of Qualitative Methods*, 5(3), 1–11.

Ewald, W. (2002). *I wanna take me a picture*. Boston, MA: Beacon Press.

Fasoli, L. (2003). Reading photographs of young children: Looking at practices. *Contemporary Issues in Early Childhood*, 4(1), 32–47.

Fernandez, J. (1986). *Persuasions and performances: The play of tropes in culture*. Bloomington, IN: Indiana University Press.

Frey, D. (1993). Learning by metaphor. In C. Schaefer (Ed.), *The therapeutic powers of play* (pp. 223–239). Northvale, NJ: Jason Aronson.

Furth, G. (1988). *The secret world of drawings: Healing through art*. Boston, MA: Sigo Press.

Gabhainn, S. N., & Sixsmith, J. (2006). Children photographing well-being: Facilitating participation in research. *Children and Society*, 20, 249–259.

Garbarino, J., Dubrow, N., Kostelny, K., et al. (1992). *Children in danger: Coping with the consequences of community violence*. San Francisco, CA: Jossey-Bass.

Garbarino, J., & Stott, F. (1989). *What children can tell us*. San Francisco, CA: Jossey-Bass.

Gardner, H. (1983). *Frames of mind: The theory of multiple intelligences*. New York: Basic Books.

Gil, E. (1994). *Play in family therapy*. New York: Guilford Press.

Gil, E., & Drewes, A. (2006). *Cultural issues in play therapy*. New York: Guilford Press.

González-Rivera, M., & Bauermeister, J. (2007). Children's attitudes toward people with AIDS in Puerto Rico: Exploring stigma through drawings and stories. *Qualitative Health Research*, 17, 250–262.

Goodenough, F. (1926). *Measurement of intelligence by drawings*. New York: Harcourt Brace & World.

Goodman, G., & Aman, C. (1990). Children's use of anatomically detailed dolls to recount an event. *Child Development, 61,* 1859–1871.

Goodnow, J. (1970). *Children's drawing.* Cambridge, MA: Harvard University Press.

Gordon, B., Ornstein, P., Nida, R., et al. (1993). Does the use of dolls facilitate children's memory of visits to the doctor? *Applied Cognitive Psychology, 7,* 459–474.

Guillemin, M. (2004). Understanding illness: Using drawings as a research method. *Qualitative Health Research, 14,* 272–289.

Harper, D. (2002). Talking about pictures: A case for photo elicitation. *Visual Studies, 17*(1), 13–26.

Harrison, L. J., Clarke, L., & Ungerer, J. A. (2006). Children's drawings provide a new perspective on teacher–child relationship quality and school adjustment. *Early Childhood Research Quarterly, 22*(1), 55–71.

Hayes, M., & Petrie, G. M. (2006). 'We're from the generation that was raised on television': A qualitative exploration of media imagery in elementary preservice teachers' video production. *International Journal of Qualitative Studies in Education, 19*(4), 499–517.

Heisley, D., & Levy, S. (1991). Autodriving: A photoelicitation technique. *Journal of Consumer Research, 18,* 257–272.

Hyde, K. (2005). Portraits and collaborations: A reflection on the work of Wendy Ewald. *Visual Studies, 20*(2), 172–190.

Ito, M., Baumer, S., Bittanti, M., et al. (2009b). *Hanging out, messing around, and geeking out: Kids living and learning with new media.* Cambridge, MA: MIT Press.

Ito, M., Horst, H., Bittanti, M., et al. (2009a). *Living and learning with new media: Summary of findings from the digital youth project.* Cambridge, MA: MIT Press.

Kellogg, R. (1970). *Analysing children's art.* Palo Alto, CA: National Press Books.

Kelly, P., Sylvia, E., Schwartz, L., et al. (2006). Cameras and community health. *Journal of Psychosocial Nursing and Mental Health Services, 44*(6), 31–36.

Kleinman, A. (1988). *The illness narratives.* New York: Basic Books.

Lakoff, G., & Turner, M. (1989). *More than cool reason: A field guide to poetic metaphor.* Chicago, IL: University of Chicago Press.

Lev-Wiesel, R., & Liraz, R. (2007). Drawings vs. narratives: Drawing as a tool to encourage verbalization in children whose fathers are drug abusers. *Clinical Child Psychology and Psychiatry, 12,* 65–75.

Lewis, D. W., Middlebrook, M. T., Mehallick, M., et al. (2002). Pediatric headaches: What do children want? *Headache: The Journal of Head and Face Pain,* H36(4), 224–230.

MacGregor, A., Currie, C., & Wetton., N. (1998). Eliciting the views of children about health in schools through the use of draw and write techniques. *Health Promotion International, 13*(4), 307–318.

Marquez, G. G. (1998). *100 years of solitude.* New York: Perennial.

Meyer, J. (1997). *Inaccuracies in children's testimony.* New York: Haworth Press.

Mahruf, M., Shohei, C., & Howes, J. (2007). Transition from nonformal schools; Learning through photo elicitation in educational fieldwork in Bangladesh. *Visual Studies, 22*(1), 53–61.

Miles, G. (2002). Drawing together hope: 'Listening' to militarized children. *Journal of Child Health Care, 4,* 137–142.

Milner, P., & Carolin, B. (1999). *Time to listen to children.* London, England: Routledge.

Mitchell, L. (2006). Child-centered? Thinking critically about children's drawings as a visual research method. *Visual Anthropology Review, 22*(1), 60–73.

Monahon, C. (1993). *Children and trauma.* New York: Lexington Books.

Nigro, G., & Wolpow, S. (2004). Interviewing young children with props: Prior experience matters. *Applied Cognitive Psychology, 18*(5), 549–565.

Orellana, M. F. (1999). Space and place in an urban landscape: Learning from children's views of their social worlds. *Visual Sociology, 14,* 73–89.

Oremland, E. (2000). *Protecting the emotional development of the ill child.* Madison, CT: Psychosocial Press.

Piko, B., & Bak, J. (2006). Children's perceptions of health and illness: Images and lay concepts in preadolescence. *Health Education Research, 21*(5), 643–645.

Pradel, F., Hartzema, A., & Bush, P. (2001). Asthma self-management: The perspective of children. *Patient Education and Counseling, 45,* 199–209.

Rasmussen, K. (2004). Places for children—children's places. *Childhood, 11*(2), 155–173.

Raynor, C. (2002). The role of play in the recovery process. In W. Zubenko & J. Capozzoli (Eds.), *Children and disasters.* New York: Oxford University Press.

Rich, M., & Chalfen, R. (1999). Showing and telling asthma: Children teaching physicians with visual narrative. *Visual Sociology, 14,* 51–71.

Rich, M., Lamola, S., Amory, C., et al. (2000). Asthma in life context: Video intervention/prevention assessment. *Pediatrics, 105,* 469–477.

Rich, M., Lamola, S., Gordon, J., et al. (2000). Video intervention/prevention assessment: A patient-centered methodology for understanding the adolescent illness experience. *Journal of Adolescent Health, 27,* 155–165.

Ring, K. (2006). What mothers do: Everyday routines and rituals and their impact upon young children's use of drawing for meaning making. *International Journal of Early Years Education, 24*(1), 63–84.

Rubin, J. A. (1984). *Child art therapy.* New York: Van Nostrand Reinhold.

Ryan-Wenger, N. (1998). Children's drawings: An invaluable source of information for nurses. *Journal of Pediatric Health Care, 12,* 109–110.

Ryan-Wenger, N. (2001a). Amela's view of war-torn Sarajevo. *Journal of Pediatric Health Care, 15,* 77.

Ryan-Wenger, N. (2001b). Hillary's no good very bad day. *Journal of Pediatric Health Care, 15,* 256.

Ryan-Wenger, N. (2002). Impact of the threat of war on children in military families. *Journal of Pediatric Health Care, 16,* 245–252.

Sagara-Rosemeyer, M., & Davies, B. (2007). Integration of religious traditions in Japanese children's view of death and afterlife. *Death Studies, 31*(3), 223–247.

Salmon, K. (2001). Remembering and reporting by children: The influence of cues and props. *Clinical Psychology Review, 21*(2), 267–300.

Samuels, J. (2004). Breaking the ethnographer's frame: Reflections on the use of photoelicitation in understanding Sri Lankan monastic culture. *American Behavioral Scientist, 47*(12), 1528–1550.

Schwartzman, H. (2006). Materializing children: Challenges for the archaeology of childhood. *Archeological Papers of the American Anthropological Association, 15,* 123–131.

Shams, M., & Robinson, L. (2005). A critical interdisciplinary analysis of culturally appropriate research approach and practices in health care and social work. *Child Care in Practice, 11*(4), 457–470.

Shratz, M., & Steiner-Loffler, U. (1998). Pupils using photographs in school self-evaluation. In J. Prosser (Ed.), *Image-based research: A sourcebook for qualitative researchers* (pp. 209–224). London, England: Falmer Press.

Sourkes, B. (1995). *Armfuls of time: The psychological experience of a child with life-threatening illness.* Pittsburgh, PA: University of Pittsburgh Press.

Stafstrom, C. E., Rostasy, K., Minster, A., et al. (2002). Children's drawings of headache pain were accurate for diagnosing migraine/commentary. *ACP Journal Club, 137*(3), 113.

Stafstrom, C. E., Rostasy, K., & Minster, A. (2002). The usefulness of children's drawings in the diagnosis of headaches. *Pediatrics, 109,* 460–472.

Steward, M., & Steward, D. (1996). Interviewing young children about body touch and handling. *Monographs of the Society for Research in Child Development, 61.*

Thomas, G., & Silk, A. (1990). *An introduction to the psychology of children's drawings.* New York: New York University Press.

UNICEF (1994). *I dream of peace.* New York: Harper Collins.

Unruh, A. (1983). Children's drawings of their pain. *Pain, 17*(4), 385–392.

Verbrugge, R. (1979). The primacy of metaphor in development. In E. Winner & H. Gardner (Eds.), *Fact, fiction and fantasy in childhood* (pp. 77–84). San Francisco, CA: Jossey-Bass.

Vronay, D., Farnham, S., & Davis, J. (2001). *Photostory: Preserving emotion in digital photo sharing.* Redmond, WA: Virtual Worlds Group, Microsoft Research.

Wang, C., & Burris, M. A. (1994). Empowerment through Photo Novella: Portraits of participation. *Health Education & Behavior, 21*(2), 171–186.

Webb, N. B. (1999). *Play therapy with children in crisis.* New York: Guilford.

Weinberg, A., & Stahel, U. (2000). Preface. In W. Ewald (Ed.), *Secret games: Collaborative works with children 1969–1999* (pp. 6–12). New York: Scalo Publishers.

Wesson, M., & Salmon, K. (2001). Drawing and showing: Helping children to report emotionally laden events. *Applied Cognitive Psychology, 15,* 301–320.

West, T. (1997). *In the mind's eye: Visual thinkers, gifted people with learning difficulties, computer imaging, and the ironies of creativity.* Amherst, NY: Prometheus Books.

West, T. (2004). *Thinking like Einstein: Returning to our visual roots with the emerging revolution in computer information visualization.* Amherst, NY: Prometheus Books.

Westcott, H., Davies, G., & Bull, R. (2002). *Children's testimony: A handbook of psychological research and forensic practice.* West Sussex, England: Wiley.

Winner, E. (1988). *The point of words: Children's understanding of metaphor and irony.* Cambridge, MA: Harvard University Press.

Young, L., & Barrett, H. (2001). Adapting visual methods: Action research with Kampala street children. *Area, 33*(2), 141–152.

Zaltman, G., & Higle, R. (1993). Seeing the voice of the consumer: The Zaltman Metaphor Elicitation Technique. *Marketing Science Institute Working Paper, 73*(114), 35–51.

Chapter 7

Baxter, J. E. (2005). *The archaeology of childhood: Children, gender, and material culture.* Walnut Creek, CA: Alta Mira Press.

Catterall, M., & Maclaran, P. (1997). Focus group data and qualitative analysis programs: Coding the moving picture as well as the snapshots. *Sociological Research Online, 2*(1).

Clark, C. D. (1995). *Flights of fancy, leaps of faith: Children's myths in America.* Chicago, IL: University of Chicago Press.

Clark, C. D. (2007). Therapeutic advantages of play. In A. Goncu & S. Gaskins (Eds.), *Play and development: Evolutionary, sociocultural, and functional perspectives* (pp. 275–293). Mahwah, NJ: Earlbaum.

Corsaro, B. (2003). *We're friends right? Inside kids' culture.* Washington, D.C.: Joseph Henry Press.

Curtis, K., Liabo, K., Roberts, H., et al. (2004). Consulted but not heard: A qualitative study of young people's views of their local health service. *Health Expectations, 7,* 149–156.

Dohan, D. (1998). Using computers to analyze ethnographic field data: Theoretical and practical considerations. *Annual Review of Sociology, 24,* 477–498.

Elliott, I., Lach, L., & Smith, M. L. (2005). I just want to be normal: A qualitative study exploring how children and adolescents view the impact of intractable epilepsy on their quality of life. *Epilepsy and Behavior, 7,* 664–678.

Forsner, M., Jansson, L., & Soerlie, V. (2005). Being ill as narrated by children aged 11–18 years. *Journal of Child Health Care, 9,* 314–323.

Giacomini, M. K. (2001). The rocky road: Qualitative research as evidence. *Evidence-Based Medicine, 6,* 4–6.

Glaser, B., & Strauss, A. (1967). *The discovery of grounded theory: Strategies for qualitative research.* New York: Aldine.

Glesne, C., & Peshkin, A. (1992). *Becoming qualitative researchers: An introduction.* White Plains, NY: Longman.

Hirschfeld, L. A. (2002). Why don't anthropologists like children? *American Anthropologist, 104*(2), 611–627.

Hunter, A., Lusardi, P., Zucker, D., et al. (2002). Making meaning: The creative component in qualitative research. *Qualitative Health Research, 12*(3), 388–398.

Irwin, L., & Johnson, J. (2005). Interviewing young children: Explicating our practices and dilemmas. *Qualitative Health Research, 15*, 821–831.

Kamp, K. (2001). Where have all the children gone? The archaeology of childhood. *Journal of Archaeological Method and Theory, 8*(1), 1–34.

Lindeke, L., Nakai, M., & Johnson, L. (2006). Capturing children's voices for quality improvement. *MCN The American Journal of Maternal/Child Nursing, 31*(5), 290–295.

Matisse, H. (1953). Looking at life with the eyes of a child. *Art Education, 6*, 5–6.

McKenna, J., & Mutrie, N. (2003). Emphasizing quality in qualitative papers. *Journal of Sports Science, 21*(12), 955–958.

Nilsen, R. D. (2005). Searching for analytical concepts in the research process: Learning from children. *International Journal of Social Research Methodology, 8*(2), 117–135.

Ruark, J. (2000). Seeing children and hearing them too. *The Chronicle of Higher Education, 11/17*, A22.

Rydholm, J. (1989). Research helps Boy Scouts of America communicate an active, adventurous program. *Quirk's Marketing Research Review, 8*.

Schmidt, C., Bernaix, L., Koski, A., et al. (2007). Hospitalized children's perceptions of nurses and nurse behaviors. *MCN The American Journal of Maternal/Child Nursing, 32*(6), 336–342.

Schor, J. (2004). *Born to buy: The commercialized child and the new consumer culture.* New York: Scribner.

Schwartzman, H. (2005). Materializing children: Challenges for the archaeology of childhood. *Archaeological Papers of the American Anthropological Association, 15*, 123–131.

Slade, A., & Wolf, D. P. (1994). *Children at play: Clinical and developmental approaches to meaning and representation.* New York: Oxford University Press.

Steinberg, S., & Kincheloe, J. (1997). *Kinderculture: The corporate construction of childhood.* Boulder, CO: Westview Press.

Strauss, A. C., & Corbin, J. (1998). *Basics of qualitative research, techniques and procedures for developing grounded theory.* Thousand Oaks, CA: Sage.

Sutton-Smith, B. (2001). *The ambiguity of play.* Cambridge, MA: Harvard University Press.

Warming, H. (2003). The quality of life from a child's perspective. *International Journal of Public Administration, 26*(7), 815–829.

Wells, W. (1974). Group interviewing. In R. Ferber (Ed.), *Handbook of market research* (pp. 2–133 through 2–146). New York: McGraw-Hill.

Winnicott, D. W. (1971). *Playing and reality.* London, England: Tavistock Publications.

Woodgate, R. (2001). Adopting the qualitative paradigm to understanding children's perspectives of illness: Barrier or facilitator? *Journal of Pediatric Nursing, 16*(3), 149–161.

Chapter 8

Alexander, K., Entwisle, D., & Horsey, C. (1997). From first grade forward: Early foundations of high school dropout. *Sociology of Education, 70*(2), 87–107.

Bradshaw, C., O'Brennan, L., & McNeely, C. (2008). Core competencies and the prevention of school failure and early school leaving. In N.G. Guerra & C.P. Bradshaw (Eds.). Core competencies to prevent problem behaviors and promote positive youth development. *New Directions for Child and Adolescent Development, 122,* 19–32. San Francisco: Jossey-Bass.

Bridgeland, J., DiIulio, J., & Morison, K.B. (2006). The silent epidemic: Perspectives of high school dropouts. Bill and Melinda Gates Foundation.

Cangelosi, J., Markham, F. S., & Bounds, W. (1998). Factors relating to nurse retention and turnover: An updated study. *Health Marketing Quarterly, 15,* 25–43.

Connolly, M., & Ennew, J. (1996). Children out of place. *Childhood: A Journal of Child Research, 3*(2), 131–145.

Csikszentmihalyi, M., Larson, R., & Prescott, S. (1977). The ecology of adolescent activity and experience. *Journal of Youth and Adolescence, 6*(3), 281–294.

Dudley, R. L. (1999). Youth religious commitment over time: A longitudinal study of retention. *Review of Religious Research, 41*(1), 110–121.

Dynarski, M., Clarke, L., Cobb, B., et al. (2008). *Dropout Prevention.* National Center for Education Evaluation and Regional Assistance, Washington DC: U.S. Department of Education.

Hale, Leslie (1998). *High school dropouts cost everyone something!* Bethesda, MD: National Association of School Psychologists.

Horn, P., & Kinicki, A. (2001). Dissatifaction drives employee turnover. *The Academy of Management Journal, 44*(5), 975–987.

Lareau, A. (2003). *Unequal childhoods: Class, race and family life.* Berkeley, CA: University of California Press.

Lee, V., & Burham, D. (2003). Dropping out of high school: The role of school organization and structure. *American Educational Research Journal, 40*(2), 353–393.

Milliken, B. (2007). *The last dropout: Stop the epidemic.* Carlsbad, CA: Hay House.

Ongori, H. (2007). A review of the literature on employee turnover. *African Journal of Business Management, 1*(3), 49–54.

Orfield, G. (2004). *Dropouts in America: Confronting the Graduation Rate Crisis.* Cambridge, MA: Harvard Education Press.

Rich, M., Lamola, S. Gordon, J., et al. (2000). Video intervention/prevention assessment: A patient centered methodology for understanding the adolescent illness experience. *Journal of Adolescent Health, 27,* 155–165.

Shacklock, G., Smyth, J., & Wilson, N. (1998). *Conceptualizing and capturing voices in dropout research.* Paper at the annual meeting of the Australian Association for Research in Education, Adelaide.

Stearns, E., & Glennie, E. (2006). When and why dropouts leave high school. *Youth and Society, 38*(1), 29–57.

Suarez-Orozco, C., Qin-Hilliard, D., & Qin, D. B. (2005). *The new immigration*. London, England: Routledge.

Sum, A., Khatiwada, I., McLaughlin, J., et al. (2009). *The consequences of dropping out of high school*. Boston, MA: Northeastern University Center for Labor Market Studies.

INDEX ⠿